SEND ME!

The Story of Salkehatchie Summer Service

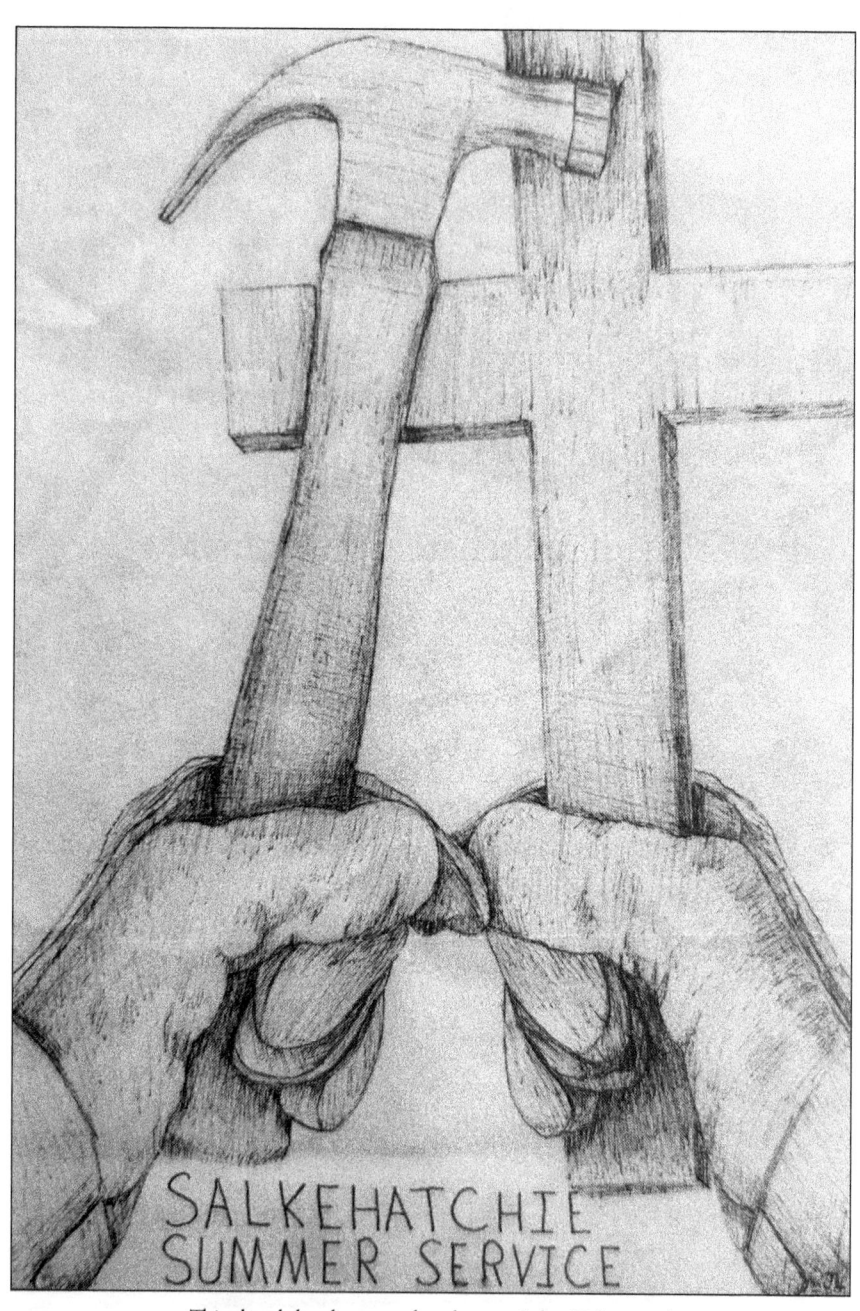

This sketch by then-youth volunteer John Liebenrood
has appeared on the back of every Salkehatchie T-shirt since 1988.

SEND ME!

The Story of Salkehatchie Summer Service

By Arlene Bowers Andrews, John Culp, Art Dexter

South Carolina United Methodist Advocate Press

South Carolina United Methodist Advocate Press, Columbia, South Carolina
First edition copyright © 2006 by Arlene Bowers Andrews
Second edition, 2024

All rights reserved. Written permission must be secured from the publisher to use or reproduce any part of this book, except for brief quotations in critical reviews or articles.

Printed in the United States of America

ISBN: 979-8-9883575-9-9

Cover photo by Matt Brodie; additional photography by Arlene Bowers Andrews, Matt Brodie, John Culp, and J. Austin Watson

Cover and page design by Jessica Brodie

Frontispiece art by John Liebenrood

Unless otherwise indicated Scripture quotations are taken from Holy Bible, New International Version®. Copyright 1973, 1978, 1984 by International Bible Society. Used by permission of Zondervan Publishing House.

Scripture quotations marked KJV are taken from the Holy Bible, King James Version, Cambridge, 1796.

Scripture quotations marked NRSV are taken from the New Revised Standard Version Bible, copyright © 1989, Division of Christian Education of the National Council of the Churches of Christ in the United States of America. Used by permission. All rights reserved.

Scripture quotations marked RSV are taken from the Revised Standard Version of the Bible, copyright 1952 [2nd edition, 1971] by the Division of Christian Education of the National Council of the Churches of Christ in the United States of America. Used by permission. All rights reserved.

Republished in the United States of America in 2024 by the South Carolina United Methodist Advocate Press.

In Memoriam

Arthur Harlan Dexter
April 21, 1923-August 6, 2004

Well done, thou good and faithful servant ...
enter thou into the joy of the Lord.
—Matthew 25:21 (KJV)

We remember Art as a prophet and saint. As a prophet, Art communicated the messages of God through his words and actions. We call him a saint not to suggest he was perfect—for none of us is perfect. Even Jesus himself said, "Why do you call me good? No one is good but God alone." We use the word "saint" according to the way of Jonathan Edwards, early American spiritual leader. "A saint," said Edwards, "is a person with an appetite for the good."

*Then I heard the voice of the Lord saying,
"Whom shall I send, and who will go for us?"
And I said, "Here I am;
send me!"*
—Isaiah 6:8 (NRSV)

Table of Contents

Preface to the Second Edition ix
Preface to the First Edition xxi
Acknowledgments xxiii
Introduction xxvii
A Salkehatchie Prayer xxxi
Chapter 1: More than a Hard Day's Work 1
Chapter 2: Hearts and Homes 33
Chapter 3: A Week: A Moment in Time 89
Chapter 4: How Salkehatchie Summer Service Came to Be 165
Chapter 5: Making Meaning: Prayers, Poems, Sermons 211
Chapter 6: The Ripple Effect: Spreading the Light 267

Appendices
Appendix A: Salkehatchie's Broader Context 307
Appendix B: Twenty-Five Years of Salkehatchie Growth 314
Appendix C: Location of Salkehatchie Camps by Year 315

Preface to the Second Edition

Ms. Johnson, age 82, carefully hoisted herself up the wooden steps to her home, one slow step at a time. She grabbed the unsteady wooden railing as she carefully avoided the parts of the steps that were rotted away. She reached the small landing before her front door with the broken door lock. She turned, smiled at the volunteers in her front yard, and said, "Come on in."

A week later Ms. Johnson sat beaming in a new weatherproof rocker on her wide deck in front of the repaired door. Inside, her home was now dry, safe, and ready for weather extremes. The Salkehatchie Summer Service crew lined up along the sturdy ramp leading to the deck. Tears gleamed in Ms. Johnson's eyes as a youth volunteer handed her the key to her now secure door. Everyone's hearts murmured, "Thank You, God. Thank You."

Much has changed since this book, *Send Me! The Story of Salkehatchie Summer Service*, was released in 2005. Still, most of the story is the same. Across South Carolina, people continue to be desperate for help with houses that are dangerous to their health and safety. Youth and adult volunteers are still eager to help, prodded by the Holy Spirit whose call to love our neighbors is eternal. Communities continue to stand ready to give support to volunteer crews as they visit their areas for a week. Together, we still pray that most fundamental of prayers, "Thy kingdom come, Thy will be done."

The book is essentially the same as it was in the first edition. The topics include family stories, youth and adult enlightenment, and the history and theology of Salkehatchie Summer Service. In this introduction, we highlight some of the innovations that have affected how the service occurs. We hope readers will appreciate the timelessness of the rest of the book.

The organization evolves

Salkehatchie Summer Service was and is a mission of the South Carolina United Methodist Conference. By the time Salkehatchie reached its fortieth year, camps were repairing two hundred homes each year with more than $1 million spent each year on construction and supplies. More than sixty-three thousand campers had experienced Salkehatchie and, miraculously, more than six thousand families had been served. As this growth trend had occurred, the Salkehatchie Steering Committee saw the need to make the mission a UMCSC affiliate with its own organizational status. In October 2016 Salkehatchie Summer Service LLC was established with a governing board.

One of the first orders of business for the new board was the expansion of the "Salkehatchie Essentials" (Chapter 1 in this book) to a handbook of Salkehatchie Policies. The informality of the early years relied on personal networks among the committed leaders to assure fidelity to the essentials of the mission. Adding multiple new leaders necessitated more formal guidelines for consistency and accountability across the many camps. Emerging leaders now have clear guidance and training, including a detailed annual retreat and periodic guidance through document updates and additional meetings. The board seeks continuous quality improvement guidance from local leaders as the policies continue to emerge.

One of the key policies to be established is one requiring compliance with the South Carolina United Methodist Conference's Safe Sanctuary policy. Since 2007, the UMCSC has required all staff and volunteers age 18 and older to be screened (criminal background check) and trained to protect children. The policy is to assure that sanctuaries, classrooms, mission encounters, camps and retreats—and all spaces where we gather to worship and serve God—are places of trust.

In 2017, the extraordinary part-time staff donated by UMCSC (especially Tammy Fulmer, Gail Corn, and Lee McMillan) were replaced by an employee hired by Salkehatchie LLC, with Bobby Romanek and Kathy Hart as the first staffers. The camp leaders, who are spread across South Carolina, can rely on the presence of a staff member dedicated solely to Salkehatchie.

Technological innovations

Technological innovations have powerfully influenced how Salkehatchie happens. In 2005, many people had cell phones, but they were not minicomputers with photo screens. At first they were portable telephones, often "flip" phones, used for audio calling. Then capacity for texting was added and in common use by 2007. The first popular smartphone, the iPhone, was released in 2007. Smartphone cameras were an immediate hit at Salkehatchie. So was GPS, which helped with locating homes and navigating from one site or supplier to another.

Often, rural communities in South Carolina, where many Salkehatchie camps operate, had no adequate cell service even as technology use was blossoming elsewhere. GPS was notoriously unreliable. Gradually, rural broadband has emerged and continues to be developed.

In 2006, Facebook was only a year old, relatively unknown, typically used on a laptop computer. Within a few years, Facebook, Twitter (now X), Instagram, and other social media platforms were part of American life.

The almost universal emergence of smartphones and social media are now fully integrated into Salkehatchie Summer Service. Prior to camps, leaders conduct organizing meetings on Zoom. They communicate with volunteers through Facebook or Instagram pages. At camp, site leaders text questions to one another, whereas in the old days, they had to wait to meet one another at lunch or drive from site to site. At the homes, site teams text orders for supplies that arrive within the day. They tell their stories through postings on social media. They record their experiences with photos and videos. And many a leader has been known to download a YouTube video for instructions on how to get a job done.

Of course, we still encourage participants to minimize media use so they can interact face-to-face with one another. Ultimately, Salkehatchie offers participants an opportunity to be in communion with God, but only if they separate from the routine urge to constantly message.

Salkehatchie Summer Service instituted online registration after years of paper applications, parental permission forms, reference forms, and liability release forms that had been gathered by mail and in-person. Registration on the first day of camp could be complicated. With online registration, camp starts (hopefully) with a completed list of registered and approved volunteers.

Communications and administration are not the only beneficiaries of evolving technology. Improved portable power tools with long-lasting battery packs and generators have replaced hand tools or earlier versions of power tools. Nail guns for roofing, with users carefully supervised, are common. Electronic measuring devices make measurement more precise.

Who knows what benefits—or risks—artificial intelligence will bring to Salkehatchie in the future? If technological innovations can benefit families in need and volunteers in service, Salkehatchie will evolve. God's world is ever-changing.

A setback

The remarkable growth of Salkehatchie Summer Service suffered a setback in 2020 when all camps were cancelled because of the COVID-19 pandemic. In 2021, the camps were again cancelled because of uncertainty about health risks to home residents and camp volunteers. By 2022, camps were beginning to re-open. And in 2023, camps were encouraged to form again. Eleven camps operated that year, with much reduced attendance. But the momentum was beginning to return.

The "contagion" about the joy and meaning of Salkehatchie participation happens often because youth pass on the word to one another over their four years of high school. In the years 2020-2022, three cohorts of youth missed the experience. The spirit of mission among youth waned.

The pandemic had other effects on youth and youth ministries, too. The rise of dependence on internet-based virtual communications intensified. Youth, as well as people of all ages, felt less of a call to be physically present at a gathering with body, mind, heart, and soul committed to interaction with other faith seekers.

Salkehatchie Summer Service is designed for participants to commit their bodies to active participation. We are the body of Christ, brought to share love and light where there is despair. Participants are called to witness poverty with all their senses—seeing, smelling, hearing, feeling, and tasting. They are likely to sweat, grow weary, get dirty, cry, suffer minor injuries, and generally be uncomfortable. They are also likely to hear angels as we sing, dance with joy, savor delicious local food, and engage in direct social contact with new friends. No virtual experience can compare. As camp director Neil Flowers said, "Salkehatchie is raw."

With prayer, we hope the trends of focus on virtual reality and avoidance of physical immersion will change. The primary purpose of Salkehatchie has always been to build youth disciples of Jesus Christ. We will persist.

More stories

In the past two decades, multiple videos have documented personal reflections and camp narratives. John Culp and the Salkehatchie board produced a DVD, *Salkehatchie: The First Three Years,* featuring the pioneer disciples who shaped the basics of what Salkehatchie Summer Service still is today.

In 2021, John Culp released *Faith in Action: Stories of Salkehatchie Summer Service* (published by the South Carolina United Methodist Advocate Press). This book features narratives from long-time Salkehatchie volunteers and adults who attended camp in their youth. They express the lasting impact that participation in Salkehatchie has had on their lives and faith.

Participation in Salkehatchie has inspired countless works of art and poetry. The crosses left at homes are likely to visually demonstrate the outpouring of love and tenderness from the volunteers.

Salkehatchie leaders are aware that the name of the service, based in the Salkehatchie River area where the first camp was planted, is Native American. As explained in Chapter 4, the translation from the Muskogee (Creek nation) language probably means "Wild Goose Creek." Mindful of cultural appropriation, Salkehatchie leaders sought and received the blessing of United Methodist Native American Ministries. In the early 2000s, Native American leaders conducted a dedication ceremony at Rocky Swamp United Methodist Church in Neeses, South Carolina.

International reach

Starting in 2006, Arlene Andrews and Kathy Hart led several annual Salkehatchie mission groups to Central America, using Salkehatchie and United Methodist Volunteers in Mission guidelines. The trips to Nicaragua and El Salvador took youth to places that broadened their understanding of God's global presence. They built homes from concrete, dug septic systems, led Bible schools for children, visited hospitals, distributed food, and served in other ways guided by the local United Methodist missionaries and their local partners.

Increasing security concerns and then the pandemic interrupted this important mission work. May God open a way for future young people to know the reality of our sisters and brothers to the south.

Based on our lived experiences in Nicaragua, in 2010 we asked home

Above, Britanny Coots, a member of Trinity United Methodist Church in Blythewood, at a Salkehatchie-UMVIM trip to Las Pasquales, Nicaragua, 2010. Below, missioners the Rev. Scott Bratton and Marty Martin dig a septic system at Las Pasquales, 2010.

In Nicaragua, Salkehatchie-UMVIM teams helped to move families from homes like this (above) to homes like this (below).

congregations to join us in this prayer:

We pray ...
... for parents who cannot find jobs or have only seasonal work
... for people who live in communities with limited food, no clean water, unpaved roads, no electricity, poor schools, no health care
... for parents whose children are sick and dying in poorly equipped hospitals with inadequate medical personnel
... for teachers and food service workers who cheerfully work under dire conditions to help children have hope for the future.
We thank God ...
... for El Ayudante bringing food, child protection, health care, schools, jobs, and the Word of God to the people of the Matagalpa region in Nicaragua
... for the privilege of traveling to Nicaragua and the Salkehatchie experience that prepared us for this mission.

Societal changes

Our changing world has affected Salkehatchie Summer Service in other ways, too.

Family needs

In the past few years, the US has seen a crisis, almost everywhere, in affordable housing for renters and homeowners. Salkehatchie is focused on homeowners who live in poverty. According to Habitat for Humanity (2023), housing cost burdens have reached their highest levels in years. Housing cost burden is defined as paying more than 30 percent of income on housing. In 2021, 10.4 percent of all homeowners had housing costs that exceeded half their income. Cost burdens were especially prevalent for homeowners earning less than $30,000 per year, and higher than average for Black, Hispanic and Asian homeowners, as well as those older than age sixty-five.

The burden of trying to afford housing and keep houses repaired is not equitably distributed. The overall poverty rate for South Carolina has come down over the years. According to the US Census data, in 2020 the overall poverty rate in South Carolina was 13.8 percent This is still high; South Carolina ranked forty-second when compared to other states. And the poverty rate varies from one area to another. York County has the lowest rate at 9.7 percent while Allendale County is at 35.4 percent.

The quality of housing where low-income people reside is a continuing problem. The US National Institutes of Health released a report in 2021 with a title that says it all: "Home Is Where the Health Is." Nearly a quarter of the homes in the United States are considered unhealthy or inadequate. Our Salkehatchie experience tells us that fewer people in poverty are living in sturdy homes (as in the early years of Salkehatchie) and more are in homes with relatively fragile construction. In the early years, more homes had no plumbing at all. These days, homes have plumbing, but it does not work because of inability to maintain the system or to pay for water and sewage services.

In short, the need for home repair assistance is greater than ever.

Race relations

Salkehatchie Summer Service was conceived in the 1970s when southerners were in the earliest years of dismantling centuries of racial segregation and degradation. As we discuss in Chapter 4, most of the volunteers were White and most of the homeowners living in poverty were Black. They encountered one another from vastly different worldviews, given their histories.

Race relations have changed considerably in the forty-five years since the beginning. People of all races mingle in most settings. People of color have made significant gains in economic assets. Yet the disparities persist. According to the US Census data, in South Carolina the poverty rate for people who identify as Black only in 2020 was 23.6 percent while the poverty rate for those who identify as White was 9.6 percent. In many geographic areas, segregation still exists in schools, housing, law enforcement, and churches. And Black people are still disproportionately among the populations suffering the effects of poverty.

At Salkehatchie, still, most volunteers identify as White and most homeowners identify as Black.

We have work to do toward unity and equity.

Women leaders

In the early years, most camp directors were men. Now, about half the camp directors are women. This is consistent with changes in general church leadership.

There was a time when participants would remark with surprise at the girl power demonstrated by youth who accomplished challenging construction work. Now, it's no big deal.

Youth culture

Even before the pandemic, fewer youth were participating in Salkehatchie. Several factors probably contributed to this change.

For one, fewer youth (and adults) were participating in church, period. Multiple social science studies are examining this phenomenon, pointing to factors such as reduced direct social connections among youth, church leadership scandals, nonreligious activities, and societal polarization. In many places school schedules have revised attendance patterns so that fewer weeks are available for summer vacation from school, which affects time for camps like Salkehatchie. Youth are pressed to get jobs over shorter summer periods, attend sports and other camps, go on family vacations, and maybe find time for mission work. They must choose priorities.

Salkehatchie is responding by offering more flexible schedules and service opportunities during winter and spring breaks. Some camps are meeting Sundays through Fridays with Saturdays left free.

As general church attendance has shrunk, churches have been less able to support youth ministers. So the core resource for Salkehatchie Summer Service—church youth leaders and youth programs—has suffered a setback. We have faith that the "pipeline" for encouraging youth participation in Salkehatchie will rise again.

Changing church structure

Salkehatchie has always been a United Methodist mission though leaders and participants have often come from many Christian denominations and nondenominational groups. As some Methodist churches have disaffiliated from The United Methodist Church, the Salkehatchie board made it clear that all are welcome.

Cost of serving

Inflation has waxed and waned, but overall the cost of building supplies has risen, in part because of global changes. Lumber is harder to get and more expensive to deliver. Oil products such as shingles are more expensive. Insurance prices have risen as liability claims increase. Thus camp registration fees have increased and fundraising efforts to support Salkehatchie Summer Service have expanded.

Alternative mission opportunities

The field of US-based and international mission opportunities has grown substantially. Many independent organizations offer short-term mission trips within the United States and abroad. Some of these offer the kind of immersion experience that Salkehatchie offers. Others are "mission tourism," more observational and cleaner when compared to work camp missions. Youth and adult volunteers have a menu of possibilities when they choose where to devote their mission commitment.

As discussed in Chapter 4, "How Salkehatchie Summer Service Came to Be," in the beginning Salkehatchie was founded to be an outreach program to help youth understand how their neighbors in South Carolina live in challenging circumstances. International missions and missions to distant parts of the United States are important. However, understanding that people in our immediate vicinity are suffering is critically important for youth development as disciples.

Still, the people come

Society is changing, but the "Send me!" response to God's call is still strong. Youth are still thirsty for the water of the Spirit.

> And let the one who hears say, "Come!" Let the one who is thirsty come; and let the one who wishes take the free gift of the water of life. (Revelation 22:17)

Many of the Salkehatchie adult leaders today were youth volunteers years ago. Often camps have intergenerational families participating. Many camps are formed around a core group of volunteers who see their annual Salkehatchie camp as a meaningful reunion with beloved friends. This is church.

Into the future

Jesus said, "Do not think that I have come to abolish the Law or the

Prophets; I have come not to abolish them but to fulfill them" (Matthew 5:17). That law is eternal. It existed long before Salkehatchie Summer Service and will exist long after. Now and into the future, followers of Jesus Christ are called to love mercy and act justly, to reach out to our neighbors who are poor in spirit and material necessities.

We discuss this call throughout the book and particularly in Chapter 6, "The Ripple Effect: Spreading the Light." Surely, over time, as the light spreads, the world will see less indecent housing, more positive youth development, and a more caring church.

While some aspects of Salkehatchie Summer Service have changed since 2005 when we released this book, most of it is and will be the same. God is good. All the time.

—Arlene Bowers Andrews and the Reverend John Culp
June 2024

Today, as in the past, volunteers are still eager to help.

Preface to the First Edition

Salkehatchie Summer Service says "yes" to life. Salkehatchie asks people to have a heart again. Salkehatchie ministers to the needy, the blind, the handicapped, the forsaken people of our society, and the ones whom Christ called "the least of these."

Our late friend Art Dexter said that if Salkehatchie participants were asked to write our biblical justification for participation in Salkehatchie, most of us would probably mention Matthew 25:35-41 (RSV), "I was hungry and you gave me food, I was thirsty and you gave me drink ... ." Salkehatchie interprets these verses, "My house was in despair and you rebuilt it; my roof leaked and you repaired it; I was depressed and alone and you brought me hope!"

Through Salkehatchie, we go as healers and become aware that the healers need healing, too. Salkehatchie devotes resources such as time, money, young talented lives, and professional adults not where the world says to go, but where Christ says to go. As Scripture says, "God chose what is foolish in the world to shame the wise, God chose what is weak in the world to shame the strong" (1 Corinthians 1:27 RSV).

Salkehatchie is an ongoing love story with a cast of thousands. How does one explain the flow of love we witness every year that transcends culture, age, race, and other obstacles?

Theologically we learn we are powerful people by the grace of God. Thousands of youth and adults have given their lives to create a space for God and to experience a new creation. At Salkehatchie, people face and absorb the pains, distress, decay, and sins of our society. Salkehatchie is a faith ministry in action as these volunteers of Christ go down dirt roads, attempt impossible tasks, work in difficult conditions, and give themselves to be the face, hands, and feet of Christ.

To the Salkehatchie youth, the occupants of the homes, the local churches, the businesses, and the connectional United Methodists of South Carolina, we give thanks.

This book is possible because of those who responded to the call. Now the miracles, stories, encounters with humanity, and the eternal are given to you. May your life be touched by the deep caring Spirit of Christ that inspires all who participate in Salkehatchie Summer Service.

Throughout this book, all descriptions of individuals and settings are based on true experiences. For the sake of privacy, some names have been changed, unless the subject has given permission to use his or her name. In some cases, illustrations of people or places are constructed using composite characteristics drawn from several real persons or situations.

—Rev. John Culp, 2005

Acknowledgments

This project has involved the direct efforts of many people, and we could not possibly mention everyone by name. We do, however, want to mention a few folks who stood by us through this project and gave it special attention. We do not intend to emphasize any one person over another the list below includes volunteers, residents of home sites, community members, church staff, and others. We are one in the Spirit.

First, we are grateful for the bounty in our lives that has given us the privilege of taking the time to pull together the information and write the book. Thank you, God.

And we particularly acknowledge our dear families, who have been our devoted supporters and best book reviewers: Stuart, Emily, and Brook Andrews; Peggy and Wes Culp, and Chris Culp McIntire; and Maxine Dexter—Salkehatchie veterans all. Our loss of Art Dexter's presence, though not his spirit, was particularly hard as we worked our way through the book. Our immediate Salkehatchie family includes Brian Rollins, Melanie Rollins Moore, Jason Moore, and Neil and Patsy Flowers, who believe in us, no matter what.

Austin Watson floated among Salkehatchie camps with Black-and-White film in his camera, capturing clear prints for us. John Liebenrood shared the logo with us. Kathy Hart shared the artwork of her late son, Robert Purcell. Erin Cline, Lauren Jackson, Marcus Sizemore, and Erin Watson worked on interviews, transcripts, and other research for the book while they attended the University of South Carolina. We are grateful to the United Methodist Church, South Carolina Conference, for support throughout the years of Salkehatchie. Recently, Tammy Fulmer, Veronica Williams, and Tameika

Green helped as we wrote this book. In the early years, Ann Walker and Mildred Oseng kept records and gave support. Jack Washington and Clark Jenkins provided coordination. And we thank the five bishops who have served during the history of Salkehatchie thus far: Edward Tullis, Roy Clark, Joseph B. Bethea, Lawrence McCleskey, and Mary Virginia Taylor.

Countless young people cheerfully helped us as we put together stories and pictures. They are the heart of Salkehatchie.

Thousands of family members from homes served by Salkehatchie helped to nurture this book. We had time to get permission from only a few, so on behalf of the others we will mention them: Rose Bostic, Elder Davis, Mrs. Dixon, Nancy Green, Irene Holmes, Annie Lee Miller, Julia and Mrs. Goins, Betty Ann Brown, Rosa Byars, John Chatmond, Lizzie Palmer, and Martha Singleton.

Jo Hood, Vivian Andrews, Maryneal Jones, and Austin Watson read parts of the manuscript and gave us helpful criticism. Ward Bradley gave us great links to adults who were Salkehatchie youth of yesteryear. Rhett Jackson was there for us when we were trying to figure out how to get the book published. Richard and Sara Hagins, John and Anna Timmerman, and Tommy Thompson sent a lot of information about history and reflections.

The Salkehatchie camp directors—laity and clergy—are a special breed of servant leaders who have our deepest respect and love. We cannot name all who have led through the years; there are hundreds. Tommy Wilkes chaired the Salkehatchie Steering Committee during much of the time this book was in development; he was immensely helpful. Several camp leaders tolerated our long interviews and let us follow them around as they performed their work: Bill Brown, Buddy Rutland, Steven Brown, Kent Daniels, Neil Flowers, Michael Henderson, Mimbee Baker, Jerry Kita, Joe and Kathy Jo Long, Steve McCormick, Bart Sistare, Matt Yon, and Jeremy and Jennifer Grainger.

We could have listened to Sister Colie Stokes, Emory Campbell, Fred Reese, Pat Goss, or Mike Vandiver talk about history for days. Our hearts were warmed as we heard Vince and Anna Brawley, Jay Gore, Hart Parker, John Liebenrood and Katie Schultz talk about being youth at Salkehatchie in the early years. Cathy Nelson and Keith Hiott shed light on Salkehatchie from a Native American perspective. Russell Smith and Richard Allen were quick to share their written reflections. And Eben Taylor, forever John's mentor and confidant, has been an inspiration throughout the Salkehatchie journey.

The folks at the Institute for Families in Society at the University of South Carolina, particularly Renee Gibson, Sheila Heatley, Deanie Stevens, Ding Su, Alina Wyatt, and John Stewart, gave technical support as the manuscript came together.

This is a book of many voices and helping hands. We thank you one and all.

—Arlene Bowers Andrews and Rev. John Culp
December 8, 2005

Introduction

Salkehatchie Summer Service is named for a river that flows from its source in the coastal plain of South Carolina to the ocean. Like the river, the service follows a course through time that is influenced by location, people, circumstances, and historical events. This book tries to capture the essence of that course with all its diverse characteristics. The sequence is not chronological like a history, though a historical synopsis is offered in Chapter 4. The story has no beginning and no end, because many of its themes are timeless. Three of us—Arlene, John, and Art—are the primary authors, although the book is filled with many voices. Participants describe their Salkehatchie experiences and reflect on the meaning they have made of it. They share their writings in the forms of stories, prayers, poems, songs, and reflections, as well as their photos and drawings.

This book can have different meanings and uses for various readers. Mostly it's a heartwarming story about how hope happens. As a devotional or educational resource, the book may be read in its entirety or in excerpts as a foundation for group discussions or personal reflection. People of faith seeking to replicate the Salkehatchie experience may rely on this book, but it will be insufficient as a practical guidebook. The only way to really learn Salkehatchie is to do it.

Chapter 1, "More than a Hard Day's Work," introduces the cast of characters involved in Salkehatchie: youth and adult volunteers, families, sending churches, and receiving communities. This mission lifts people from their daily comfort and hassles and places them in a challenging new reality that offers them an opportunity for transformation.

Chapter 2, "Hearts and Homes," introduces the families whose homes we serve. On the surface, Salkehatchie seems to be about fixing old houses. Dig deep, and it is clear Salkehatchie is mostly about repairing and sustaining the spirits of the families and volunteers. Salkehatchie is not just about helping the poor. It is about building relationships among people who have names and life stories: Emily, Ms. Rose, Nathan, Mr. Quick, and so on a thousand times over and over again. In this chapter we created a collage of portraits, using words, depicting representative people from among the many who have made Salkehatchie what it is.

Chapter 3, "A Week: A Moment in Time," provides a context for what happens during a typical week at a Salkehatchie camp. The opening describes the broader environment, with its disparities and injustices, and the call of the church through the social gospel. This chapter addresses pragmatics: how do all the pieces come together to make a Salkehatchie week? The Spirit seems to tap different people in various places, and they all converge to make a miracle. This chapter includes youth perspectives, from signing up to coming home; and adult volunteer perspectives as they balance challenges like finding homes, organizing work, nurturing youth, and managing the budget. Reports from families who live in the homes describe what it's like to anticipate the arrival of the workers and live with them for a week, and then reflect on the experience after they are gone. We hear about how churches prepare the youth and adult volunteers, support them, and learn from them upon their return. And community members illustrate what Salkehatchie has done for the greater community.

Chapter 4, "How Salkehatchie Summer Service Came to Be," examines the history of the program. Salkehatchie emerged in the mid-1970s in the rural Deep South at a time when the church was struggling to bring harmony to communities torn by vestiges of racial segregation, a failing war on poverty, and a nuclear arms race. We tell the story of how founder Rev. John Culp organized adults who believed that young people can change the world. We trace how one camp of forty participants in 1978 became forty-one camps of more than 2,700 participants in the summer of 2004.

Chapter 5, "Making Meaning: Prayers, Poems, Sermons" focuses on the fruits of the work. This chapter includes examples of the reflections Salkehatchie inspires. Here, participants grapple with the raw force of poverty and the healing words of scripture that come to life while the work is done. The expressions of the youth—the "children," as most site families call them—are interspersed with the words of the adults. The selections range from the whimsical to the profound, from heartwarming to heartbreaking.

Chapter 6, "The Ripple Effect: Spreading the Light," describes how participants carry their Salkehatchie experience into their lives and into the world. For this chapter, we interviewed people who participated as volunteers more than twenty years ago and families served in the past. We tell the stories of pastors who received their call at Salkehatchie and couples who married after meeting at a camp. We hear from people who haven't attended a camp in fifteen years but feel its spirit in their daily lives. We put Salkehatchie into the broader context of biblical tradition and world trends, and challenge the reader to help shape the future.

This book was conceived as a celebration, a silver anniversary gift. We offer it as commemoration of what transpired across more than twenty-five years and as a promise for the future. Salkehatchie is still being created. The participants of the future will shape its destiny. Until justice comes, people will live in family homes that disintegrate around them. Until then, Salkehatchie will promote faith and hope, fellowship of the church, and outreach to the world.

Jesus calls us to minister to the hungry, the naked, the strange, the sick, and the imprisoned. We know God wants Christians to do the kind of things we do at Salkehatchie. We don't understand why the world is the way it is, or how, each year, miracles seem to happen. We may not always know how to do what we need to do, but we know God knows. So we say, "Here we are, Lord. Send us."

A Salkehatchie Prayer
Art Dexter

We pray for people
Who keep pictures of Jesus and Martin Luther
    King on their smoky walls,
Who look on the bright side, though we can't
    see why,
Who love the Lord,
Whose smiles and laughs touch our hearts,
Who have faith we'll return after tearing off
    their roof,
Who wave at us with tears in their eyes when
    we depart,
Who never forget us.

And we pray for those
Who bathe in a dishpan
Who listen to the rats in their walls at night,
Whose toilet is a slop jar,
Who share a house with eleven others,
Who look at the outside world through the holes
    in their walls,
Whose children eat grits with their fingers from a
    communal bowl.

And we pray for those
Who don't have enough pans to catch the roof
    leaks,
Who sleep with a knife beside their beds,
Who "pass it on" and abuse their children,
Who in their old age care for abandoned "grands,"
Who have no one to lend a hand,
Who farm their children out in winter to friends
    with heat,
Who live in homes we wouldn't be caught dead in.

And we pray for those
Who have outlived family and friends,
Who work on plantations all day and never see
    their children till night,
Whose bodies are broken like communion bread,
Who never get medical care,
Who struggle as single parents,
Whose children's greatest treat is going to lunch
    with us,
Who never had a White friend,
Who go to bed hungry.

And we pray for those
Who work by our side in heat and filthy conditions,
Who serve the crippled, blind, elderly, palsied,
    and intellectually disabled,
Who help us see we're one in Christ,
Who shed tears and share hugs at evening
    reflections,
Whose own families are not without problems,
Who delight in learning to toenail and use a
    circular saw,
Who build sandboxes and rope swings for children,
And smother them with love.

Chapter 1

More than a Hard Day's Work

When Bryan's crew arrived at Ms. Mattie's house, they were amazed at what they saw. The house and shed were covered with crosses. Outside, there were crosses made of twigs, branches, and scraps of wood and vinyl. Inside, the crosses were of paper, straw, sticks, anything. They were tacked on, stuck with tape, fastened in many ways.

Bryan said, "Ms. Mattie, we can fix your house, but we'll have to take down your crosses, and I don't think we can replace them just the way they are."

Ms. Mattie smiled and replied, "That's okay. I put them up to mark my prayers. When the rain fell on my head in the house, I would pray to the Lord for help. Then I would put up a cross. When the freezing wind blew through my walls in winter, I would say a prayer and put up a cross. Now you have come. I won't need these crosses anymore."

"They won't understand." That's what Rev. John Culp, founder of Salkehatchie Summer Service, tells the volunteers at camp. He says, "When you go back home, the people there aren't going to understand what you did here and what Salkehatchie is all about." Those of us who have been to Salkehatchie for many years still don't understand, at least not fully. Understanding implies that we've extracted the meaning, and it's clear and finished, somehow.

But nothing about Salkehatchie is ever really finished. It's like the world we live in. God's not finished with this creation yet.

Kurt Vonnegut included a creation story in one of his novels that went something like this: God created heaven and earth, and when he was done, he wanted someone to witness what he'd done. So he reached down, pinched off a piece of clay, formed it into the shape of a man, and breathed life into it. And then God said to the little man, "Look what I've created!" The little man looked all around and said, "Wow! It's great, Lord! But what's it all about?" God replied, "I'll let you figure that out," and he walked away, leaving the little man alone.

Without faith, we could experience the same fate—wandering around, wondering what life is all about, feeling rebuffed by a presumed vain and uncaring creator. Experiences like Salkehatchie reveal a profound truth—we are not alone and God will guide us to figure it out.

It is difficult to explain the Salkehatchie experience and why it exerts such a powerful influence in so many lives. We yearn for the confidence of Mother Teresa of Calcutta, who, in a life of faith and good works, offered a brighter perspective on what life is about. She simply asserted, "This is the true reason for our existence: To be the sunshine of God's love, to be the hope of eternal happiness. That's all." We believe each person, during his or her time on the planet, can find a way from that dazed and confused state to the bliss of solidarity with God.

Salkehatchie Summer Service, a mission of the South Carolina Conference of The United Methodist Church, brings together teen and adult church volunteers with families from the poorest communities in the state for a week of hard work rebuilding homes and spirits. Week after week, in many communities, Salkehatchie workers gather on Saturday, divide into home site teams, worship and build community on Sunday, and spend sunup to sundown Monday through Friday tearing down broken structures and building new ones, taking time for worship and reflection. Along the way, the families share their wisdom and gifts and forge bonds with the workers. As the houses are repaired, the workers and families feel healing in their own lives.

Somehow, Salkehatchie Summer Service helps young people on the journey from confusion to solidarity with God. Over and over we asked youth volunteers, "When you tell other kids about Salkehatchie, what do you say?" And they responded, "I just say it's awesome. You can't put it into words. You have to do it." Words in print cannot capture the fullness of the experience of being immersed—body, mind, and soul. You have to be there, at a

Salkehatchie home site, to feel it, smell it, move through it, hear it, taste it, and see it to begin to comprehend it. Still, we've been at this for more than twenty-eight years, and we feel called to tell the story, to create a record of what has been and hopefully to inspire others toward what can be.

> I expected to work hard and give of myself. What I didn't expect is how much the families would give me.

—Vince Brawley, 2004, who served as a youth, 1978–1984

What is Salkehatchie?

In 1978, a group of forty United Methodists, most of them between the ages of fourteen and eighteen, left their comfortable pews and stepped into the lives of four families affected by some of the worst poverty in America. While restoring dilapidated houses on the Sea Islands of South Carolina, they discovered their lives transformed by the gifts of grace from the families who lived there. The feeling was mutual; the families at the home sites were awed by the love of the volunteers. That small group inspired a contagious movement. In the summer of 2002, the twenty-fifth anniversary year, the South Carolina Conference of The United Methodist Church sponsored thirty-six Salkehatchie Summer Service camps involving 2,396 adult and youth missioners at 216 homes. Each year, the youth live together in camps for seven days, working in small groups at family homes by day, and sharing reflections and building community by night. By 2006, there were forty-one camps, including camps in North Carolina and Georgia, with more than 2,700 volunteers, and for the first time, a team of 18 Salkehatchie veterans went abroad for a work week at El Ayudante in León, Nicaragua.

Salkehatchie is similar to other intensive youth missions that involve teamwork, hard labor, and spiritual reflections. Still, when participants talk to people who have not gone on missions, it's hard to say just what Salkehatchie is like. People say, "Salkehatchie? Isn't that like Habitat?" Many of us have also worked at Habitat for Humanity. No, it is not the same. At Habitat sites, things are clean, walls are plumb, workers are somewhat skilled, the work is planned and organized, and the families have steady incomes. Probably the only similarity is that at Salkehatchie, we are also grounded in faith. Habitat founder Millard Fuller calls it the "theology of the hammer."

At Salkehatchie, we use a lot of lumber, roofing shingles, and power tools. Otherwise, we begin with major demolition. The homes are almost always a mess. Workers are primarily young; they are earnest but easily distracted. Some site leaders have no formal training or experience with building construction, and the work proceeds according to necessity and whim. The families are among the poorest of the poor, that is, those who cannot afford monthly house payments. The process at Salkehatchie sites looks and feels more chaotic than at Habitat sites, but by week's end, stability and order emerge. The main difference, though, is that each Salkehatchie home has a history. As the youth work, the house reveals—and the families share—bits and pieces of their stories, so the youth come to know them in

Salkehatchie sites are homes, first.

familiar ways.

Some people call Salkehatchie Summer Service a youth camp. This conjures images of teens singing songs around a campfire, playing cooperative games, and engaging in heavy dialogue about curriculum-based topics. Well, it isn't like that. Is it community service learning?[1] Salkehatchie does promote civic engagement and social responsibility, those hallmarks of civilized democratic societies. We see youth develop self-efficacy, leadership, and a clearer sense of their own futures, which are known to be effects of service learning. Youth often get credit for community service through Salkehatchie, but it's not designed for that. Unlike certain civic service, though, no one can be required or even expected to attend Salkehatchie; the participation must be truly voluntary. Young people don't participate in Salkehatchie because they are supposed to, they participate because they want to.

Salkehatchie could be classified as experiential education, which is an approach to learning based on the student's discovery by doing, rather than receiving instruction. Young people from predominantly suburban middle-class homes learn about poverty, aging, race, rural life, and how to work with their hands. But no one has articulated these educational goals or created a system to assure that these students learn the lessons. At Salkehatchie, young people lead by identifying and creating solutions. They try on new skills, relationships, and values. They share their new knowledge and beliefs with one another. The week is filled with teachable moments, as insight passes from youth to youth, adult to youth, youth to adult, and so on.

Is Salkehatchie about Christian character education? Yep. Could Salkehatchie be a mission? Not if that means people who "have" reach out and touch people who "have not." Sure, most of the workers at Salkehatchie have toilets that flush and roofs that don't leak, but many have not the unwavering faith or wisdom of many of the people we come to serve. Those who have and those who have not quickly become blended at Salkehatchie. Those who come to give always receive. Likewise, those who receive the service of home repair usually give all they can. It is a mission of mutual support.

Salkehatchie is definitely church, albeit without the conventions of

---

1. A. W. Astin et al., *How Service Learning Affects Students* (Los Angeles: UCLA Higher Education Research Institute, 2000).

liturgy, preaching, proper dress, or sanctuary. The most inspirational speaker of the week may lead with "Lately, I don't know what I believe about Jesus … " and follow with a profound reflection that helps all on their journeys to closer relationships with Jesus. At this church, young people explore their faith with each other, in their own language, both in organized settings and informal conversation. They feel safe expressing emotions. They cry, laugh, argue, hug, and show fear, bravery, confidence, doubt, and humility. What

> Salkehatchie is an ongoing love story with a cast of thousands.
>
> —*Art Dexter*

many young adults remember most about their teen Salkehatchie experience is their late-night talks with one another. They build bonds of Christian community that can last a lifetime.

Salkehatchie Summer Service is an autonomous mission supported entirely by its participants, the communities it serves, and the South Carolina Conference of The United Methodist Church. It aims to reach families in need who live not in distant lands but in neighborhoods and communities near the volunteers who serve. Salkehatchie creates experiences for youth to discover their own faith and to share faith while accomplishing good works. It takes people out of their comfort zones and thrusts them into alternative life spaces. The implicit theory of learning at Salkehatchie starts with the premise that for sustained learning to happen, participants must have autonomy and be able to make spontaneous discoveries about themselves and the world. Adult and youth participants dive in with minimal instruction and develop substantial trust in one another. They place heavy confidence in the Holy Spirit. Given that most adult volunteers are not experts about house renovations or family concerns, the skills and problem-solving capacities of youth come to the fore. Their responsibility is critical and they have stature rarely achieved in other settings of their lives where adults rule. At Salkehatchie, youth are treated as human beings, not human becomings whose full worth is yet to be recognized.

The values of Salkehatchie began in the early years, when the adults, youth, and families simply discovered and implemented them. They derive from the essence of John Culp, whom many regard as Salkehatchie's prophetic founder and ever-present shepherd. Some say John doesn't have a clue how to fix plumbing or roofing rafters but will doggedly try anyway. He does have a knack for finding people who do know how to do the job and convincing them that God needs them to do it. John humbly and powerfully attends to the spirits of the volunteers while they diligently try to keep him from getting hurt or breaking something. This is the playful way love gets expressed, with the result being amazing expression of confidence and ability by the youth.

Founder John Culp.

Over the years, various Salkehatchie camps have replicated the creation of opportunities for spontaneity and discovery through subtle structure, servant leadership, and a few simple guiding principles. Each year in camps at various sites, among all the diverse groups involved, we see spiritual, social, moral, and life skills developed, sometimes by leaps and bounds.

In 1977, John presented a proposal to the South Carolina Conference of The United Methodist Church for resources to support a "Work Camp Project" for this purpose: "To provide a group missional experience for youth." What an understatement! When we tell you what Salkehatchie is, keep in mind that behind the words lives a mystery that cannot be fully understood. We perceive this mystery and feel it in our hearts and have faith that it is of God, full of love. Most of us call it "grace," like John Wesley did.

The People of Salkehatchie

While Salkehatchie is about building family homes, it's also about building church—that is, promoting faith, community, and outreach to the world. The experience builds community among people whose lives seem different on the surface. In The United Methodist Church, we speak of our unity within our diversity. Salkehatchie week brings together people whose lives may never cross otherwise because their typical life spaces are segregated and different. Each participant is special but representative.

The youth

It's summer. Justin, a rising tenth grader, wakes up about ten-thirty in the morning to the sound of music that has played all night from the computer on his desk. His room, all his own, is filled with his stuff: a guitar, two amps, a skateboard he rarely uses, books, magazines, posters, art supplies, handheld games, scattered clothes, leftover food, an old boom box, and a CD player. He stretches his arm across the bed and feels around until he finds his cell phone. He calls his friend. "Whazzup?" They agree to meet in an hour. He rolls out of bed, shivers from the chill of the air conditioning, wanders to the kitchen, and gets aggravated after rummaging through the boxes of cereal and breakfast toaster treats because the kind he likes is all gone. "There's never anything to eat in this house," he grumbles. He finds a note his mom left before she went to work: "Mow the lawn!" No way, he says to himself. It's too hot today.

An active participant in his church's youth fellowship, Justin lives in a middle-class suburb with his mom, stepdad, and two younger sisters. A White person with English and Scottish roots, he's a good student at a racially integrated school. He plays on the school's golf team, although his mom is upset that his matches are often scheduled on Sunday morning. He knows Christ calls Christians to reach out to poor people. He's gone on CROP walks to raise money for hungry people and wrapped packages at Christmas for children in faraway lands. He's seen videos about starving children in Somalia and Iraq. He's also heard adults and friends talk about people in America who rip off the welfare system and refuse to work like everybody else. Sometimes, on the way to the beach or to golf matches out of town, he sees shacks alongside the road, but he never really thinks about

> "Sony's smallest Walkman: Can you live without it?"
>
> —*On the cover of STUFF magazine, April 2003*

the people who live there.

Three months ago, a car wreck killed a friend of Justin's and put his cousin, Brent, in a wheelchair; they don't know if Brent will walk again. Brent's accident shattered Justin's view of the world as a safe place. But now that the shock has passed, Justin tries not to think too much about it. He's a pretty happy-go-lucky guy. He's got lots of friends, and they talk to each other about life. He stays connected to the world through the Internet. He e-mails Brent, who lives in another state. He tries to watch a movie a day in the summer, to catch up on what he misses during the school year. Except for people like his mom, stepdad, and teachers always trying to tell him what to do, and some nagging concerns about car wrecks, he knows he's got a pretty good life. Justin knows God is watching over him, and sometimes he prays, mostly before a test or golf tournament, and of course, at church. Justin heard about Salkehatchie from friends at church and decided to go this year; it sounds like fun. The older youth were so excited when they returned last year, they couldn't stop talking about it. Something in his heart tells him he should go. And it will get him away from his parents' hassling for a while.

The family

Mrs. Sandra Chapman, known to her neighbors as "Ms. Sallie," rises before dawn every day, which has been her habit throughout her seventy-seven years of life. In the summer, she tries to finish her chores before the intense heat of midday, when she rests near her box fan. For the past thirty years, Mrs. Chapman has lived in the middle of a tobacco field. Her husband's lifelong employer, who owned a farm, deeded the old wood frame house and an acre of land to her. Mr. Chapman worked as a tobacco hand

and supervisor of pickers, and performed odd jobs on the farm until his death. Mrs. Chapman cleaned houses and sat with elderly people until her arthritis and diabetes got so bad that she couldn't do the work. Some weeks, Mrs. Chapman worked around the clock for five or six days at a time. The Chapmans raised four children, two of whom have survived. One died in Vietnam, and one had complications from sickle cell anemia. A son, who has a serious alcohol addiction and has been in and out of prison, lives with Mrs. Chapman. Her daughter lives up north with her family and visits at Christmas.

Jobs are hard to find in their rural county, which has an 18 percent unemployment rate. Various grandchildren, both teenagers and young adults, stay with Mrs. Chapman for weeks at a time, but they mostly make a mess, according to her. Since Mr. Chapman died four years ago, Mrs. Chapman can no longer maintain the house. The roof leaks everywhere; she catches the water in pots. The house has no running water, just a pump outside the back door, and an old rotting outhouse about fifteen yards from the house. Friends from Mrs. Chapman's church give her rides to places she needs to go, and the Medicaid van takes her to doctor's appointments. She can't afford a telephone, but a neighbor about a half-mile down the road shares hers.

Mrs. Chapman, who is African American, lived her first forty years under strict segregation. In those days, she and her husband could not register to vote, could not get a loan from a bank, and could not rely on the sheriff for protection. They didn't eat out often, because most places would not serve them, but sometimes they stood in line at the back door to pick up barbeque from the place that served White folks at tables inside. And she and her neighbors always had their church picnics. She was happy when civil rights came, and she has pictures of the Reverend Martin Luther King Jr. and President John Kennedy on her wall, alongside Jesus.

Mrs. Chapman never knew any White youth when she was young. Later, young people came and went in the houses where she worked, but they never seemed to notice her except to occasionally ask her to do a task. No White people have ever been inside Mrs. Chapman's house, except the owner of the farm. Mrs. Chapman likes to watch TV, but she doesn't have cable and sometimes her antenna reception is weak. She loves to crochet and sings hymns to herself throughout the day. Friends say she is the best cook in the county.

One day, a man and a woman knock on her door and say they are from a church. They ask if she needs help on her house, and tears spring to her eyes.

The adult volunteer

Thomas, a thirty-five-year-old accountant, arises earlier than usual in the weeks before he goes to Salkehatchie. He has extra work to do to be sure his office will run smoothly when he leaves for a whole week. Well, it takes more than a week, really. It takes about two days to gather up all the tools and equipment, make a supply run through the hardware store, pick up first aid, snacks, and other supplies, pack clothes, personal and "just-in-case" items, and load the truck. It will take a day upon return from Salkehatchie to do all the laundry, clean the gear, and put everything away. He knows he needs to have everything in order ahead of time so the home site crew can hit the ground running when the work begins. He needs to be sure to spend extended time with his young children and wife before he leaves. He was hoping his wife could come with him this year, but she cannot be away for a whole week. He knows she'll be praying and eager to hear his stories when he returns. And Thomas's nephew is going, although Thomas's brother won't be coming. His nephew told his dad, "It's time to stop making excuses. Next year make a plan to get away, and let's go."

Thomas has been a site leader for eight years, so he looks at the list of reminders he made for himself last year: "Bring some devotional books that the young people can use to prepare for site devotionals. Bring a blank notebook so they can keep a journal." And so on. Overseeing the young people's group dynamics, faith development, and work can be quite a challenge. Last year, he hardly got to know the family at his site because he spent so much time under the house doing plumbing. This year he'll organize things differently so he can be sure to reach out to the family. And, of course, there's the house to be repaired.

Thomas feels quite confident about his carpentry skills, but last year the house mostly needed plumbing, and he had to learn as he worked, teaching a young person at the same time. He's been praying for patience. He's not a regular youth counselor, and he knows that Salkehatchie is about helping the young people to lead and do the work, but it's hard for him to step

Roofers in the rafters.

back while they do a job slowly that he could do in no time. He's learned a lot over the years about how creative the youth can be and how splendid the finished product can be, even when he doesn't instruct them every step of the way. The young people's perspectives on what they are doing always touch him. They seem to be goofing off half the day, but the work gets done, and in the evening, they have the most profound things to say! He's glad that Mary Tyson will be an adult leader on his crew, because she seems to know how to encourage the youth to reflect on their experiences and share devotionals in the morning. She can't hammer a nail worth a hoot, but she sure knows how to get the youth to do it!

The church

The Rev. Doris Millard has never directly participated in Salkehatchie, but at least six youth from her church and a volunteer youth counselor attend each year. She knows its value as a mission of The United Methodist Church. Since the time of John and Charles Wesley, Methodists have been

> Some of the worst poverty, the poverty of spirit, is in America's middle class.
>
> —*John Culp*

known for putting their faith into action. When people join the church, they agree to "accept the freedom and power God gives you to resist evil, injustice, and oppression in whatever forms they present themselves" (United Methodist Baptismal Covenant I). Salkehatchie is one way the church helps youth and adults put this belief into action.

In the winter, when the time for Salkehatchie registration arrives, Reverend Millard makes sure all youth receive an application, and she creates a time during a worship service when adult and youth veterans can share their experiences and encourage youth and adults to apply to serve. She hopes one day her church will be large enough to support a youth minister, who can help reach more young people with the Salkehatchie experience. The volunteers register as a group for a camp located across the state. The youth cook and serve spaghetti suppers on the first Wednesday of each month to raise money for their registration fees. The church's finance committee sets aside funds to help as well. The youth Sunday school teacher plans a lesson on Jesus's call to minister to the poor and Dietrich Bonhoeffer's vision of life together in Christian fellowship. A women's circle stocks first aid kits for each volunteer with antibiotic cream, bandages, sunscreen, and insect repellent. An adult Sunday school class prepares notecards with prayers for each volunteer to take to the camp. The worship committee plans a "Salkehatchie Sending" time during a service in late May, to recognize the volunteers who will be going forth as missionaries during the summer. Reverend Millard calls for prayer each week in support of the Salkehatchie workers throughout the state. Reverend Millard also prays earnestly for those church members who just don't understand it, those who seem to avoid coming on youth Sunday and to Salkehatchie services.

When the volunteers return, the church devotes an entire worship hour to the testimony about Salkehatchie, which is shared in pictures, songs, stories, and prayers. The young people bring back a fresh image of God. The church feels uplifted and renewed by what is shared.

The community

Long before the summer, during the cold winter months, Yvette Jacobs, a home health worker at the county health department, prepares a list of families who might need help from Salkehatchie when the camp comes to their community. She talks to colleagues in the schools and at the welfare department, and meets with Rev. Christopher Jones at the local United Methodist church to go over the list. They talk often by phone with their community's Salkehatchie camp director, who lives a hundred miles away. The camp director comes with other adult volunteers three times during the year to visit homes and select the sites. Sometimes they drive along country roads and if they see a house that looks like a "Salkehatchie house," they stop and introduce themselves. They talk with the family about its needs, assess the extent of damage to the house, and gain assurances that no one other than the resident or a family member owns or is responsible for repairing the home. With time and prayer, the list of "maybe" houses becomes a "will do" list. When the final list is complete, the camp leaders seem to know in their hearts where they should go.

Yvette talks to the local school superintendent to get the paperwork in place so that the camp can stay at the school. There are only three showers for each gender, and there will be about forty-five males and the same number of females, so they'll have to be quick! She talks to the mayor to get access to the town warehouse; throughout the year, the town allows items of furniture and building supplies to be stored there for Salkehatchie. She checks with her friend Ralph, a building contractor. He has already contacted area businesses and building supply stores, who are eager to help by offering discounts. A member of Reverend Jones's church volunteers to coordinate meals, and calls churches in the area to see if they will take turns providing meals for the ninety-five camp participants. Churches from the Methodist, Baptist, AME Zion, Catholic, and Presbyterian denominations sign on. The United Methodist Women gather donated paint and brushes, and arrange for free ice from the local soft drink distributor. The Men's Club members plan a hearty cookout for Friday night, when the home sites are finished. One church circle prepares eight large first aid kits, one for each site. The community is ready for Salkehatchie to come.

For one week each year, these people, and scores of others like them, will come together. They form the cast of characters at each camp. Somehow, this convergence in time and place produces transformations in personal faith, church, and community.

The work at hand

Ostensibly, Salkehatchie Summer Service is about fixing houses. We know, though, that the roofs we repair will eventually crumble again, and the houses will fall apart. But the family's memory of the love that was shared will last forever and be passed from one generation to another. And the lessons the youth learn about the spirit of humankind in the face of oppression and how faith can make a difference will stay with them throughout their lives.

The physical structures

Salkehatchie generally serves only families who own homes, because landlords are legally responsible for their rental property. Sometimes the landlord is so poor that the camp works on her or his house and the rental unit, too. Occasionally camps will work on rental property if the landlord agrees not to raise the rent. Otherwise, the house will stay in disrepair, because the landlord who must borrow large amounts of money to repair homes must have enough rental income to cover the loan repayment. Poor tenants could never pay the difference, so the landlords opt to leave things as they are. If codes were enforced, some landlords would simply evict the tenant and stop renting the property. Salkehatchie is about helping people have a decent and affordable place to live, so they arrange what they can with homeowners.

The houses include a range of structures. Most are simple frame structures with wood siding. Some are so rickety you can see the ground beneath the floorboards and the sky through the wallboards. Others, incredibly sturdy with frames of huge logs laid more than a century ago to make a tenant farmer's shack, could be listed on the National Registry of Historic Places. The cinder block houses are like large roach hotels; they seem to retain moisture and attract pests. Some structures are the standard brick ranch houses built in the 1960s. Others are fragile mobile homes. Some

> Before I came to Salkehatchie, I thought of poverty as an abstract idea.
> Now, poverty has names and faces.
> There's a story in each face.
>
> —*Austin Watson, camp director*

owners built their houses haphazardly over many years, one room at a time, with bits and pieces of leftover materials acquired from building sites. Most of the structures are too small for the service they have given. They often include two-bedroom houses where a family raised seven or eight children. They rarely have built-in closets or sufficient storage capacity.

The houses have been acquired in various ways. Perhaps a couple bought or is buying the home by mortgage over many years. Some houses have been deeded by White landowners to longtime African American tenants who worked their farms, or houses have been given as a life interest to those who reside there. Sometimes the house is owned outright by direct inheritance from a parent or spouse. One lady lived in a house that was a wedding present from her father in the 1940s.

Another lived in an old World War II barracks that had been moved to her rural property. In some cases, the structure is "heirs' property," owned by several descendants of someone long deceased. Poor people rarely have wills, so when they die, any interest they have in real property is divided among their descendants. When this process is repeated over multiple generations, identifying who has rights to the property and resolving conflicting interests can be highly complex. Some heirs' property can be traced back to the deeds that were granted to freed slaves after emancipation.

Most of the houses need basic infrastructure work, including repairs to roofs, rafters, ceilings, floors, joists, plumbing (including major drainage and sewer work), electrical wiring, exterior siding, doors, windows, and steps. Some houses have settled too much and must be jacked up so that the foundation can be properly aligned. Rarely is the basic structure plumb, that is, level or aligned at right angles. The foundation must be redone for some houses. For example, one house should have had about fifteen supports in the foundation; it was built with only five. Amazingly, it was still standing, though the entire frame twisted and the roof was about to collapse. Salkehatchie volunteers become adept at using car jacks and hydraulic jacks to lift houses and insert new foundations.

Some houses need a room added on, such as a bathroom or bedroom. Many have rotten or broken windows and doors. Even in 2006, in the richest country in the world, some houses have water only from an outside spring or well and an outhouse for a toilet. Some have no toilet facilities at all, just buckets and trees beyond the house. Occasionally people live in houses that have never been wired for electricity. Many houses have faulty or insufficient wiring. Most families have no air conditioning and need a nice porch, preferably one that is screened, to provide relief from the steamy summers. Older houses are drafty and need insulation and weather-proofing (such as storm windows) to keep people warm and heating costs down in winter. Many homes need to be adapted for wheelchair accessibility, including adding ramps, widening doorways, installing support bars, creating low shelves, and moving walls.

Salkehatchie homes sometimes suffer the effects of years of hoarding things that might one day be useful. These things form piles until they are so thick they impair movement through the house and become a haven for vermin, mold, and other health hazards. Sometimes the home needs closets, shelving, or a way to create order. Families on limited incomes find waste disposal services to be simply too expensive. One youth observed, "Their front yard, they had, like, eighty bags of garbage. They had nowhere to put it. It was a massive amount of trash inside and outside the house." The yard may be cluttered with the carcasses of rusted cars and appliances. Family members are particularly pleased when the site crew assists with new functional appliances, cleaning and organizing, and cheerful painting.

The families have many stories about how they reached the point where they could not maintain the houses themselves. Some people might wonder why the families stay in what could be called squalor. It's because their houses are their homes, the places where they have roots. The houses feel familiar, even with all their problems. To leave would be to give up a part of themselves, even if other affordable options were available, which is rare.

And so they stay. They make adaptations to make a place livable, although by the time Salkehatchie gets there, their patience is often frayed. As Ms. Mattie told us, "I heard a sound—it was the refrigerator cracking through the floor—and I said, 'Lord, how much more can I take?'"

Low-income homeowners simply cannot afford to keep up their properties and cannot afford to pay back home improvement loans. Many families built or renovated their own homes when they were able, sometimes working with scraps of lumber and building materials that they found or were given as they worked on construction crews. For years, they did their own painting, repairs, and upkeep. Sometimes, they paid the lowest amount possible and received shoddy services, as when a man paid to have his roof replaced, and the installers aligned the shingles in straight lines—a pretty, albeit leaky, grid. We often discover mistakes made during plumbing or wiring installation. The families cannot afford termite treatments, so they suffer infestations and the wood crumbles.

In many cases, the family members have developed frailties associated with old age and can no longer do extensive manual labor. Their adult children may live far away, or have disabilities themselves and cannot do the work. In other cases, they are single mothers or young adults with physical or mental disabilities that restrict their capacities to do manual labor. Each year, several of the families we help are comprised of grandmothers rearing

Wall waiting for whitewash.

multiple grandchildren; they don't have the energy to do the heavy work of house repair. Some family members know how to do the work and are willing but have no tools. In all cases, the cost of materials is beyond their reach on their meager incomes. These problems can seem insurmountable. Without help, they would be.

The faces of poverty

Most families have shown remarkable creativity and resilience in coping with the decline of their environment. We have worked in homes where the broom was worn to stubble on the concrete floor as the owner tried relentlessly to keep the place clean. Many families still sweep their dirt yards, a custom gone from most communities since irrigation and chemicals allowed the spread of lawns. Good old versatile duct tape covers window cracks, welds broken pipes, patches floor linoleum, secures walls and ceilings, and holds doorknobs in place. The pots and bowls placed to catch rain leaks can appear artistically arranged. They sometimes even sound musical. Cinder blocks prop wrecked steps and brace falling walls. When tacked to a roof, tin plates from TV dinners can help stop leaks. Neighbors allow cords from their homes to provide occasional electricity to the house next door, and hoses run from one house to another for water. Even though managing a house that is falling apart requires constant work, many families handle the challenge with remarkable good cheer.

Many homes are occupied by elderly people who live on fixed incomes and cope with frailties associated with aging. They have suffered strokes, heart attacks, kidney disease, cancer, respiratory problems, crippling arthritis, or mobility limitations. Most have Social Security and Medicare and get by as best they can.

It can be hard to tell just who lives at a house.[2] Extended family members come and go, staying for a few days or weeks at a time. Generally at least one person or couple are the primary residents of a house. Most families happily share their space, but some elderly family members have told us they feel their house is a dumping ground for their younger kin's possessions.

Like the houses, many of the families have wounds, scars, and perhaps even damage to their very foundations. While many families demonstrate strength in the face of adversity, Salkehatchie volunteers inevitably see the

---

2. The families tend to say, "stays at."

harsh cruelty of problems commonly associated with poverty. These include:

Fatherless homes

Single motherhood is common across all income groups in the United States, but in middle class families, often a father provides financial or emotional support, even if he lives apart. In poor families, single moms are likely to be on their own, because the dads are often dead broke or moved away. Many are in prison. We often see multiple generations of families with moms, grandmas, and great-grandmas living in the same household.

Chronic physical health problems and disabilities

Many families have members with serious disabilities. Some are developmental, as was the case for Dottie, a twenty-one-year-old who lived with her mother in an old mobile home with broken sewage pipes, four kerosene heaters, and mildew everywhere. Dottie could not see, hear, talk, or move. She spent her days at an adult day care center while her mom worked.

Young poor people, especially men, must often work in dangerous jobs. They run the risk of work-related injuries or disabilities, like the man who was blinded at a local sawmill. Others suffer financial problems precipitated by health crises.

Mental illness

Families will often tell you that a member has a problem with "nerves" or is "not right in the head." People with chronic, serious mental disorders like schizophrenia may end up in poverty, sometimes dependent on another family member. Poverty commonly causes depression, and having a depressive disorder can cause someone to lose the will to work, so they go into poverty. It's a vicious cycle.

Intellectual disability

Adults with mild intellectual disability typically work in minimum wage jobs with no hope of advancement, or they live on disability income. They sometimes own homes given to them by family members or parents, but have no wherewithal to do the upkeep.

Educational and employment challenges

Many family members are unable to work or cannot find work for which they are qualified. Employment affects family lives in many ways. Often younger family members have moved far away, where more jobs can be found, leaving older family members home alone. Perhaps when they left, the elder was capable, but over time their health has deteriorated, and they need help with the house. The younger family members are often unable to come because of lack of transportation, work demands, and needs of other family members.

Alcohol abuse

Too often, someone who lives in or near the home clearly has a drinking problem. This is evident by the stench of alcohol, the piles of beer cans in the yard, or the person's groggy behavior. We can often detect the psychological effects of addiction by the chaos in the physical environment.

Drug abuse

Drug use is sometimes less obvious, but often we learn about what is going on. A family member may tell us someone at the house has a dope problem, or the community police officer mentions it. Sometimes we find drug paraphernalia. At one site, volunteers found crystals of crack cocaine in the cottage of a military veteran with post-traumatic stress disorder. We sometimes can smell the acrid presence of marijuana. And we see people who stay in the shadows or on the sidelines as the work goes on. We also meet people effectively on the road to recovery who are actively recruiting

> Salkehatchie is raw.
>
> —*Neil Flowers, camp director*

others to do the same.

Crime

Some homes are occupied by families whose primary wage earner is in prison. At one home, the young mother of a tiny child was trying to keep a regular job after working for several years as a prostitute. During Salkehatchie week at another home, a young adult family member stabbed and killed her drug dealer.

Family violence

Some families are referred by the Department of Social Services Child Protective Services, the county agency that tries to help parents learn to care for their children without beating or neglecting them. At some homes, women disclose how they fear their boyfriend or husband because they have been beaten. Sometimes they are trying to fix up their home after escaping from a violent relationship.

The Spirit responds

The youngest volunteers, who have heard about poverty's harshness but have rarely encountered its reality, are sheltered by the older volunteers, who help them process their responses to what they are seeing and learning. They learn that the families are not defined by the problems they have. They learn, for example, that Joseph is not just a "drunk." He is a witty, caring auto mechanic who loves his children but also has a drinking problem. By getting to know the families and respecting their dignity, the volunteers learn that people may have life circumstances that are unlovely, and they may have been unloved, yet they are not unlovable.

Salkehatchie volunteers come not to cure problems, but simply to share love and compassion. When the families feel their love, they sometimes are moved to take a step toward managing their problems differently.

Sometimes, early in the week, the less experienced volunteers express their dismay and judgment about the condition of the home. They feel disgusted that people live under such conditions. They imply that some family members are not worthy. Experienced volunteers listen to these concerns with patience, and help the new volunteers be open to understanding and loving without judgment. By week's end, their tone has typically changed. We come not to judge, but to serve. Everyone is worthy of God's love.

The volunteers also gain a personalized appreciation of problems that they sometimes know only in the abstract. After all, they must ponder such questions as:

> *"What would I do if my best buddy got blown up in war? How would I feel when I got home and he wasn't around anymore? Would I use drugs to dull the pain?"*

> "What would I do if I had mild retardation and two children to raise while my husband served time in prison, particularly if I had been sexually abused as a child and never wanted to see my own family again?"
>
> "What would I do if I don't even know who my father is, and my mom is an alcoholic, and my grandmother, who raised me, had a stroke?"
>
> "What would if do I work on my farm all the time, 24/7, but have no health insurance, and then have a massive heart attack and pile up a half-million dollars in bills and then my house burns, but I have no house insurance?"

The volunteers often don't understand. We leave with more questions than answers. We do, though, gain a richer comprehension of the teachings of our faith. Luke 4:18-21 tells of Jesus speaking at the Temple, reading from Isaiah:

> The spirit of the Lord is upon me, because he has anointed me to proclaim good news to the poor. He has sent me to proclaim freedom for the prisoners and recovery of sight for the blind, to set the oppressed free, to proclaim the year of the Lord's favor.

During Salkehatchie week, the volunteers are the good news messengers, although the families are, too. They enlighten the volunteers and help free them from prejudice and brokenness. They help them take the next step in their faith journey, if they are open to it. The spirit of the Lord is upon them.

Faith and community

Lila Watson, an aboriginal woman in the Australian outback, once said to some missionaries: "If you come to help me, you are wasting your time. But if you come because your liberation is somehow bound with mine, then stay, and let us work together."

Salkehatchie connects people who, in their everyday lives, have little to do with each other. The prevalent world order separates the economically poor from the rich, the old from the young, the sick from the healthy, country folk from city folk, those with disabilities from those with typical abilities, those with a formal education from those without, the privileged from the deprived, and the adored from the abused. The forces that divide us contradict Christ's view that all believers are one (see John 17:22-23).

When families allow Salkehatchie volunteers to immerse themselves in their lives for a week, the ordinary world turns topsy-turvy and relationships get rearranged. Visually, this change becomes manifest in the tearing apart of the old house and the rebuilding of the new. Socially, the shy hesitation among strangers early in the week gives way to new friendships and mutual love and appreciation. At the end of the week, most volunteers and site families say, "we are family now." Spiritually, a parallel transformation occurs in the hearts and souls of the participants. The walls that divide us come tumbling down, replaced by bonds of shared faith and awareness that we are one in the Spirit.

That's not to say that every participant experiences a revolutionary transformation each year. The participants, in their own ways, at their own paces, absorb the experience into their life journeys. The volunteers do not descend on the camp like angels. They bring with them all their frailties, sufferings, bad habits, and temptations. Some volunteers are dealing with hardcore issues of their own: divorce or break-up, depression, death of loved ones, school failure, terror, loneliness, rejection, car wrecks, alcohol and drug abuse, mental illness, disabilities, or separation from loved ones who are at war. They come anyway. Some volunteers have serious health problems or disabilities of their own, like head injuries, cerebral palsy, diabetes, heart conditions, mental retardation, or recent surgery. They come anyway.

The families who open their homes do so with blind trust, expecting relief from the physical distress of their houses. They often are stunned when they realize that what the family gets extends far beyond house repairs. As with most spiritual matters, the transformation is a mystery. Something about combining all these ingredients yields a predictable pattern of growth and renewal, although the experience at each home is unique and special.

Being open to mystery and discovery fits with how young people see the world and forms a foundation for lifelong learning. Nowadays, most middle-class young people (adults, too) spend their lives in regimented environments or plugged into electronic devices. Many do not know life without electronic stimulation. They have been monitored in utero and with baby monitors in their cribs, constantly in one environment after another with the quiet hum of some kind of motor in the background. They spend far more time in online virtual community than in spiritual community. Only a few have ventured with their families or groups into the solitude of Earth's wild areas. They have never known true silence. They can barely hear the still, quiet voice of God if he speaks to them.

In addition to the need to go unplugged, today's young people need environments they can freely explore. Much of their time is at schools that teach for the test, with right or wrong answers, and demand hours of homework time in addition to school time. Most sports activities are organized, not spontaneous, and aim to produce competitive success. Too often, it is about whether you win or lose, not how you play the game. Artwork gets judged instead of simply shared and appreciated. Young people are understandably reluctant to express themselves for fear they'll get it wrong. They have doubts about their faith but may feel insecure letting anybody know, for fear they will be judged.

Many adults roll their eyes about young people and treat them as if they have a long way to go before they will be full members of society. Youth respond in kind, saying adults "don't get it—they don't listen and they don't understand." Many families succumb to the multiple demands of life outside the home and have little time together. Contemporary life in the United States moves at a rapid pace. Young people have few safe arenas in which to ponder the critical questions, "Who am I? Why am I here? Who is God? What is my relationship to God? What am I supposed to do with my life?"

Dietrich Bonhoeffer observed that Christians cannot always live among other Christians, and that, in fact, much of our time as Christians feels solitary.[3] He calls Christians to learn to live together so that we can understand what it means to be in Christ. In the fellowship of believers, we learn mercy, forgiveness, righteousness, truth, gratitude, and sacrifice. By practicing the virtues of Christian life with one another, we learn to spread those gifts into the rest of the world.

Salkehatchie creates opportunities for young people to confront one another in anger and love, to share sadness and joy, to explore justice and evil,

---

3. Deitrich Bonhoeffer, *Life Together* (New York: Harper & Row, 1954).

and to differentiate that which is trivial from that which is profound in life. Christians rarely have opportunities for such demanding experiences that integrate their minds, hearts, bodies, and souls.

Salkehatchie strips youth of their familiar roles for one short week each year. They go unplugged, with a limited regimen and few obvious answers. At first, most youth at the camp know only each other's first names or nicknames. They know little about each other's families, grades, social status, or reputation. Youth are free to reveal as much or as little of their regular selves as they choose. They can try on new names, different clothing styles, or alternative hairdos. As they labor, they listen to one another's music: rock, country, oldies, praise, soul, and others they might never hear otherwise. Salkehatchie offers novel experiences to them. It is an open learning environment in which they are encouraged to do things themselves and to learn from one another. The work is so urgent and so demanding that there's no time to focus on self, which is a great relief for most adolescents. It is really easy to do as Jesus said and not be anxious about what you eat, drink, or wear (Matthew 6:31).

Tackling interior work.

Adult volunteers try to refrain from lectures, sermons, and giving answers during Salkehatchie week. They step back. Perhaps the youth have never used power tools or believed they were afraid of heights and could not stand fifteen feet above the ground on a roof. They try, and discover they can. They learn to teach one another. They become physically and emotionally

> The fruit of silence is PRAYER.
> The fruit of prayer is FAITH.
> The fruit of faith is LOVE.
> The fruit of love is SERVICE
> The fruit of service is PEACE.
>
> —*Mother Teresa*

exhausted, but learn how to cope and handle stress.

At Salkehatchie, young people arise early and witness daybreak outside, which gives new meaning to the fact that Christians changed the convention of timekeeping to mark the start of day at sunrise rather than evening, which was the way of their ancestors. Each day is a new resurrection, but that's hard to appreciate if the day is half over when you first arise. The youth's schedule and environment at camp are totally different from their everyday lives. The youth who, the week before camp, says to his mother, "Why do I have to mow the lawn? I'm busy. I'll do it another day," says at the Salkehatchie site, "Let me do it! It's my turn!" when a new task arises.

We know that young people learn more from one another than from adults. Perhaps the most valuable parts of Salkehatchie are the periods devoted to personal and group reflections. At group time, the youth talk to each other, sharing their discoveries and disappointments, and acknowledging the mysteries and the miracles. They talk about how their Salkehatchie experience relates to what is happening in their regular lives. They make the connection, in their own ways, with gentle (or not-so-gentle) prompts from the Holy Spirit.

Of course, most Salkehatchie volunteers are Methodists, so there is a method behind the apparent chaos. At Salkehatchie, we practice all the basic methods of our faith: prayer, Bible study, journals, small group reflections, mutual support, and performance of good works. In addition, the camp leaders create structure and processes to make Salkehatchie what it is. Few participants are aware of the work of the shepherds who form the Salkehatchie Steering Committee, the network of camp directors and youth who organize the camps, oversee administrative matters, and support the camp leaders.

The methods of Salkehatchie, which emerged from discoveries at the earliest camps and have been refined from the experiences of 437 camps over twenty-eight years, are crystallized into a list of principles and practices known as "The Essentials of Salkehatchie." That, and a ten-page notebook for camp directors that emphasizes the fiscal accountability and safety needs of camps, as well as the steering committee bylaws, make up the formal written foundation of Salkehatchie. The rest is about relationships.

Salkehatchie essentials

Salkehatchie Summer Service happens in multiple places with "a cast of thousands," as Art Dexter would say. The Steering Committee identified the following list of "Essentials," principles and practices that are expected in each camp for maintaining the spirit of Salkehatchie and consistency across camps.

1. Regularly Scheduled Time Each Night for Spiritual Reflection

This could be fishbowl discussions, small group conversations around a Bible verse or theme, skits, large group devotional, or other formats. This is time for the kids to reflect on who they are, whose they are, and what exactly we are doing at Salkehatchie that is kingdom building. These reflection times should not be crammed into marathon sharing sessions, but should have parameters of time.

2. Work

Each participant should be required to do what he or she can to help accomplish the physical goals set before each home site. Each camp should include a time for basic safety training, i.e., wearing safety glasses, not putting the metal ladder around power lines, etc. (Longtime volunteer Ward Bradley would add, "Don't do stupid stuff.")

3. Music

No camp should be without musical leadership. Music is such a vital part of Salkehatchie and should be secured early in order to promote group bonding and worship. If you need help securing music, you might try going to a church or a magnet church in the area of your camp and try to recruit a music or youth leader. You might consider, like many camps, having a special music program for one night to share and lead the group in a special way.

4. Fun

Salkehatchie is not about just having fun and/or entertaining kids. We are about something much greater. However, it's OK and necessary to provide places and spaces within the camp experience where the youth can bond, enjoy, celebrate, laugh, and share. Many camps provide some kind of activity on the Sunday of the camp.

5. Structure

Every camp struggles with structure and where and how we go. At a minimum, a camp booklet with contacts, site family names and numbers, guidelines for your camp, maps, and a schedule of events should be provided. Samples from other camps are available.

6. Prayer

Let's not wait till Wednesday to pray for the camp, the campers, and the Lord's will to be done! Let's undergird all that we do in prayer.

7. Volunteers

Please make sure you secure donations from area businesses, churches, etc. Salkehatchie will not make it unless we continue to access the support of the community for meals, workers, and other gifts. People want to give, so ask them, and let them be a part of Salkehatchie.

8. Friday Night "Symbol Sharing" and Communion

This is the night when each person should share a symbol with the full group that represents their Salkehatchie experience. The camp will then share in the Sacrament of Communion as a community in Christ.

9. Sharing of the Salkehatchie Story

This happens when the campers return to their home churches. Each church will handle this differently, however, we strongly encourage every church to create a forum for Salkehatchie missionaries to share their stories upon their return.

10. Initial and Final Tour of Homes

All youth and adults will witness the before and after of the homes worked on that year.

11. Getting to Know the Families We Serve

Time spent with the families is important. One of the major parts of Salkehatchie is to establish and build relationships with the families we have the honor to serve.

12. Other Ideas

Many camps have moved to creating themes for the week, such as "Faith Like a Rock," "Standing on Holy Ground," or "Be Transformed."[4]

Each servant leader interprets these essential principles as the camps evolve. The leaders must tackle multiple challenges during Salkehatchie week: intimidating construction jobs; supervision of active and excitable young people; logistics of food, transportation, and shelter; acquiring and managing equipment, supplies, and funds; and facilitating a spiritual environment in which faith, hope, and love flourish. As servant leaders, they generally accomplish these awesome responsibilities with minimal use of authority. They don't have all the answers, and rely on the ingenuity of youth and adult camp participants and site family members to make the process happen.

The families who live in the houses give as much as they receive. On rare occasions, Salkehatchie crews have worked all week at houses with no one there. Perhaps the resident was too ill to be around the dust or their work schedules kept them away. In these cases, the crews say, "It's just not Salkehatchie." The volunteers love getting to know the families. When family members are able, they work as hard as or harder than any member of the crew. When they are unable to do the physical labor, they share ideas and wisdom and offer support in the form of smiles, hugs, and occasional good-

---

4. Provided by the Rev. Thomas B. Wilkes III, 2003-2004 chair of the Salkehatchie Steering Committee.

ies from the kitchen.

Somehow, it all comes together, again and again. Each home, each crew, each camp, each year is similar, yet special. Of course, the common presence is the Holy Spirit. At Salkehatchie, we realize with refreshing perspective that, indeed, what seems to be the least may actually be the greatest. One of our guiding biblical foundations for Salkehatchie is in Matthew, where Jesus talks about the righteous, who ask:

> "Lord, when did we see you hungry and feed you, or thirsty and give you something to drink? When did we see you a stranger and invite you in, or needing clothes and clothe you? When did we see you sick or in prison and go to visit you?" The King will reply, "Truly I tell you, whatever you did for one of the least of these brothers and sisters of mine, you did for me" (Matthew 25:37-40).

Leaving our mark on the doorstep.

Chapter 2

Hearts and Homes

The people of Salkehatchie are typical human beings with gifts and burdens. After twenty-eight years, we can barely begin to describe the thousands of volunteers and site families. Together, they make the Salkehatchie week happen and create memories whose images stay bright in our hearts.

Houses and homes

Every house has a history. Just by looking at it, we can read the structure. We examine the substances of which it is made (most often, wood, cinder block, brick, metal, or plastic). We recognize construction patterns such as fine craft, shoddy workmanship, or cobbled together over time. We can detect where rooms were added or walls removed. We can date the house, or parts of it, by the type of materials used and building processes. We can see how the house fell into disrepair. The roof or the plumbing leaked, fire damaged a wall, or perhaps violence broke the door or shot holes through the windows. The building shows its wear and tear.

Likewise, every family has a story. The house contains all the physical manifestations of their home. Home has tremendous meaning for people. Physically, a home offers security and protection from danger and weather, a source of food, comfort through heat in the winter and shade in the summer, and a place to rest. The United Methodist Resolution on Affordable Housing notes that a house is a means to preserve and protect the human body, which the apostle Paul characterized as the temple of God.

A house also shelters and displays family heirlooms. Its decor expresses what the family values; walls tend to be covered with photographs of family members, family crafts, and expressions of faith. So people form identity and a sense of history through the place they call home. A person's home sets a major foundation for her or his self-esteem. People need to feel pride in and have positive feelings about their homes. Problems in their physical environment can cause them to feel helpless, hopeless, and stripped of their dignity.

Home also has powerful social and psychological meaning. Home is where people spend most of their time. Their most important and intimate relationships occur there. Adults do the tender work of nurturing and interacting with infants and children in their homes. They care for people with disabilities of all ages at home. People study, play, practice creative arts and crafts, meditate, and otherwise engage in private and social activities. When a house is falling apart, home life can be strained. Residents can be grouchy and wear on one another's nerves.

Sadly, home can also be the source of our gravest problems, even our terror. Families express their best and their worst features in the home. Troubled families may suffer from addictions, domestic violence, child abuse, financial exploitation, or failure to respond to each other's needs. In some areas, families may feel fine in their own houses, but anxious about threats from the neighborhood. Home can become a lonely or fearful place.

Building and maintaining a house is hard work, but building and maintaining a home is even harder. At Salkehatchie, we glimpse how families are maintaining their houses and their homes. By repairing the house and sharing God's love in the home, Salkehatchie helps to relieve some of the family's anxiety. When the family can devote less time to maintaining the house, the family can devote more time to positive interactions and maintaining the home. When the house is in good repair, the family feels less stigma and stress, more order through organization, and a greater sense of mastery over the physical environment. This empowerment can transfer into the work of nurturing the family and home.

The people in our hearts

Over and over, the families in the homes have captured our hearts and shed light on our souls. We go to offer help with houses and homes, and the people who live there offer gifts to us in return. They know they are helping us to learn and grow. As we read in Hebrews 13:2, if we reach out to a stranger, we might meet an angel. This passage certainly comes to life at Salkehatchie.

Everyone involved in Salkehatchie has stories to tell. The families tell stories about the workers, the workers about the families and each other, and so on. In the following passages, we tell a few stories. This collage of word portraits depicts a few of the thousands of family members we have met and loved over the years.

Each person has a name. In some cases we have changed the names because we were unable to find the person to get explicit permission to use his or her name. In other cases, we have permission or the person is deceased and we feel confident he or she would have been honored to be included here. We have blended the stories from various times, because when a family touches our hearts, our memories become timeless. The stories and portraits are written from the perspectives of volunteers, most of whom are middle-class White people of various ages. We are viewing people from other cultures through our own lenses. Each selection reveals something about both the writer and the subject.

Sea Island Soul
Art Dexter

*for Maxine and
the beautiful people of the islands
with whom my heart dwells*

JOHN CHAPLIN

His possessions are few.
Even his name isn't his own.
It belonged to the man who owned his great-grandfather.

His crippled body propped up by a crutch
carved from a sapling,
he stands beside the road
with his wish in his eyes,
for he works in Port Royal ten miles away.

One day he saw an ad that said
"If you can read, you should teach another."
After work he will stay in Port Royal
and share his talents with three others.
God willing he'll hitch home to St. Helena in the dark.

But rides aren't easy to get.
Folks are put off by the spastic way he moves, he says,
and he understands their reluctance.

Reuben[1]

On rainy nights and on cold days
when I sit cozy within my home,
I am saddened by thoughts of my friend Reuben
in his roofless, floorless dwelling,
the rickety walls of which
lean at a forty-five degree angle
and would fall if not for the tree limbs
he props them with.
Even so, he must abandon his lair
when the wind rises and shakes the decrepit ruin.
The man on whose land he lives
tolerates his presence
and hopes he'll move on.
But he's been there for years now.
Would Reuben be consoled if he knew
that his name means
"God has noticed my troubles?"
Would he ponder it perhaps as he warms himself
and cooks a scant meal
over a few sticks of wood?

To people along Highway 21

---

1. Reuben kept alive the age-old craft of weaving fishnets.

he is "the shrimp-net man,"
one who is wonderfully adept
at weaving circular cast nets,
works of art that he sells on occasion
but which must now compete
with cheap Korean imports
of synthetic monofilament construction.
As he hustles up and down the highway,
neatly dressed in his white cap,
he sometimes stops,
takes a partially completed net
from the bag he carries,
ties it to a stop sign or tree,
and proceeds to add to it,
weaving with incredible speed,
like a spider working
in anticipation of his next meal.

Reuben, my brother,
you are "the least of these,"
the lamb that God calls us to tend,
the ache in my heart
on rainy nights and on cold days.

Florence[2]

She sits alone in the small clearing
beside the hand-operated pitcher pump,
washing her dishes in a pan,
stacking them on a scrap of plywood to dry.
Her husband left her years ago,
before arthritis froze her left hip

---

2. Florence's plot of land, with its tar paper house, bordered a sumptuous private golf course and gated community on a sea island.

leaving her bent and in need of a cane,
long before malnutrition
turned her black hair red.
But time has left untouched
the beauty of her ready smile,
the bright sparkle of her dark eyes,
the soft Gullah accents of her speech.
To know her is to love her.

Her tar papered, two-room shack
is both home and prison
with neither room big enough
to swing a cat in.
A wood stove fills one,
a bed the other.
The dishpan suffices for bathing,
a slop jar serves as a toilet.
Beneath her bed she retains a stack
of Playboys that her son left
eight years ago, when he moved to town.
He hasn't returned to see her since
but he may return and want them some day.
At night when the surrounding woods move closer
and her sense of isolation
and vulnerability fills the cabin,
she sleeps with a butcher knife beside her bed.

Regaining her feet is a special kind
of agony that makes her wince.
Now leaving the dishes to air dry
she crosses to the cabin
and dons her Sunday-best dress
—the floral print one—
retrieves her bulky purse
from the only chair
and steps out into the yard

where egrets and water birds
pass overhead in their travels
to and from the lakes
of neighboring condominiums
and golf courses.
Gentrification has come to Lady's Island.
By some irony
the grassy trail from her cabin
intersects the paved road
at the sentry house of a posh enclave.
With a rolling gait
she proceeds along the road,
cane tip punctuating her walk,
hoping someone will stop
and give her a lift
for she must pay a small electric bill
in Beaufort eight miles away.
Later, she'll enjoy the pleasure
of window shopping on Bay Street.

'Lizabeth

Day and night are much alike for her,
she is blind.
She doesn't know how old she is.
She thinks either 80 or 85.
She's never had a birthday
and doesn't know when she was born.

The small, blue travel trailer
that is her home
was a gift from a lawyer
who lives in Beaufort.
On summer days

the inside temperature
reaches 120 degrees or more.

The long rope
strung between trees and posts
is the umbilical cord
that links her to her neighbor Daisy's house
and the shady bench under the live oak tree.

Sam Doyle[3]

His yard was an art museum
of primitive paintings
executed in bright colors
on pieces of tin that he had collected
or that friends had given him.
He was prolific and his paintings
leaned against every tree, post, and object in the yard.
Here was a painting of
the first Black doctor on St. Helena Island;
the first car;
a famous Black midwife;
the baby found in the top of an oak tree
after the hurricane of 1893
(no one knew if the mother put it there
for safe keeping or if it had been blown there);
the Old Hag, a legendary obese woman
who came in the night
and sat on your head

---

3. Sam Doyle (1906-1985) grew up on St. Helena Island, South Carolina, in the same community where his grandparents had been slaves. The Penn School, where he was a student, nurtured his creativity and artistry. He painted the story of the island people: its history, traditions, idiosyncrasies, and special residents such as the root doctor and partygoers. Mr. Doyle painted on pieces of wood, roofing tin, and other scraps. He once said, "I paint the spirit of the person, yeah." His work has been featured in the Smithsonian and the High Museum in Atlanta. For more information, see Louanne LaRoche, *Art Random: Sam Doyle* (Kyoto, Japan: Kyoto Shoin International, 1989).

cutting off your breath
(she was painted in bright red);
and there were many Black notables
who were Sam's heroes:
Ray Charles, Joe Louis, Jackie Robinson.

What wasn't obvious in a painting
Sam supplied as docent
for he was also the local historian.
He proudly showed a clipping
that related how the Smithsonian
had held an exhibition of his paintings
in Washington, D.C.
He was equally proud of a photograph
taken there, which showed him
with First Lady Nancy Reagan.
But like so many artists
he lived in poverty.
His friend Emory tried to act
as a manager for him
so that the lady art collectors
who came to his yard
would not take advantage of him
for he was no businessman.
It was said that Sam's son
was a successful psychiatrist
somewhere up North.
But no one could ever recall
seeing him nor had anyone
ever heard of him helping Sam.

His old house gradually decayed around him.
Porches and additions fell away.

A Methodist church group
made some repairs in an effort
to alleviate the years of neglect.
Sam passed away soon after,
victim of another kind of neglect,
and his outdoor art museum
reverted to an empty piney woods.

Bessie

Visitors to her house are surprised
to be looking at the outside world
through the holes in the walls.
It's then that they become aware
of the missing panes on the windows,
the lack of furniture,
the absence of running water.
If they'd been around earlier
they would have seen the children
eating grits from the one communal bowl,
grits scooped up with fingers.

When winter comes
she'll farm the children out
to neighbors and friends
so they won't suffer the bitter cold.
She lives in quiet desperation.
A line from an old blues song
runs through her head;
"I been down so long
that gettin' up
ain't even on my mind."

Gertie Mae

When Gertie Mae stopped
by the clinic one day,
she heard a pitiful man relate
that he would not go back
to the halfway house
from whence he'd come.
For he had been beaten
and mistreated, he said.
Filled with compassion
she'd said, "You don't have to!
You can come home with me!"
Afterwards, she phoned John
at work and timidly said,
"John, I brought a man home
with me today."
He said something in reply.
Screwing up her courage
she continued, "John,
he's mentally handicapped."
He said something further in reply.
Finally, she put it all before him,
"And John, he's White!"

Years later, he's still their guest.
They've taken in many others
and built a home,
with hard to come by money,
to house them all.
John declares that they live well,
for Gertie Mae is the best cook
in all of South Carolina,
and God,
acting through their friends,
provides all manner of gifts of food.

Their love for each other
and for their charges
is a tangible reality.
Gertie Mae is proud
of what they've done
and pleased to give the visitor
a tour of their home.
While showing a modern bathroom
she explains,
"Most of the people make it to the toilet.
Only one man fails to
but at least he gets to the bathroom
and it has a tiled floor
so I don't mind mopping up after him."

FRANCINE

At first acquaintance
Francine shocks
one's sensibilities.
Her appearance is alien.
Her face is long
with protruding teeth
that are perpetually bared
and her eyes seem fixed.
She salivates continuously
so that her blouse is always wet.
She has no language
and can only utter
monosyllabic grunts.
People say that she
is severely intellectually disabled.
And yet, she understands

what is said
and patiently tries
through gestures and signs
to communicate.
Suddenly, the tables are reversed
and it is I who lack
the interpretive skills.
I am intellectually disabled in her world.
But if I observe closely, her
message becomes clear
and I perceive her satisfaction
in finally reaching me.
It is at these times
that I sense the presence
of something gentle and divine.

Here is my beloved sister.
I embrace her in greeting
indifferent to my wet shirt.

The Rev. Greene[4]

His boyhood ambition
was to be the pastor
of old Brick Church
erected in 1855
with a unique gallery
where slaves once sat.
He wanted nothing more,
nothing less.
And God granted
his supplication.

---

4. Slaves built the Brick Church at Penn Center, which has hosted a Salkehatchie camp since the early 1980s. Reverend Greene was pastor of the church when the camp started.

Smartly dressed
in his ministerial robes,
handsome of countenance
benevolently beaming down
upon his congregation
in their hard, cushionless pews
rich articulate voice
filling the small church,
he is truly magnificent.

His smile is beatific,
his gestures perfect,
even to the way that he
pats at the perspiration on his brow
with a neatly folded white handkerchief.
To everyone's pleasure
he may stop in mid-sermon
and deliver an apt hymn
or spiritual
in an exquisite baritone voice.

Today his sermon
relates to finding
a woman of his flock
and her small children
living in abject poverty
without benefit of plumbing
or beds and other necessities
just a few hundred yards
behind Brick Church.

He berates himself
for having his attention
focused elsewhere
and relates—with tears

flowing down his cheeks—
that it was like God
speaking to him
from a burning bush.
We are touched
and filled with compassion.

They say that with his qualifications
he could lead some elite church
on Riverside Drive or elsewhere
but he is content to work all week,
selling insurance and collecting bills,
to supplement his income
so that he can minister
to his cherished "Brick."

Rebecca

In the grey dawn
near the praise house
I encounter Rebecca
walking toward the crab factory.
She gives me a hug,
we exchange a few words
and go our separate ways.

I remember once
when we gave her a ride
from the crab factory,
she was carrying
a small pail
of crab scraps
to feed to her chickens.

It was a hot day

and John said, "Ma'am
would you please hold
that bucket out the window."
She laughed and complied.

She and Floyd
live close to the land.
They either make do
or do without.
After someone stole
their chickens
they did without
for awhile.

Sometimes things work out.
When we dropped in
last spring
they'd just slaughtered
their sole hog
and a scene of such carnage
in one tiny kitchen
I've never witnessed!

Every pan, crock, dishpan,
bowl, countertop,
pail, and jar
had been pressed
into service.
They were awash in
neatly sorted hog parts.

Some all too recognizable,
others mere parts
of an anatomical puzzle.
It felt good
after a proper interval

to step out the door
into the fresh air.
We politely declined
their generous offer
to share their bounty with us.
As one who shops in supermarkets
I not only lack
their survival skills,
but their survival stomach.

Sister Mary[5]

Everyone knows her,
she is everywhere.
Small, energetic,
compassionate,
she is the bright
weft thread of love
that runs through
the social fabric
of these islands,
touching the lives of many
but especially
the impoverished.

After prayers
in the small chapel
her work begins:
Firewood and a bag of pears to Florence.
A cook stove to be located for Bessie.
Food, clothing, and an oil heater
for a penniless migrant family.

---

5. Sister Mary was among the network of Catholic nuns who lived in the South Carolina Lowcountry and challenged John Culp to do something about poverty. He created the Salkehatchie camps.

Help Maggie with craft classes
for senior citizens
at the Leroy Brown center.

Grab a bite to eat
then run to arrange
a wheelchair ramp
for an amputee.
Must remember to work
on the Christmas gifts
for the children.
Funds so short
but God will provide.
Galvanized tub for a family
of seven to bathe in.

Look in on lonely old Ethel.
Visit Rose's brother
who has MS and can do
no more than blink his eyes—
brush away
the gnats and mosquitoes
that torment him.

Hurry through
a quick supper.
Hurry to Mass
in Beaufort
and home again in time
to give two guitar lessons
before bedtime.

Hurry, Mary,
so much need to be met.
It is in giving
that we receive,

St. Francis said.
Hurry,
try to be a light
in the darkness.
Hurry
but try not
to let yourself
burn out
in the process.
Hurry.

A Requiem for Miguel[6]

Was it inattention or miscalculation
that caused the bike and its rider
to fall into the green maw
of the abandoned, half-filled
swimming pool that had patiently
lain in wait for just such a six-year-old
as Miguel—child of the poorest
of migrants, who had each day
watched his pregnant mother, Lydia,
scrub three loads of laundry
(for a family of eight)
in the backyard galvanized washtub?

When grief immobilized Angelo, and he sat
staring with unseeing eyes,
it was Lydia who said,
"I must be strong
for the sake of the family."

---

6. Miguel's family emigrated from Central America. After living in the fields where his parents picked crops, Miguel's family moved into town because his mom had health problems. They lived in a little house down the street from a house that had an abandoned pool covered in weeds in the backyard. Apparently, Miguel, who could not swim, rode his little bike right into the pool. As rescue workers attempted to revive Miguel, his young sister said to his mother, "Some lady is here for Miguel."

At the funeral home
for the last time
she cradled the one
she had birthed
and dressed him
in the suit newly purchased
from K-Mart.
And she prayed,
asking God's forgiveness
for there had never been time
in all their travels
to have him baptized.
Surely, He would understand!
But she had been forewarned
and his death had not come
as a total surprise,
for curly-haired Toya
her pretty, dark-eyed four-year-old
had said, two days before,
"Mama, the Lady says she
is going to take Miguel away!"
The next day, Toya had called
Lydia to an empty room
and said, "See Mama,
the Lady is here!"
When the fireman
located him
beneath his coverlet of algae
she'd said, "See Mama, I told you so!"

Unconversant with English
they sat impassively
that night of the wake
while Father Laughlin
said the Rosary and,
when at last he finished

they went to Miguel
in his donated coffin
—small brown hands folded
for eternity.
And they crowded together
the little ones climbing
upon the prayer bench
and reached out to stroke
the cheek that had lost its warmth
and felt the crisp curly hair of one
who never in life could have
remained so still.

Their questions were many
and when Lydia answered,
"It was God's will," their brows
furrowed in incomprehension.
Loathe to leave, they lingered
for they were told that tomorrow
the coffin would not be open.
While the mortician fidgeted
they gave their final kisses
and whispered, "*Vaya con Dios*, Miguel."

When the tomorrow they had hoped
would never come arrived,
Toya and Maria stared in fascination
at the gift of shiny Mary Janes—
the first new shoes they had known.
As 11 o'clock approached, Maxine hurried
to hem the hand-me-down
dress that someone had given
grandmother Dolores.
There was no time to press it
and it billowed at the bottom.
It was brown and matched

her thin legs and the flip-flops
on her feet.
By contrast, small Roberto's new shirt
gleamed whitely
against his coffee-colored skin.

Seated in the front pews
of small St. Peter's church
their eyes flitted from the small casket
to the bas-relief of The Last Supper
beneath the altar, to the colorful
stained-glass windows, and back
to the priest as, unassisted, he
performed the Mass
alternately uncovering and covering
the elements, swinging the smoking censer,
serving the elements to the faithful
who had come to offer moral support
to the grieving family they did not know.

When all formalities had been met
the small casket was wheeled
to the double doors that opened
onto the simmering heat
of Carteret Street, and gently
carried to the waiting hearse.
As the small procession crept
through the tropic heat of Beaufort's
noontime traffic, in slow pursuit
of a flashing blue light, they crossed
a busy intersection where traffic
was blocked for their passage.
Someone remarked, "Wouldn't he have smiled
to see all the cars stopped for him!"
and Denise broke down
and sobbed uncontrollably.

At Anderson's Cemetery
where the canopy-shaded chairs
stood in orderly rows
the journey ended.
The outlines of the donated grave
were softened by blankets
of artificial grass that were soon surmounted
by the four-foot long coffin
topped by a spray of flowers
Jeanette had sent.

As Father Laughlin
took his place
and Lydia and Dolores
in their flip-flops
crowded close for one
last touch of good-bye,
thoughts like, "Blessed are the poor"
and "Suffer little children
to come unto me"
ran through Arturo's mind.
But these thoughts
were cut short
when the priest began
"Our Father ... " for simultaneously
a beautiful yellow butterfly
came out of nowhere
and landed on the spray of flowers
where it sat with pulsating wings
until the prayer was through
and—as everyone watched
in fascination—
it flew slowly off
while little Toya pointed.

> Salkehatchie is a twelve-letter word for love.
>
> —*Youth at Santee Camp*

Miss McCain: A Week of Unconditional Love
Amy McConnell, Youth Volunteer, 1988

Nothing could have prepared me for the initial shock of Miss McCain's house, a small, two-room structure blackened with soot from fires built on the ground beneath a large hole in the floor. The whole house leaned to the right. The bedroom floor was termite infested. The boards that supported the structure were slowly decomposing from water exposure. There was no garage, no phone, no car, no grass in the yard, no running water, no mirror, and there were no screens on the doors and windows. I saw only one light bulb.

And then there was her face. It was a face of hope, and yet a face of neglect and fear—fear of what might or might not come. I know she must have been alarmed when one hundred teenagers inspected her home and gawked at the severity of its condition. But that face spoke to me—I knew from first glance that I was to help improve her life.

The story began a year earlier when two church members returned from a United Methodist Church mission project, Salkehatchie. Their excitement was contagious as they told of sharing God's love by helping to rehabilitate homes of the poor. When this year's mission began, I knew I had to be involved.

The first morning, we went over every inch of her house and made a record of the materials needed to make repairs and improvements. By ten o'clock, we were tearing down boards, removing furniture, and scraping walls.

It was amazing to see how she lived. She had only seven pieces of furniture and a dilapidated refrigerator. The interior of her house was very damp, making it a haven for black widow spiders and cockroaches. Life for Miss McCain meant surviving from day to day, just making do with what little she had. Her closest friends were her cat and its kittens. She had never been to a doctor and had never been off the island on which she lived. She had no family and spoke only in Gullah, a local dialect.

Yes, our visit that first day must have been terrifying, but probably no more terrifying to her than it was to us.

Our first work day ended at six o'clock in the evening, but the best was yet to come. Nights were always devoted to group-wide reflections about the day's experiences. At the first session, we learned that the symbol of Salkehatchie for 1988 was the butterfly, one of God's beautiful creations. The butterfly was chosen in remembrance of a young boy whose house had been repaired by Salkehatchie last year. He drowned when he fell into a swimming pool. On the day of his funeral, a monarch butterfly landed on his coffin and stayed until the service had ended. Butterflies took on a special meaning that day to the people who had helped his family.

Broken, boarded windows

Imagine the wonder and excitement I suddenly felt when I recalled that, just that day, a butterfly had landed on Miss McCain's chimney while we were beginning reconstruction! I suddenly knew that God had hand-delivered a blessing to my group. He was telling me that I had chosen the right worksite to share his love. My dedication to helping Miss McCain and rebuilding my relationship with God became very firm that day.

As Reverend John asked for two members from each of the nine rehabilitation sites to come forward to share the thoughts and experiences of their day, my father persuaded me to reveal my feelings of when I saw the butterfly. Through Reverend John's questions and discussions, I realized that the butterfly was like Jesus because of its beauty, while the cockroaches we encountered each day were like Satan and evil. Also, some people are treated like cockroaches, stomped upon in society—yet these people, like Miss McCain, are beautiful butterflies. I was overwhelmed with emotion that two of God's creatures could help me realize the good and bad, and the happy and sad, in our lives.

Miss McCain's home slowly began to transform. We replaced her kitchen floor, put in new windows, and refinished her furniture. We painted the interior and exterior of her house and bought her household items and food—even a cover for her couch. We laid linoleum in both rooms and added a porch so she could sit under her large oak tree on hot days.

The most rewarding benefit of the week was seeing Miss McCain's transformation. At the beginning of the week, she isolated herself inside the neighbor's house and would not even step into the yard as long as we were there working. Each day she appeared to relax and accept us a little more, and by Wednesday she sat at a distance and watched. On Thursday, she actually came over to ask if she could help and told us she appreciated all we had done for her. I was touched by her words; they put the entire week into perspective. Through our labors, love shined through. The lack of sleep, the heat, and the food that I had complained about suddenly seemed selfish concerns.

Friday, the final working day, arrived. That afternoon, everyone from all the different sites loaded into cars to view the changes that had been made during the week. Miss McCain's house was the last one of our before-and-after tour, and as we pulled up, a sense of extreme joy welled up in me. I experienced the greatest sense of personal closeness with God that I had ever known. He helped me to realize many things about myself and his purpose in bringing people's lives together. He helped me to use the talents he had given me to help someone less fortunate than I. I cried my first tears at Salkehatchie as I walked through her home and felt the love of Jesus Christ surrounding me and all the people who had given a week to the Lord. Salkehatchie was not only a week of hard labor, but a week of unconditional love.

As a result of attending this mission project, I have felt a transformation in my own life. I no longer take a nice home, warm meals, clothing, and a caring, loving family for granted. More important, I now know the meaning of unconditional love, the true love of Jesus Christ! As I see a monarch butterfly in flight, I envision his love being spread around the world—even to that small, two-room house on an island off the coast of South Carolina.

Thirteen Years of Salkehatchie Enlightenment
Arlene and Stuart Andrews

1993

Each day, Ellie and Joe Thomas drive 150 miles round trip to their jobs on Hilton Head Island. She cleans rooms at a hotel and he maintains grounds at a golf course. They live in a spotless and tiny two-bedroom house with four teenagers and need space for their only son to sleep, along with repairs to the roof, plumbing, windows, and floors. Their tight budget makes repayment of a home improvement loan impossible. "When you come to the island for vacation," says Ellie, "You won't even notice me."

1994

Lucy lives far in the country with no car and her only income is welfare. The DSS caseworker tells us Lucy is at risk of losing her two young children because poor sanitation, caused by the broken toilet and dysfunctional bathtub, threatens their health. Lucy's husband can't help because he is serving an extended prison sentence. Lucy, who attended special education classes when she was in school, knows several of my friends in Columbia because she stayed in shelters they operate there while she was homeless.

1995

About midway through the week, I realize Ms. Sonya cannot read. She lives with her aging mother (who has Alzheimer's), her eighteen-year-old daughter (who works at a diner; the local cop tells us she has been a prostitute), and her precious one-year-old grandson. There are no signs of any men in the family except the baby. The rotting roof has created a haven for roaches and damaged the wiring. "It's a miracle that no one in this house has been electrocuted," says our electrician.

1996

Ms. Juanita, whose daughter succumbed to the seduction of crack cocaine, is raising her four grandchildren, plus the fifteen-year-old's baby, her great-grandchild. Ms. Juanita's ancient home has seven layers of shingles on the leaking roof, requiring a removal job that would cost a fortune even if she could afford it. While we work, Ms. Juanita shows me the crack house down the street and worries about how she will protect her grands from temptations in the neighborhood. On Wednesday morning, Shawn, a local police officer who has been working on our crew, meets us with numbing news: Ms. Juanita's adult daughter has stabbed her drug supplier to death.

1997

Annette, who seems to be in remission after recently losing a breast to cancer, lives in a rusting trailer with her four teenagers. Everything leaks: the roof, the pipes, the faucets. One daughter invites me to eat "chalk," a clay she digs up in a nearby field. Another tells me about how she would like to go to technical school to learn construction, so she can teach others and help them get jobs.

1998

When they were young, Ms. Mabel knew Marion Wright Edelman, head of the Children's Defense Fund and one of my heroines. "Sure, everyone knew the Wrights; we went to their church," the retired custodian says. Ms. Mabel's adult children all live in other states. Ms. Mabel's kidney disease recently confined her to a wheelchair and she is staying with church friends until she can get her kitchen and bathroom adapted and a ramp built.

1999

Dan, a member of a local United Methodist Church, used all his savings to pay an inept roofing company to re-shingle the house he inherited from his father. The shingles are neatly lined in even, not staggered, rows, causing leakage and related damage everywhere. Dan works as a full-time custodian but can't get a loan to fix the roof. His house is deteriorating around him.

2000

Ms. Beatrice "Bee," age fifty-nine, worked all her life in other people's homes, cleaning and caring for elderly people, sometimes around the clock. She is no longer able to do heavy labor or move adult bodies and has no retirement income and no health insurance. Ms. Bee is too young for Social Security, and her only car is a rusted heap with four flat tires. She dreams it will actually run one day. No one in the tiny town where she lives needs her services or can hire her. She lives in a house inherited from her parents and gets occasional help from her adult children, who work minimum wage jobs. She has no water service, because she cannot pay the bill.

2001

Ms. Mary, long a diabetic, is on kidney dialysis, and her husband, Mr. Rudi, has a brain tumor and arterial blockages. They are anticipating that after his scheduled surgery, Mr. Rudi will be unable to walk ever again. They live on disability income. The roof of their brick home has all but caved in. At night, when they lie in bed, rain falls on their faces. Mr. Rudi needs a wheelchair ramp. He used to do all his house repairs himself; now he shuffles up the new ramp on Friday with tears streaming down his face as he admires the finished work of the Salkehatchie crew.

2002

Ms. Wilma cooked for the local schools for thirty years, until she retired. She cannot bend her knees, but she does manage to barely walk. She and her husband bought the house decades ago, but after he died, she could no longer clean or repair her house, and the mess piled up. Her plumbing and heating systems are broken. She has young adult grandchildren who sometimes live with her when they have no place else to stay, but they do not help. "We don't get along," she says.

2003

We thought cheerful Ms. Maggie simply needed a new roof, just as her brother Donald did. He lived in a tiny cinder block house behind hers. At first, Donald avoided us and told us never to go inside, though he did agree we could put on a new roof. He has suffered post-traumatic stress disorder since he returned from the Gulf War in the early 1990s. Ms. Maggie worries about his drinking. During Salkehatchie week, his ceilings collapsed after a storm blew tarp off the exposed roof. He reluctantly let us into his dark and dingy two rooms. It was so cheerful when we finished. He was all smiles and joy. Ms. Maggie said she had not seen him like that in years.

2004

When we arrived at Ms. Lillie's house on Monday morning, it seemed there were little sleeping bodies scattered everywhere, on the floor as well as the beds. She is raising her grandchildren, three teenage girls who share a double bed, and five boys, ages four to nine. They have no place to sit down for a meal; they simply go to the kitchen when they are hungry and walk around or sit on the floor while eating. Their heating system is broken. Randall, the eight-year-old, says in the winter he can see his breath when he wakes up. I look around and cannot imagine where a child can find a place to do homework in this house.

2005

Though Ms. Katherine's roof was caving in, her biggest problem was her broken heart. Her husband of twenty-seven years died after a terrible car accident. She still grieves and cannot get over her depression. Her house is spotless and decorated with hundreds of cute figurines. She has a darling goldfish pond in the front yard. She clearly has had a life filled with happiness and beauty. She speaks tenderly of her husband as she caresses his picture. After the site crew took over her house and yard, Ms. Katherine said she laughed more in a day than in the years since her husband died. She slept through the night for the first time.

Mr. Napoleon Quick
Neil Flowers, Youth Minister and Camp Director

This year in Bennettsville, South Carolina, I was honored to work on an eighty-two-year-old saint's home. He is a sweet, loving, and kind Christian man named Mr. Napoleon Quick. He has trouble walking and his sight is 90 percent gone, but you would never know that he had any problems at all.

He would take his stool and sit down and talk with us. He sweeps the yard every day, starting in the backyard, doing a little each day until he works his way around the house by the end of the week. He said he has worked every day of his life. He takes Sundays off.

Each morning at six o'clock, he would be waiting for us to do our devotional and was ready to be a part of our prayers. We would stand around in a circle in his yard, ask him if he had anything to say, and he would always have a word for us. It seemed every breath he took was a witness for the Lord. He amazed us so much with his way of telling about his personal relationship with God that it was hard to just not sit there and listen to him all day long. His witness and stories will stay with me all my life.

He said to us, "This wonderful work that you are doing is not your work, but the Lord working through you. We are the Lord's hands and feet."

I never will forget how he told about his wife, who passed away a couple of years ago. They were married for sixty-two years. He loves her and misses her so much. They have more than fifty children, grandchildren, great-grandchildren, and great-great-grandchildren scattered in all fifty states. He said, "If my wife is not in heaven when I get there, I am going to ask the Lord to let me trade places with her." Talk about love and devotion! Wow!

It was hard to tear ourselves away from him, but there was work to be done. He needed a roof and a lot of repairs to his old house. We built him a front porch, and I told him that we wanted to see him in his rocker, sitting and chilling out, when we ride by next year. It was a miracle that we were there that week, because his well dried up and we helped him dig another one.

On Friday, Mr. Quick's house was the last to be visited when the whole camp toured all the homes. We got to Mr. Quick's home about seven-thirty that evening. We were tired and hungry and wanted to go back to the camp, but we brought him out on the porch and asked if he had anything to say. He started to preach, and no one wanted to leave.

With tears in his eyes he said, "I never thought that I would live long enough to see the day when there would be so much love shown as there has been this week—that you would come and love and care for an old Black man like me."

George
Elizabeth Webber, Youth Volunteer, 1983

It was a hot Saturday afternoon in July, the kind of hot that makes you want it to snow. The kind of hot that covers you in sweat. The kind of sweat that attracts dirt and filth and makes you feel uncivilized.

Carpenter at work.

These were my feelings as my parents dropped me off at a rundown old house on a small sea island. I was here to spend a week fixing more rundown old houses because my parents thought it would be good for me. All I could think was how much I wanted a shower, how I knew I was going to hate it, and how I could get them back for sending me to this concentration camp.

They left, and it was me, myself, and I, along with a lot of other people probably feeling the same way. After we had all settled in, we gathered for a get-acquainted meeting. I immediately made some friends and began to think perhaps I could make the best of it. I was adjusting.

The next day was Sunday. I had become good friends with two guys. The three of us shared a corner of a pickup truck as we traveled to all the different sites. When our little pickup caravan stopped for the third time, my heart jumped. I wanted this house. Later that night, the director of this program gave a brief history on each of the sites; I knew for sure that the third one was for me. I convinced my new friends to join me.

Site Three was a small house inhabited by a man who used to run a vegetable stand on the side of the road. Strangely enough, I've traveled this road all my life on the way to the beach. My mother and I used to stop at these little stands quite often, but there was one in particular that I always liked. The man who ran the vegetable stand always talked my mom into buying watermelons for me and my sister. The man at Salkehatchie Site Three was hit by a car a couple of years ago and lost his right leg. My vegetable man had vanished about the same time. I thought it impossible that they were the same person, but I would find out.

Bright and early Monday morning, my group arrived at the house of George M. I was nervous about seeing him, fearing he'd be the man I thought he was. As soon as I saw him, I felt it. I kept telling myself it had been years and I could be imagining the resemblance. I introduced myself and told him to let me know if he needed anything. As strange as it sounds, I actually loved him, even though we'd just met.

As the days went by, George and I got really close. Whenever the heat would get to be too much, I would sit down and talk with him. One day we sat on the porch and snapped beans together and traded recipes. He still had his little garden and his friends would come over and pick vegetables for him. I told George how my mom and I used to stop at his stand. He said he remembered but I found that a little hard to believe. He told me all about his accident and his court settlement which he had still not received after three years. One morning he asked me to sit down for a minute before I started work. He pulled out a newspaper clipping with the story of his accident. He said he wanted me to see it because he knew I cared.

George said that he loved listening to our wild music and to us arguing with each other. Sometimes he'd listen to our teenage nonsense and just laugh. I think he really enjoyed us being there. I know I enjoyed it.

On Friday night, all of us Salkehatchie people piled into the trucks and went to see all the work done on the sites and to say good-bye to the people living there. When we got to George's, I ran inside. I found him cooking in the little kitchen and warned him that I'd talked about him so much that everyone wanted to meet him. I stood behind him with my hands resting on the wheelchair handles as everyone crowded in. Faces filled the doorway and the lucky ones that managed to get in shook his hand. It was as if all they wanted to do was catch a glimpse of him.

Saturday morning was a complete rush. We were all running around trying to pack and get addresses. I was really going to miss the heat, the dirt, the fighting for showers, and our meetings. I loved these people and it was really hard to part with them. When father finally picked me up, I could only thank him rather than get revenge! We drove over to George's for one more good-bye. I gave him my address and telephone number and he gave me his. We hugged each other and I promised to come back.

I did. Not too much later, my family and I went to the beach. Our place is only two islands away from George's. My sister and I went over and took him some crabs we had caught. He was very appreciative, as always. He and I talked and caught up on things. I called him the next day before I went back home. Not much later I received a letter from him. It was the sweetest letter I'd ever gotten.

I didn't keep in touch with George like I should have. Not long ago I was thinking of him and I wrote him a letter. The next day I put the letter in our mailbox to be mailed. That night John, the Salkehatchie director, called. When he said he'd been down George's way, I knew something was wrong. I was right. George had died.

Although I closed my eyes tightly, the tears found their way out. I was so choked up I couldn't speak for a minute. John was very sensitive and tried to ease the pain. I was really glad I'd heard it from him.

As I sat in my room and cried, I realized it was probably better for George because I know he's in heaven. Then I asked God to let him have both his legs, a little garden, and the new car he'd picked out of a magazine to repay him for the misery he had endured.

Then I went and got the letter out of the mailbox.

Gifts from Ms. Jane
Brantley McConkley, Youth Volunteer

I don't think that I ever actually got to say thank you. I gave her a hug as she sat on her couch wiping the tears from her eyes. I remember how the fresh paint stung my nose for the last time. She hugged all of us, one by one, as we stood in the small room. I remember the way she smiled at us that day. I will always remember that smile. Seventy years of wrinkles couldn't hide the love in her face. The long years of isolation and pain seemed to have disappeared in this one week. As she looked around the room, her eyes sparkled like a child's on Christmas Day. Yet, I could only think of the time when those eyes weren't so bright.

When we arrived that first morning, it was unnaturally cool for June. The air was heavy and damp. I was so nervous when I walked into that dark room. One lamp in the corner gave the room a sinister appearance. We found her as we would leave her, sitting alone on the couch with her walker by her side. She kept telling us how wonderful it was to see young faces again. We squeezed in tightly and found places to sit on the dirty floor. I didn't say much that first day; I listened as she told us about her life.

Her husband had left her a number of years before. She said he had a drinking problem and a gambling problem and was never faithful to her. There was a certain chill that came to her voice when she spoke of him. "He used to slap me around a lot," she said. He had remarried and she hadn't heard from him since. She didn't like to talk about him; I didn't blame her.

In those seven short days we tore down, sawed, nailed, painted, and cleaned. When I went inside, I understood the impact that we were having. "Ms. Jane," I would say, "how are you doing today?" She would always smile and say, "This is the happiest I've ever been. I just don't know what I'm going to do when you children leave me." More than anything else, she cherished the conversations. She talked from the minute we arrived until the minute we left. Every morning when we would return, she'd be waiting for us at the door.

I probably slept about five hours every night. Our lack of sleep didn't stop our drive to keep working. Her house was condemned by the state, and we had to fix and rebuild it to get it off the condemned list. What originally seemed impossible was now being completed with great speed. Slowly, we realized that there was so much more to this than just work. We realized that we weren't just working on a site, we were working on a home. What we were doing was far greater than mere construction work. I knew this was an experience that I would never forget.

I remember taking a break one day out on the newly built porch. Ms. Jane sang an old hymn from her childhood. We all sat quietly while she sang. I hadn't ever heard the hymn before; it was simple but nice. She said she couldn't remember the last time people had listened to her sing. She cried again, but this time they were tears of joy.

While we did many things to help her, I don't think she knew that she was helping us. Ms. Jane opened my eyes that summer. I walked into her home with a nail apron and a hammer, but I walked out with so much more. She showed us that no matter how poor a person is, the human spirit will always persevere. At one time I might have believed that we were a miracle sent to her, but looking back now I see that she was the miracle sent to us.

A Sample of Volunteers and Families

Every year, at every camp, at every home site, individuals with unique and special characteristics come together to build community. We particularly remember ...

- When we found Samuel, a one-hundred-year-old man lying on plastic bags on a pallet in his back room;
- When we went to Ms. Russell's house and she told us her three-year-old granddaughter had fallen through the floor to the ground;
- Those people who called us "the people with the straight hair";
- The sisters whose former-slave grandmother bought their beautiful land "four years after freedom";
- The youth volunteers who begged Mr. Jefferson to stop drinking and tried to pry his bottle from his pocket;
- Watching from a rooftop, in horror and outrage, as a burly man next door whacked a little child with a thick leather belt;
- The adult volunteer, a man with retardation, who comes and works faithfully each year;
- The home where only one wall stayed dry during rain; that's where Elvis's picture hung;
- The Heyward family, who trapped coon, salted them into "petrified coon," and sent them to relatives in New York, who would soak and eat it.
- Swatting roaches with a stuffed animal;
- Mr. Drayton, who was too weak to go to the outhouse so he relieved

himself in the corner of the room or through cracks in the outside wall;

• The volunteer with diabetes who struggled to maintain her glucose balance in the evenings as her body adjusted after sweating all day;

• The roaches crawling all over the floor of a cinder block house more than an inch deep in some places; when we first set off a roach bomb, the roofers yelled, because a brown cloud of roaches flew through the chimney and scurried across the roof;

• Ms. Tybee, a mother who punched a hole in a dime and hung it on a string around her baby's neck to keep the baby from getting sick while teething;

• The college student volunteer awaiting his trial for drug possession;

• The front yard covered with a massive amount of trash that filled eighty large garbage bags;[7]

• Girl volunteers covered in paint, mud, and tar during the day who wouldn't leave their cabins in the evening without makeup and finely coiffed hairstyles;

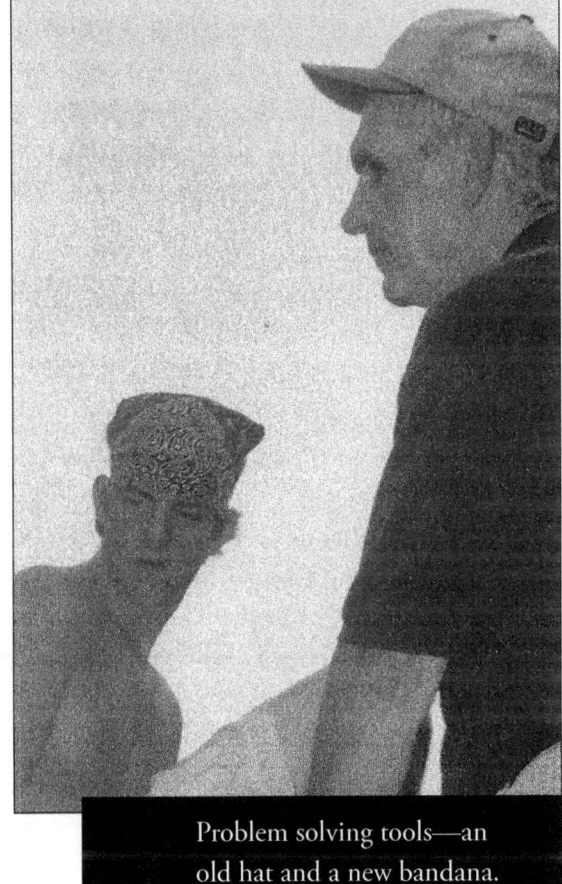

Problem solving tools—an old hat and a new bandana.

• A boy who said his name was Nigger, and a man who said his name was Darkie. More than one person said, "I can't call him that!";

• Trips to the ER with volunteers for nails in the foot, dehydration, and bumps on the head;

---

7. In some rural communities, trash pick-up costs between $15 and $30 a month, an impossible amount for poor people.

- Ms. Anderson, an elderly lady whose neck was broken in a car accident, who still managed her home and kept her animals in spite of the screws in her skull and the brace on her shoulders;
- The youth volunteer who got irritated often and aggravated others in the process; he was coping with his parents' never-ending conflicts after their bitter divorce;
- When we took out a mattress, mice went everywhere;
- Home after home where children have been raised to serve their country, as indicated by their photos on the walls in military uniforms;
- Watching Ms. Cooper give a demonstration to fascinated youth about how a washboard works;
- Ms. DuBose, who crushed the head of a snake after she killed it, because she believes the Bible says to; otherwise, the snake will crawl into the baby's mouth to get the mother's milk;
- Eating pigs' feet stew at the end of the week because it was a feast prepared in gratitude by the site family;
- Freeing Ms. Myers, a blind lady, from the confines of her trailer by simply running a rope that she could follow to her sister's trailer across the way;
- Eighty-year-old Ms. Simpson, who has 156 children, grandchildren, great-grandchildren, and great-great-grandchildren;
- Working on a house in McClellanville after Hurricane Hugo, where two of the family's eight children had drowned during the storm;
- Ms. Holmes, an African American lady who said that when the whole camp of predominantly White volunteers came to look at her house, "the whole place out there was looking almost like snow and we stood out there and took pictures";
- Catching fleas from the dog under the house;
- The young adult volunteer with an eating disorder who tried to lose weight by not eating or drinking much and ended up in the emergency room on IVs;
- Camp director Dave Dillon's pants suspenders that are bright yellow with ruler markings; and John Culp's "CAT" (Caterpillar) hat;
- Walking on floors that feel like sponges, they are so rotted with moisture.
- Metal carcasses all over the yards: old rusty cars and trucks, appliances, wheelchairs, bicycles, farm equipment, and mobile homes;
- A rusted stove with only one working eye (burner), where the daily grits

get cooked;

• Mr. Beasley, who described mosquitoes on his sea island this way: "Oh they're bad. They don't even talk. You see, I'm originally from Kentucky and we had mosquitoes, but you'd hear them coming, making noise, but out here they don't say nothing. They just sting you";

• Jesus walked on water. So did our site family. The kitchen had about a half inch of standing water most of the time;

• The Hires family, who ate from one communal bowl with their fingers;

• Ms. Miller, who remembers paying two dollars a week for rent when she and her husband first married;

• Sammie, a little girl who, when we gave her toothpaste, said, "But I don't have a toothbrush!";

• The picture of The Last Supper with all African American figures;

• Ms. Cromer, who called Buddy Rutland first thing on a frigid Christmas morning after her house was repaired in the summer, just to let him know she was warm;

• Youth volunteers who manage to make light of work that involves "toilet juice";

• More than one African American elder who calls her neighbors "White people" without ever giving them a name and says, "I've been good to them and they've been good to me";

• Ms. Branham, a ninety-four-year-old lady who lived in an old World War II barracks building that had been moved to her property; even in 2004, she had never had a well or running water and got her water in jugs from a neighbor; and

• Mr. McCormick, a retired farmer who does all the cooking, sewing, and cleaning as well as care for his wife, who had a stroke ten years ago; in 2003, they live one hundred fifty yards from a United Methodist Church, but it's a White church; they drive a ways to go to a Black UMC.

The Goins
Arlene Bowers Andrews, 2002

The flowers were taller than I am: bright pinks, purples, and reds, bordered by pots with smaller yellow and white blossoms. Dwarfed by a huge fig bush that rose at least twenty feet into the air, they surrounded the house. Happy butterflies twittered from one bush to another as we stepped down a short path to the front porch, where Mother Pauline Goins sat quietly snapping fresh green beans on the spacious new screened front porch built by Salkehatchie volunteers. Her husband of more than fifty years, Elder James Goins, rocked nearby.

A carpenter, Elder James built this house himself, starting with a two-room house a White man gave him. He disassembled and moved the house from Columbia to this lot in the woods, near a small town. Using free materials that he gathered from here and there over the years, he gradually added rooms to the house to accommodate their growing family. They raised seven children in the house that eventually had four bedrooms, two center rooms, a bathroom, and a kitchen and laundry room, all covered by a tin roof. In recent years, Elder James had become less able to repair the house, so by the time the Salkehatchie crew arrived, the floor was unstable in several places, the roof was starting to leak, and the plumbing was out in the bathroom.

The Goinses had one condition when asked if they would like work done on their home: no one could work on Saturday, their Sabbath. Elder James, who turned eighty-two during Salkehatchie week, pastors a small church, where he and Mother Pauline share their musical talents. Their traditional gospel music, sung to the accompaniment of guitar and clapping rhythm, has carried far beyond their little community. They've produced a CD and sung in New York City.

The couple tells the story of how a man came to their yard and asked, "Do you have a cow?"

"Yessir, we do."

"Do you have butter?"

"Yes, we do."

"Can I buy some?"

"Yes, you can."

So they sold him some, and he invited them to come to his restaurant in the town up the road from their house. He said he had heard about their music and would like for them to play in the restaurant. They did, and later made a recording of their music. Then someone came and offered to pay their way for a trip to perform at the New York City Public Library. They took the train on a Friday, sang on Saturday, and came home on Sunday.

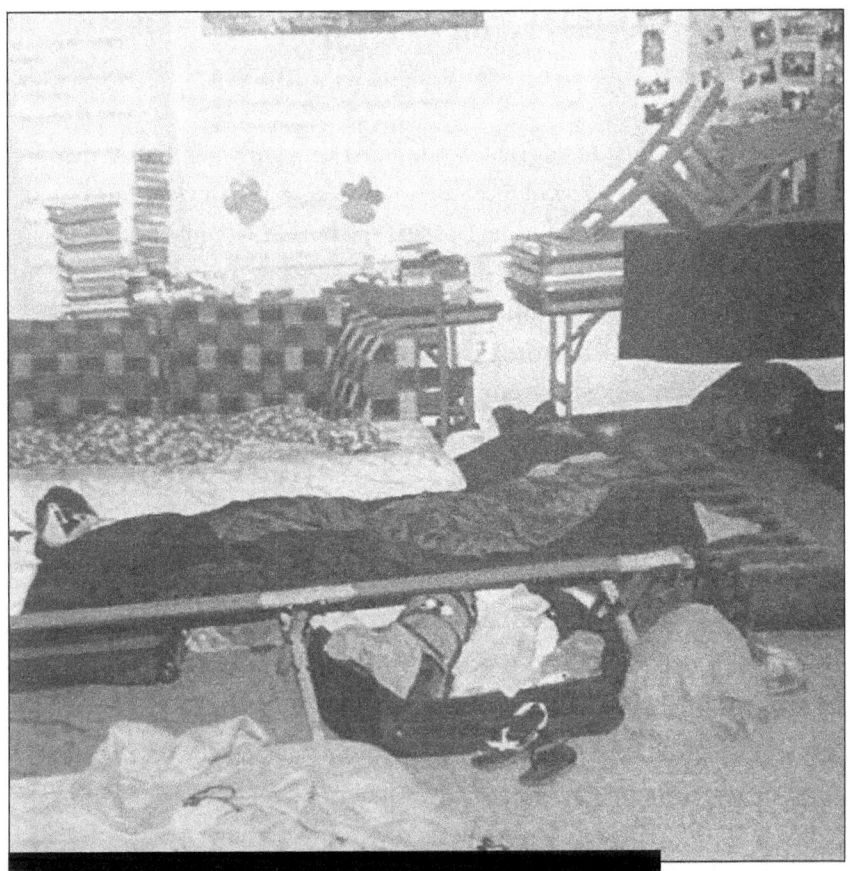

A place for volunteers to lay their weary heads.

Now some people want them to play in Switzerland, but the Goinses aren't too sure they want to ride on an airplane. They're thinking about it.

They were grateful for the offer of help with their house and expected the workers to do only minor repairs. Mother Pauline says, "I thought they were going to just fix the rotting sills around the bottom of the porch. When I came around the corner, I saw they had taken the whole porch off!"

"Those were the hardest working children I ever did see. I know they were teenagers, but I call them children. Sweat was just pouring off them."

The Goinses live a life of devotion to Christ. Their conversation is peppered with the heartfelt refrain, "Thank you, Jesus." With lyrics like, "Children go where I send thee" and "Have you been faithful to Jesus?" their music celebrates his leadership and the call to be faithful.

Ms. Boykin and the Salkehatchie Rosebush
Katherine Thomason, Youth Volunteer, 1994

Stop and smell the roses. That was my first thought when I arrived at my Salkehatchie site. A beautiful rosebush grew next to the Boykin house, and I promised myself that each time I passed the bush, I would pause to smell one of the fragrant roses. And I did.

It's the little things that you remember that add up to form the experience of Salkehatchie—the roses, the people, the trees that shade your skin from the burning rays of the sun. It is amazing how it all fits together.

This past summer, I worked on the Blind Faith site. I had never seen it when I picked it; I just trusted the site leader, Hart Parker. I asked him two questions. "Is it a big roofing job?" He answered, "Yes." And, "Is there enough to be done to keep us busy, plus some?" He answered with a smile, "When isn't there enough to be done?" I volunteered for the house along with seven other girls and two guys. We were ready for anything.

On Sunday, we went to visit the site to see how much work we'd have to do. The main thing I remember was the trash, or what I thought was the trash. As I walked through the house, everything was piled with bags full of stuff. There was barely room to move about the house. I found out later that it wasn't trash at all. The roof leaked so badly that they put all of their belongings in trash bags. They didn't have much, but what they did have, they wanted to keep dry.

All week everyone worked hard. On Monday we tore off the sunbaked, rotten shingles and prepared the house for the repairs. We worked all day in the heat of the sun. We met the family—Mary Boykin and her two daughters, Toya and Gail. Little did I know that many other relatives would arrive by the end of the week.

We got a lot of work done that day, and at six o'clock we headed back to the camp. That evening, disaster struck. Heavy rains in the area tore at the tar paper that covered the otherwise unprotected roof of the Boykin house. As I watched each raindrop from inside my watertight cabin, my heart was torn to pieces. I knew that Mary and her daughters and all of their treasured trash bags were being drenched by the heavy rains. I have never been so terrified to return to a site as I was on Tuesday morning. Would the house be redeemable? Would we be able to fix the rotten ceilings? Would Mary ever trust us to complete the work on her house? My fears were confirmed as we pulled up to the house and saw that the tar paper had been blown from the roof. Everything must be soaked. An instant calm came over my heart as Mary walked out of her house with a smile on her lips and kindness in her heart. She was a true believer and she trusted us, whether it rained in her house or not.

Tuesday afternoon it rained again. We had begun to shingle, but we were nowhere near finished. Large droplets of rain poured into the house and there was nothing we could do. I went back to Toya's bedroom and sat on her mattress under one of the large leaks, trying to absorb the majority of the water with my shirt. I began to cry. I cried for Mary's faith and unconditional love; I cried for Toya's drenched belongings; I cried for their need and our inability to stop the rain from falling. Toya found me in the back room and sat next to me on the bed. She was as calm as the sky after the storm and sat there quietly next to me watching the water fall into her room. I smiled at her through my tears and made another promise—really to myself more than to her. "Toya, I'm not going to leave until we fix up your house. I promise you we will get it done." Her answer came softly. "I know. I believe in you." We stood up and walked back to the others.

On Wednesday there was more disappointment. As I rounded one corner of the house, I noticed a short, stubby thorn branch. The rosebush was gone, and only a few thorns remained. Someone had cut it down. I was torn. I didn't know what to think. It was explained to me that it was to make it easier to paint the house, but I still felt that the beauty had been stolen.

The family was great. They were always willing to help, and we really got a lot accomplished. We shingled the roof, built floors, hauled trash, reworked the plumbing, and put screen on the windows. Amazingly we still had time to replace boards on the house, paint the house and the ceilings, and build a couple of closets and a back stoop. We were also able to wallpaper the bathroom, put down rugs and linoleum, and put up new blinds. The house looked wonderful.

It is amazing how close you get to the people on your site during the week. We would laugh together, and sometimes cry together. We had some great times and some sad times, but everything we did, we did together. The strength everyone has during the week at Salkehatchie is unbelievable.

We work for five days, ten hours each day, doing tasks we have never even attempted before. Some may think that the strength comes from the loving friendships, Jesus Christ, or even God the Father. I believe that it is maybe a combination of all three, but one thing is for sure. The strength is real, and it gets the job done on every site.

The last day we made a gift for Mary's grandson, Jamal, who had helped us all week. We constructed a basketball goal for him and gave him a basketball. As we hugged everyone good-bye, I watched Jamal playing basketball with his cousins. I was overwhelmed with joy. We had finished. It was a wonderful feeling.

On the final house tour, I remember something that one of the other homeowners said. "My house had fallen, and you picked it up. At the same time, you picked me up with it." And as she described the shape of her house before the week had started, she claimed, "It was rain'n inside and leak'n outside." So often it is the rain that comes inside our lives and it seems that when it rains, it pours. But, for once, the people we serve have a dry place to live, a floor under their feet, and an understanding of the love Salkehatchie can bring.

By the end of the week, I finally understood the significance of the rosebush. At the beginning we had destroyed the bush, just as we had torn apart the house in an effort to rebuild. We encountered thorns throughout the week from the heat, the sun, and the work. But just as the house was rebuilt, so will it be with the rosebush. It is with faith we are assured that the beauty of the rosebush will return. In 365 days I will return, just like the roses. And it is the hope of the rose that instills in me the beauty of life and unconditional love. Next year the rosebush will have blossomed, my faith will have flourished, and I will reunite with all of the loving friends I have made through Salkehatchie. We made a difference, and we made it together.

Daniel
Arlene Bowers Andrews, 2000

What a smooth week. We had Greg "Squirrel" Bridges, Nate "Moose" Cannon, and Jonathan "Doood" Rollins, steadily on the roof until it was done. Courtney "Skeeter" Durden and Jennifer "J-Bay" McKay started on the roof and moved to interior decorating for mildew control. Chad "Fishman" Fish and Tamara "C.O.D." (Catch of the Day) Fentress persisted with floorboards, vinyl, and carpet, as well as interior decorating. Stuart "Boss Man" Andrews handled plumbing, ceiling, and fascia. Rick "Tool" Goss showed up to lend his gear and a hand for the day. And Dennis "Doc" Fish, a first-time adult counselor, became our Floor Meister. The amazing Linda "Shop Till You Drop" Honeycut ran the truck for us. And I worked on windows.

Everybody worked on other jobs, too, until the house had a new roof, blessed running water, nice white ceilings, unstained walls, fresh carpet and stable floors, new vinyl floors (bathroom, kitchen, and back porch), whole windows, new doors (with knobs and locks), fresh exterior paint with nice blue trim, new refrigerator, and no pile of debris because we hauled three huge loads to a site where it would be picked up. Ms. Bee did the interior cleaning, which was a challenge, given that the water wasn't turned on and working until close to quittin' time on Friday.

We had extra help from Ms. Bee's five-year-old grandson, Daniel.

"Miss Arlene, do you have any jobs for me?"

"Yes, Daniel, but you'll need to go home and put on shoes... and wear this pair of safety goggles. . . this pair of gloves... this nail apron..." The roofing crew fixed him a cap like theirs, made from a tee shirt sleeve.

Daniel proudly wore his outfit while he picked up nails, scraped paint off the exterior walls, tested our snacks, and ran to find a tool or give a message to someone on the other side of the house. He spent most of one afternoon with his new set of blocks, made from numerous discarded pieces of two-by-fours. I've never worked with such a smart and polite child. He knew all the crew members' names in no time. He especially loved the guys on the roof. He took breaks with them and sang and danced with them.

He and his sister Samantha and their friend Ashley got into a fight over who could play with the blocks. This wasn't your typical in-your-face-I-don't-care-about-you tough kid fight. They really cried—they didn't want to fight with each other. It hurt to argue. While they were each tearfully trying to tell me what harm the other one did, I let them know that I didn't want to hear about what they had already done, I wanted to know what they would do next, because one of our site rules is that everybody shares because we're a team. We huddled and stacked our hands on one another and said,

"Go, team!" Within minutes, they had invented a cooperative game with the blocks and they were laughing and running and having fun. I didn't teach them that—they already knew how. They just needed a little prompt.

"Who's the boss man?" asked Daniel. "Is it Mr. Stuart? Is it you? Ross?"

"No ... No ... No ... It's God, Daniel."

"Oh."

Jennifer and Courtney talked to Daniel about how we are all brothers and sisters, in God's way.

Friday, after our 140 friends came to view the work we had done, it was time to say good-bye to the Clifton family. Daniel had been fooling around with the guys, but he looked all around with big eyes and trembling lips. He was trying not to cry. I was stunned that he understood we were going away and wouldn't come back for a long time, if at all.

"Are you sad because we have to leave, Daniel?"

He nodded.

"We're sad, too. We love you. And God loves you."

We were so frantically busy throughout the week, I hardly realized how much this family had touched my heart. It was hard to say good-bye. Ms. Bee was truly moved. She said "I just wish I could cook a meal for all of you. I make the best biscuits! God bless all of y'all. I'll remember you in my prayers, and you remember me. And come back to see me!"

Glimpses
Mike Vandiver, 1984

Tom and Ella Jones are an elderly couple who lived without running water all their lives. Last spring, Mrs. Jones was almost bitten by a rattlesnake on her way to the outhouse. A deeply religious couple, the Joneses shared their faith journeys with the site crew. One of the young people said, "They taught me that God is already present and at work ahead of me. God is already with the suffering. I don't take God anywhere, I run to catch up."

When the crew finished, Mr. Jones, moved by what he saw, said, "I hope heaven looks just like this, but for now this my little heaven." The young people made a sign with "Our Little Heaven" on it and hung it over the door.

Grace and beauty.

Everyone took a piece of heaven with them when they left the Jones's home.

Sam Hyatt, an elderly gentleman with mental retardation, lives alone in an old sharecropper's cabin with no electricity or running water. Mr. Hyatt lives a simple life; he taught the crew a great deal about what is really necessary to live. The crew raised and resupported the floor, built a new outhouse, covered the floor of the living room, and painted. They wrapped the exterior of the house in rolled roofing to stop the wind and rain. Mr. Hyatt had only a box to sit on, so the crew found a cushioned chair for him.

Lily Smith is an elderly lady who lives alone. Her house was literally falling down around her. Even so, she seemed to spend a good bit of her time scrubbing it clean. As poor as she was, Ms. Smith donated the chair to Mr. Hyatt.

The large, extended **Sims family** lives in three trailers on one plot of land. A Salkehatchie crew fixed the grandmother's trailer last year by installing running water and building an extra room. This year, we worked on the daughter's trailer, which had neither running water nor electricity. We fixed that and added a porch and new outhouse. As the crew worked, at least eight children were always present. The crew taught the family about how to take care of their house themselves. One of the young people observed that the crew helped to "restore the lives and hopes" of the family. The crew became quite attached to the family and made many tearful discoveries as they connected with the family's sufferings.

Clyde Pinckney and his sister, **Aurora**, live in a large old house. Mr. Clyde uses a wheelchair. The crew started the week with trauma, because the house is located in the backyard of the local liquor store, and throughout the day, customers cast critical remarks about the crew's work. The Pinckneys were elated with the changes in their house, and by the end of the week, neighbors had brought the crew boiled peanuts and soft drinks.

Ms. Rose
Arlene Bowers Andrews, 2003

Ms. Rose, at age eighty-nine, lives in an unpainted wood frame house owned by "White people" (her words, she doesn't give them a name). She worked for the family all her life, in the fields and in their house. As she says, "I was good to them and they are good to me." They say she can stay in the house as long as she wants. The house has electricity and water from a cool, clear well that comes up through a rusty old pump outside the back porch door. The bathroom facilities are down an overgrown path behind the house, in a new outhouse the Salkehatchie crew built for her. Ms. Rose has raised six children and has countless grandchildren and great-grandchildren. She lives in the house with her young adult grandson and her son, who is "sick in the head" and stays in bed most of the time since he returned from a Columbia institution.

The house sits under a tree in the middle of a field at the end of a dirt road. Ms. Rose doesn't get many visitors, and when cars drive up, she doesn't go out to meet them. She watches from her front room. The day Pee Dee Camp Director Neil Flowers drove up for the first time, she just watched. She said he called to her through the screened doors and windows, "How ya doing?" He made no move to come to the door, he just walked around the front yard, looking up and all around, examining the house.

Ms. Rose says, "I can tell when I meet someone if I'm going to like them.

I liked Neil right away. He's plain-talking."

When Neil asked if she would like work done on her house, Ms. Rose said, "I've got to show you something. Stay right here." She went inside, and came back with a smooth little stone.

She said, "When I'm feeling good, I go to church. We've got a nice big church. A few weeks ago, the preacher had a box full of these stones. He said that if we have faith like a rock, God will answer our prayers. He gave me two stones. This stone has been good luck to me, because I prayed for help with my house. I had faith, and here you are. Here, I pass one of the stones on to you."

Neil's theme for the year was "Faith Like a Rock," and he gave every Pee Dee camper a stone.

Ms. Rose observed, "Those children were all over this house—working so hard! I always worked hard; I didn't know what sitting down was. I think hard work is good for your body. I used to get up, work in the fields, take a bath, put on clean clothes, then go to work in the house." For a while, she lived in New York, working for rich people who furnished all her clothes.

Ms. Rose smiles all the time, gazing at her listener through bright eyes covered with thick cataracts. Her voice quivers with palsy, yet she talks with enthusiasm as she describes how she teased the children and sprayed them with water. I realize she is extraordinarily beautiful as she says, "I love to leave people happy."

Wilma
Arlene Bowers Andrews, 2002

This year I'll start at the end, which is, as all endings are, really a beginning. After our site family left on a hot Friday afternoon (the temperature was almost one hundred degrees), Stuart and I returned for a moment and found Ms. Sarah Jo, the eighty-five-year-old mother of Ms. Wilma Ford, sitting in the yard under the tree. Ms. Wilma was inside, enjoying the now-functional air conditioning, and Ms. Sarah Jo could have sat there or on the newly refurbished screened porch, in the new rocking chair. But from her perch on the old folding chair in the clean, freshly raked yard, Ms. Sarah Jo could behold the wonder of the outside renovations. And she seemed to be at peace, sitting alone, facing the house.

A week ago, when we arrived on Sunday, we asked Ms. Wilma what she would like for us to do. She simply said, "Anything you can do to fix up this place." When we urged her to be more specific, she said she would like to be able to sit outside her house. A sturdy deck that is completely accessible by way of a gently sloping ramp now wraps the front corner of the house. One end of the deck leads to a screened porch with comfortable chairs. The porch was there before we came, but it was mostly a storage area, loaded with old stuff. About half the screening had fallen. The side door to the house, inside the porch, was completely blocked off and the concrete steps to the porch had been smashed. So we cleared the porch and fixed the screens and built a little step from the porch into the door.

Ms. Wilma, age sixty-three, suffers from kidney disease and receives dialysis three days a week. We thought we arrived early each day, at six-thirty, but on Monday, Wednesday, and Friday, she had already risen and left for her treatment by that time. She didn't return until after noon. She also has severe joint pain, especially in her knees, making it hard for her to climb steps, bend, reach, or rise up from a chair. Our goal for the week was to improve her quality of life by making the simple motions of daily life easier for her.

> I know that my life will be over soon. I don't have much longer ... maybe a year or two. I accept that. I pray that all those young 'uns and you will have a long life and that you will be blessed.
>
> —*Wilma, house renovated 2002*

Her ceilings were leaking in a few places and we traced the problem to inadequate flashing around the chimney; otherwise her roof was in good condition. She had been unable to bathe (except by hand towel) for quite some time, and she said she would like to be able to shower, but her tub plumbing didn't work. We also noticed access to the toilet and tub was hindered by a narrow passage, less than eighteen inches, between the bathroom sink and wall. So we fixed the plumbing and knocked out part of the wall to recess the sink and open the passageway. The bathroom and kitchen floor coverings had crumbled and elsewhere the carpets rotted, so we replaced those. And we widened the access to the rear of the house, where the bathroom is located, by removing part of a kitchen cabinet to open the space between it and the stove.

We saw signs that Ms. Wilma and her family had struggled to keep the house warm in the winter and cool in the summer. The family had added several improvements to the house over the years, including storm windows and (remarkably) a central heating and air conditioning unit. The windows had deteriorated; many were broken and, in some places, plywood or duct tape had been used to patch them. Several wooden windows had rotted around the casings. We replaced as many windows and storm windows as possible. The ducts for the air conditioning leading to the combined kitchen and living area had fallen under the house, so when the air conditioner was on, the area under the house was being cooled (at great expense), but the rooms were stifling hot. The bedroom air vents were blocked with stuff and the central vent had a filter that was rendered thoroughly useless by layers of dirt and dust. The family had installed ceiling fans but bought the kind that are meant to be hung from a high ceiling, so they hung low and conked you in the head as you walked through the room, or if you are tall, in the throat. We replaced the main one with a ceiling hugger.

Ms. Wilma was also concerned about being secure from the crackheads who live in the neighborhood, so she asked for a front door that could lock. When we arrived, her front door was just a glass storm door with a loose flip handle. We installed a sturdy exterior door with bolt lock.

All of the work described so far was the easy part. The hard part was that this was a tunnel house. Last year, John Fooshe talked about how the house they worked in was like a tunnel when they arrived: dark, piled with stuff, with a narrow walkway through it. Ms. Wilma's house reminded me of caves I had just explored a few weeks before. Piles of clothing and bedding were everywhere. The closets were overstuffed - enormous mounds of fabric rose like new volcanoes as we tossed stuff out. Some of the stuff was in large bags, some just lying folded or loose. There were mounds of new and used drapes and bed coverings gathered from the factory where a family member had worked. Her grandchildren of all ages had brought clothes and other items to the house; these were lying all around.

Ms. Wilma resisted letting go of much of the stuff. She clung to her things like we all cling to the treasures we have built up on earth. To her, each item had a potential use, and seemed important for the moment when it was acquired. Over time, the accumulation of these valuable objects had rendered them worthless, impaired the process of basic living, and created dangers (not the least of which was fire and health hazards, given that these piles were havens for roaches and vermin). Ms. Sarah Jo became an official member of our crew, overseeing the disposal of these piles while her daughter, Ms. Wilma, was at dialysis. It was a tedious, three-step process: first we screened—if it looked like trash, we tossed it. Otherwise, Ms. Sarah Jo got it, and she helped create "give-away," "toss," and "maybe-keep" piles. Then Ms. Wilma went through the maybe-keep piles and chose what to keep and what to give away. Joseph and Thomas, Ms. Wilma's adult sons, were the most efficient. They simply said, "Toss it all," and, at one point, Joseph converted the old, useless car sitting in the front yard into a storage shed by stuffing it with bags.

The window doctor, author Arlene Andrews.

We tried to respect Ms. Wilma's emotional needs. As the week progressed, letting go became easier for her. The hardest part was the morning when she went through her husband's clothing. He had died a year-and-a-half earlier, after forty-three years of marriage. Ms. Wilma broke down and cried and talked about him while the sorting continued. We tried to honor Ms. Wilma's desire to give to others by donating useful items to the Heaven Sent thrift store. We tossed or gave away about three truckloads of stuff but never finished going through it all; we didn't touch one room and only went through about half of the other. Thomas says he will finish and send us a picture of the place; we think he's inspired! Ms. Wilma now has a hanging rod in her bedroom with her best clothes on it, a dresser and mirror, and easy access to her bed.

The kitchen was a story in itself. Ms. Sarah Jo is a professional cook, and she taught all her children to cook. Ms. Wilma also loves to cook—when we arrived on Sunday, she was baking a hen and making a huge pot of dressing. But she had no counter space. All surfaces were covered with tin cans, jars of food, spices, dishes, paper products, old hams, cooked food, and leaking and rotten items.

The cabinets were stuffed with more cans—many of them institutional size—and jars and other things. Many of the cans were ancient, dented, and rusted. In the shelves were Mason jars of mysterious preserved food that had been put up by Sarah Jo's mother, who died ten years earlier. Who knows what sort of organisms lived in them. Rat poison was scattered around, and lay on items like country hams. The drawers were stuffed with paper, rags, and utensils.

Odors came from the overstuffed refrigerator. A deep-freezer was on the side screened porch and another in the laundry room. We defrosted one and tossed the old items. We kept good items in the other. Both are now accessible since we removed a lot of the things that were blocking them. Perhaps Ms. Wilma hoarded food because she thought it would be useful one day, or she could share it. Over time, she had lost her ability to bend down and even see what was in the cabinets, much less lift and use items or keep the cabinets in order. Her physical condition had seriously reduced her ability to clean.

Now, she has plenty of counter space, a table at which she and others can partake of a meal, a shiny new floor, and cabinets and drawers that are organized by items.

I think I understand how Ms. Wilma's house got to be so congested. As her health deteriorated, she was less able to keep it up. Her husband was ill for a long time before he died, so she lost the help she had from him. She had good intentions when she acquired things that seemed valuable at the time, but couldn't follow through on the intentions. She stored food and then couldn't use it and didn't have the will or capacity to get rid of it.

The massive clean-up effort this week was true servant work. Salkehatchie sites always include many jobs. Many have benefits associated with them: you can get a tan, learn a skill, or get immediate gratification, like when paint converts a wall. Some jobs bring glory because they look so impressive when they are done. But some are jobs that no one wants to do. No one wants to clean up other people's messes, whether it's forty years of trash or the stuff we spread around the yard and house during the week while we work. Every year, you can watch Salkehatchie volunteers try to wiggle their way out of doing clean-up. This week, we could tell that Ms. Wilma's family avoided doing clean-up. It's easy to think someone else will do it, because that's how we live our daily lives.

Of course, at Salkehatchie we are called to be servants, not heroes. I thought a lot about this on the ride home, as the odor of ripe laundry wafted forward from the back of my minivan. I thought of how Christ washed the dirty, stinky feet of his disciples. His disciples were stunned, because they believed such a task was beneath them, and certainly beneath their leader, because such tasks are meant to be done by silent, lowly people. Christ bent down and put his nose right near their feet, in a posture like the one our site family members assumed when they stuck their noses and hands into those messy kitchen cabinets. Christ did it for love and in respect of his disciples. I pray that I can have even an iota of such humility.

At the final site tour, Ms. Wilma shared with the group that she has been a Christian all her life. She prayed, "Help me, Jesus," and we came. She thanked God for sending us and said she loved every one of our crew. Ms. Wilma made a great witness to her own children this week, by showing them that prayer can produce a miracle. I pray they realize this mother's gift to them.

On Friday, after Stuart and I left Ms. Sarah Jo sitting in the yard, we went inside to say good-bye to Ms. Wilma. She was sitting on her chair, sipping a Pepsi, listening to the police band radio and watching TV. She was obviously comfortable and content. She told us that she was so thankful to God for all of us and that she was praying for us to have a long life. She said, "I know that my life will be over soon. I don't have much longer ... maybe a year or two. I accept that. I pray that all those young 'uns and you will have a long life and that you will be blessed." She seemed ready to let go. I am thankful that

God sent us to help her get ready. We assured her that we are blessed and that spending a week with her was a part of our blessing.

Each year, on Friday, at the closing communion service, we bring to the altar a symbol of what the week has meant to us. I didn't find my reflections symbol this year ... it found me. The yard had been covered with piles of trash and debris that either existed before we came or that we created. We loaded most of the trash onto the wheelbarrow and moved it to the dump pile by the street. Before I left, I picked up small pieces of trash and debris that were scattered around. I lifted a wad of something, and under it was a metal crucifix. It was about two inches long and was the kind that would be worn on a large chain. There, in the dirt, under debris, in front of the house where cars could drive over it, was an image of our servant Lord, in all his agony and humility, suffering for us, before his resurrection. There, after removing all that stuff, his hidden image was revealed.

I have barely begun to reflect on what the discovery of that crucifix means. Some would see it hanging around someone's neck and think it tacky, commercial, meaningless, or maybe even stylish. When I see someone wearing one, I never know if it's a declaration of convinced belief or just a mustard seed, signifying a bit of faith that, with encouragement, can grow. I do know that my daily routine can get so cluttered with gotta-do lists that I often lose sight of the risen Christ. I forget the spirit of Salkehatchie, though I would love to feel it all the time. I need to clean my own spiritual house, let go of a lot of trivia and garbage, and put my life in order. I need to remember Christ's sacrifice and rededicate my life to service. I need to figure out how I can join with my fellow believers and support the Holy Spirit in spreading unity through faith, hope, and love across this world where hate and selfishness are causing so much agony. That's just the beginning. Who knows where this reflection will lead? So, I'll end with a beginning.

Lisa
From a presentation by Hart Parker

Lisa, a young college student with cerebral palsy, was confined to a wheelchair because her muscles were always contracted. She always wore a smile, though her speech was garbled. She had the most caring mother you can imagine.

Their home had water, but no bathtub or electricity. Lisa would drag herself around the home. Her house was not equipped for the wheelchair that she had been given. Her fiftyish mother would pick Lisa up and drag her from room to room to bathe her or to help her go to the bathroom.

We worked the entire week in Lisa's home. We took doors down. We built ramps. We built a bathroom that I'll bet was the quality of any in a hotel. We changed the home dramatically.

Lisa was always there with a smile. The last day, as we were leaving, all of the 160 volunteers were standing there. In her garbled speech, she said two things: "You're special" and "I love you."

I received a Christmas card from Lisa every year until she passed away. We touched her life and she touched mine.

Closing

Salkehatchie is first and foremost about people and their relationships. We come to the homes of strangers; we leave feeling as if we are family torn by a bittersweet need to separate. The volunteers return to their own land. In the days between our meeting and our parting, we see glimpses of the family's feelings and wisdom. Our volunteers, with their determination, energy, and vulnerability, witness the joy and tragedy of the setting. The family members say the "children" have blessed them. The youth say it's the other way around; they feel blessed. Their hearts are in the homes of the families they leave behind.

Chapter 3

A Week: A Moment in Time

Christian faith calls believers to a life dedicated to the relief of poverty and oppression, with Jesus as a role model. What difference can one week possibly make in the big scheme of the universe? The answer is: Mucho.

Salkehatchie happens in various times and places with different participants. Although each camp week is unique, we'll try to capture the essence of how a service week evolves by describing representative events. We describe how families and volunteers get connected, the work, the reflections of volunteers and families, and the transformation of both the physical structure and the people.

Words like "busy," "hectic," or "hyperactive" are insufficient to describe the level of activity during a typical Salkehatchie week. The work manifests as physical labor and material change in the structure of the houses, though much of the work is unseen as it is in the hearts and souls of the participants.

Making the connection

Families connect to Salkehatchie in various ways. Salkehatchie Summer Service does no formal advertising or recruiting for homes. Most often, the families are not seeking help; rather, someone notices they need it. Their friends, pastors, health workers, or others know how to contact a camp director or the local host church. Some camp directors simply drive around the areas they intend to serve, looking for homes that are visibly in disrepair. They boldly walk up to the front door and knock, introduce themselves, and say, "Do you need work done on your house?"

Some people who have never done mission work feel they don't have permission to intrude into another person's life. The Reverend John Culp has a pat response to that. He says, "I give myself permission—I have a mandate from God." He will quickly quote Isaiah's message in chapter 1, verse 17 that we are to rescue the oppressed, or James's admonition that faith without works is dead in chapter 2, verse 17. He observes that Salkehatchie gives young people confidence and permission to do amazing things with their lives.

> The time we take for this week is little compared to the time people take waiting for someone to help.
>
> —*Bill Brown, Fairfield Camp director*

Often, someone in a formal agency knows the family, such as a Department of Health and Environmental Control home health worker, or a Department of Social Services child protection worker, or someone at the Area Agency on Aging, or a community center like Penn Center in Beaufort. Sometimes families hear about Salkehatchie through an announcement at their churches. Sometimes a neighbor is familiar with Salkehatchie because they know someone whose house was repaired before. These people tell the pastor at a local United Methodist church about the family, and their name is passed on to the camp director or a community volunteer associated with Salkehatchie. In each community, the list grows during Salkehatchie week as people come forward to ask for help. They must wait twelve months, unless another community group helps them.

Consider how Ms. Barnes came to know about Salkehatchie. She is a widow who worked for years as a live-in sitter for elderly people. She earned whatever the people could pay her, which sometimes was very little, because the people she sat with had very little. She talked about how her house started to fall apart over the years after her husband died.

> My medicine was $139, but I've gotten now, the last few months, I've a friend of mine to help me, I've got it to where I can get it

> cheaper now. But I was drawing $629 and they took out $128 for supplemental insurance. They have to have that 20 percent. And then life insurance of $35.88 taken out of that, I didn't really have but $400 something a month. That's what I had to live on, besides what little bit Sam [her fifty-year-old son with partial disability] would give me, and that's just probably to buy his food, I would say. Telephone, homeowner's insurance, I had to borrow some money because I just could not make everything. ... the car out there, the taxes on it, liability coming up, and all these things, I just could not. ... I just did the best I could. When anything broke down, I just left it until I could get it fixed. The Lord see fit for me to get it fixed, I will. So I tried to be content with what I had under the circumstances.

She talked about old friends in the neighborhood and how they help each other.

> So she, this girl in North Carolina, J. W's wife's sister, had told me, we were just talking one day, that she knew Habitat for Humanity had done some work in North Carolina to help somebody. So Dorothy got to thinking about it. ... You know what, she had been in the hospital, had been real sick, had a blood clot. And I didn't want her thinking about my welfare or anything because I didn't think she was getting along very well.
> So she started, she said the Lord just led her to call some churches here in town. ... She said she had to think, you know, I haven't called the Methodist church yet. So she called the church and talked to the preacher there. She said he was real nice, she asked him if he knew anything. He said yes, that he knew this program. The preacher came out here and talked to me. He was very nice, I never met him before he came out here. He asked me if I wanted him to fill out an application for me. I told him I'd be very pleased if he would. ... I didn't know I could get help. The preacher said, "Ma'am, I would have helped you long years ago if I had known."

Many families express confidence that the Lord sent somebody to help them. They approach the week with awe. Ms. Irene Holmes, a pastor who suffered a stroke after her husband died, tells how she was at the local food pantry getting supplies to help a family. She happened to get in a conversation about work on houses and mentioned that her own had roof and plumbing problems. The pantry worker connected her with the local Salkehatchie camp director. She says, "It wasn't nothing but the Lord. I couldn't have gotten it done by myself."

The camp director's toughest job is selecting the families to help. Camp Pee Dee Director Neil Flowers often had referrals for as many as seventy homes, and could only choose twelve each year. In February and March, he would work with local community members to visit homes to assess needs and feasibility. Sometimes the selection team can refer the family to another faith-based volunteer group that does smaller projects, perhaps a roof or ramp only. Sometimes the applicants misunderstand the program's intent, thinking the program is to give jobs to youth, and they ask for unnecessary home improvements like a deck or paint job.

Sometimes the family needs far more than Salkehatchie can do, as in the case of the mother in Fairfield County whose carport was piled high with a mountain of beer cans. The house was structurally sound (it had been repaired by Salkehatchie volunteers years before), though filthy, and the power was off because she had been unable to pay the bill. Her family had desperate needs, but they were not of the kind that Salkehatchie could meet. The selection team left with tears in their eyes and prayers on their lips.

Some families are hesitant to accept help. Neil told the story a couple of elderly sisters, both almost completely deaf, as they pondered his offer to help. One said, "How much will it cost?" He yelled, "It's free!" and the whole neighborhood could hear. It's free. Just like God's grace.

Feeling the call

Each volunteer comes to Salkehatchie for his or her own reason. If you ask a group of younger volunteers, they'll say:

"My youth minister said I needed to go."

"I heard it was tons of fun."

"My best friend was going and I didn't want to be at home alone all week."

"I heard it is a good place to meet babes."

"My whole family comes. This is what you do during the summer when you turn fourteen."

As they make return trips, the youth are more likely to say:

"I learn more in a week of Salkehatchie than I do the whole rest of the year."

"I come because I feel closer to God here than anywhere."

"Salkehatchie is like family. I come because I want to see the friends I've made at this camp. We have a bond."

The spiritual work starts back in the volunteers' home communities, when they respond to the call. That usually happens when the youth or adult listens to someone talk about his or her Salkehatchie experience at a church service or program. The speakers generally talk about the house renovations, the community of friends, the love for the families, and the sense of closeness to God.

One camper told us, "I grew up in the Methodist Church, so we had Salkehatchie Sunday for many years. I was waiting until I turned fourteen, and I started that summer and have been going ever since. I'm twenty-six now. They can't seem to get rid of me. It has become a real staple in my life."

A rookie adult volunteer from Georgia observed, "We had these guys in our youth group who never said anything. They came back from Salkehatchie and spoke in church. Then they couldn't stop talking. They went from being pew-sitters to go-getters. I had to come and see what this was all about."

To be honest, we might ask these questions, from a reflection written in 1989 by youth volunteer Paul Robinson:

> Have you ever had to wake up to a cold and damp house and know you have to take a cold shower because there is no hot water?
>
> Have you ever woke up late at night and had to walk a hundred yards into a cornfield to go to the outhouse?
>
> Has your dad ever come home so drunk that he beats you black and blue, then in the morning he can't figure out why you are covered with bruises?
>
> Have you ever walked through your house and fell through your floors because they are rotten from the rain coming through the roof that is full of holes?
>
> Did you have to drop out of school so you could go work just to pay the rent that month?

Have you ever laid next to the wall at night and listened to the rats and cockroaches run around?

Have you ever come home and your mom is so high on crack that she can't even say, "I love you?"

Most volunteers could thankfully answer no to these queries. But rarely are they asked. Camp veterans who give the talks often glow with the joy of the experience and describe the desperate conditions in only brief terms. Volunteers are left to discover them after they arrive at the homes. Volunteers do not have to anticipate fear based on people's differences or judgment about their worthiness. Salkehatchie volunteers are called to focus on people's assets, not their deficits, and to love them just because they are.

Signing on

Volunteers sign up in the springtime and pay a registration fee that covers their room, board, camp overhead, and materials for the house renovations. They submit medical forms and receive a list of supplies to bring (hammer, gloves, safety glasses, Bible). They generally come in groups from their churches. Because Salkehatchie is a youth ministry, about 75 percent of the volunteers at any camp are between the ages of fourteen and eighteen. The adults come to teach and supervise. Before they come, they are asked to prepare. They receive a letter that includes the following:

> This information is for each volunteer! Everyone who plans to participate in the Salkehatchie Summer Service Project should read and study this information. This includes counselors, workers, and pastors.
>
> With all due sensitivity, we ask each applicant to consider our philosophy to see that he/she can relate to us and to the project in a positive and creative manner. Otherwise, he/she should seek other activities.
>
> We come to serve the people of South Carolina in the Christian sense of the word. When we commit ourselves to service, we are making a covenant with God to put our own needs and desires aside in order to share our talents, love, and concern with our sisters and brothers. If we do come with our own selfish desires (i.e., to be

appreciated, to erase guilt, to practice our own construction skills), we may as well stay home.

We do not work on empty buildings, but rather on homes where real people live. People who need love, a sense of ownership, an avenue for creativity, and a desire to belong. ...

Why Salkehatchie? Our neighbors in South Carolina live in homes needing repair and Jesus has called us to love our neighbor (Luke 10:29-37). The teachings of the Bible and the *Discipline of The United Methodist Church* challenge us to respond to the needs of all:

> "And he said to all, 'If any man would come after me, let him deny himself and take up his cross daily and follow me'"—Luke 9:23 (RSV).

> "And the King will answer them, 'Truly, I say to you, as you did it to one of the least of these my brethren, you did it to me'"—Matthew 25:40 (RSV).

> "He has showed you, O man, what is good; and what does the Lord require of you but to do justice, and to love kindness, and to walk humbly with your God?"—Micah 6:8 (RSV).

Social Principles (*The Discipline 2016*, para. 166, page 145):

> We believe in the right and duty of persons to work for the glory of God and the good of themselves and others and in the protection of their welfare in so doing; in the rights to property as a trust from God, collective bargaining, and responsible consumption; and in the elimination of economic and social distress.
>
> It is our hope that participants will experience discipleship in action as taught by the gospel and that by being open to learning, developing skills, and accepting grace, they will continue to be used as instruments of God's love.

We do not come to judge or change value systems. We come simply to serve and show God's love. The rest is up to God.

The volunteers come from all walks of life. A rare few are professional contractors or are skilled at carpentry, electricity, or plumbing. Most have do-it-yourself skills, desire to learn, and willingness to solve problems and ask for help from someone who knows more than they do. All come ready to engage in a meaningful relationship with the family.

For repeat volunteers, eventually the time comes when they have matured and they are tapped to be a site leader. Jason Moore (age twenty-five) reflected on what it was like the first year he led a site:

> I wasn't sure what to think when I found my name on the list of site leaders. I suppose I should have felt honored. After all, someone thought I was capable of pulling together a group of teenagers to fix this house and minister to Mr. McDonald. But honored wasn't my initial reaction. "UH-OH" was more like it.
>
> You see, I'm not a carpenter or roofer or contractor by trade. In fact, until my first year of Salkehatchie, I'd never used a power saw, much less repaired a floor or shingled a roof. Back then, I'm not even sure I could change a tire. Tim Allen, I'm not. But this was my sixth or seventh year (I'll have to go back and count my T-shirts), and I'd learned quite a bit in the interval. Like how to raise a floor with car jacks or how to use scrap board to shim in a new window. Still not what you would look for in a home repairman. Certainly not professional grade.
>
> So I was worried. Concerned. Overwhelmed. What if I screwed up? What if the kids found out how little I really knew? You can only fake it for so long at Salkehatchie. Sooner or later, everyone's true colors show through.
>
> There were more than a few times that week when, I confess, I didn't want to be the answer man. I didn't want to have the last word. I would have been just as content to haul shingles up the ladder all day, because I didn't have all the answers. And I really didn't know exactly what I was doing. More than once we gathered on the roof to pray because I was so frustrated I couldn't see straight. More than once I felt inadequate.

Salkehatchie weeks open with site tours.

I've asked around some since then. The feeling is not uncommon. After all, we're attempting the highly improbable and almost impossible: to repair a home in less than five days, using mostly inexperienced laborers, with little money. It's a daunting task at best. At times, it seems a recipe for disaster.

Then again, this is Salkehatchie. This is where miracles are expected. Where they are almost commonplace. So I've come to expect things will work out: the kids will bond; they will get at least a coat of paint on the house while they're painting each other; the rain will hold off long enough to get the roofing felt down; from a distance, the shingles might even look properly aligned; ultimately, we will leave the family better than we found them; and we, too, will leave as better, more compassionate people than when we arrived.

Jason speaks for many site leaders. They bring all the tools and resources necessary to do the physical work at the homes. Yet often, they are afraid. The challenge is awesome: they guide the transformation of the youth, the family, and the house. They also bring their faith, courage, and a can-do attitude. After all, they come from a long line of disciples who know that, "I can do all this through him who gives me strength" (Philippians 4:13).

Camps form as experienced site leaders feel called to lead. No one can direct a Salkehatchie camp until he or she has served as assistant director at a camp. All camp directors have a story to tell about how they stepped up to lead at Salkehatchie. Some will say they felt a call in their hearts. Others will say, "Reverend (fill-in-the-blank) asked, and I couldn't say no to a preacher." A few stepped in by accident, when a director became ill or otherwise unable to come. They knew if they didn't lead, the camp would not happen.

And so they come. Directors, site leaders, and adult and youth volunteers sign on. The Salkehatchie Steering Committee encourages churches to commission their Salkehatchie volunteers in a service that recognizes them as ambassadors of their congregation and Christ. The service also reminds the volunteers that the people they leave behind will offer prayers and other resources as they perform their mission.

Leaving the comfort zone

When volunteers leave home for camp, they let go of material comforts and familiar supports, as well as routine responsibilities.

Arlene has gone to the same camp in a rural community each year. She finds the trip from home to camp is detoxifying, as she leaves her busy urban life and enters a different world:

> I love the drive to camp. There's no air conditioning in my truck, and it's ninety degrees outside, but the breeze feels cool as we drive down the interstate early Saturday morning. We cross the Wateree River and its swampy bottomlands. We pass through historic Camden with its quaint little houses, blooming crepe myrtles, and antique shops. Then we travel for miles through pine forests, lots of pine forests, broken only by a peach orchard, where we always stop to get a bag of fresh peaches for snacks during the week. The road parallels a railroad track, and I wonder what rail transports these days. We pass through Bethune (home of the Chicken Strut), McBee, and Patrick, where we once wound up in the Pinestraw Festival parade as we passed through town. We pick up sub sandwiches

in Cheraw and get gas at the Wallace crossroads. By the time we get to camp, I feel like I was just here yesterday, not fifty-one weeks ago. I go to my timeshare, a bunk in Cabin Six. It's like coming to a family reunion at an old vacation home. My entire focus is on the Salkehatchie camp experience. We work in places like Clio, where we feel like we've experienced time travel. The town seems much like it might have been fifty years ago, except some of the stores are closed. For the week, I hardly hear any news of the outside world.

For a person whose life is dominated by the fast pace of urban living, the quiet, slower atmosphere of the rural South is refreshing.

Some camps are in urban communities. Some volunteers go to camps close to their homes. Wherever they are, the volunteers let go their routines and shift into mission mode, absorbed by the interactions and work of the camp.

Getting started

The camp headquarters tend to be at church recreation centers, church camps or schools. Everyone arrives, checks in, and finds a place to lay their heads at night, which typically involves a bunk, cot, or spot on the floor in a crowded room. They wander around the campsite among piles of ladders, paint cans, carpet rolls, toilets, water coolers, and other paraphernalia for the week. As volunteers arrive, they are likely to see someone getting a lesson in how to drive a dump truck or assemble a scaffold.

On Saturday, the entire group gathers to get acquainted and get oriented. The camp director goes over basic rules of communal living at the camp. That may be simply, "Do unto others as you would have them do unto you." Some are more explicit: "Act like a Christian. Love God. Love one another. Love yourself. No alcohol, drugs, sex, or smoking." One director held up a book and observed, "In case you are not familiar with this—it's a Bible. It's our guidebook for the week."

Many of the youth are from middle-class or affluent homes and the week ahead predictably contains elements of culture shock for them. The camp leaders present a theme for the week and begin a discussion of the spiritual basis of service. Leaders encourage participants to set aside their own needs and desires so they can share their talents, love, and concern with their brothers and sisters.

Mimbee Baker, Black Swamp Camp director, includes this statement in a packet for each camper:

> What is Salkehatchie Summer Service? For those of you who are returning, you have your own definition. For those who have never been, soon you will have your personal working definition, too! For most of us, we would agree that Black Swamp Salkehatchie is the hottest piece of heaven we have ever known. It is the most meaningful spiritual life experience many campers ever know. That is why so many return year after year.
>
> It has been said, "Our spiritual self is our greatest possession." Salkehatchie is certainly a place where Christian service develops our spirit by challenging us with difficulties we could never imagine facing alone at home. At camp we can discover the power of God and his children at work overcoming unbelievable obstacles through his miracles and the endless random acts of kindness shown to and through this Christian family of brothers and sisters we call Camp Salkehatchie.
>
> There will be times when you find yourself between a rock and a hard place ... under stress ... and literally wearing mud (if you're lucky!) on your face! ... Tar and Kool Seal take an entirely new meaning ... and no experienced camper would leave camp without their Bounce sheet ... bandanas become a badge of courage and pride ... and crying in public is no longer shameful!
>
> Now, as you prepare to begin one of the greatest, hottest, most frustrating, successful, stressful, longest, shortest, most spiritually strengthening, and humbling weeks of your life, here are a few key pieces of Scripture to lean on!

And the statement continues with the verses from the application as before.

So the campers at Black Swamp are forewarned!

John Culp has been known to put himself in a tall plastic trash can, telling the youth that we all live in trash cans. He observes that many people regard the houses we work on as "trashy." As he stands in the can, he says,

"It's easy to get in our trash cans—but it's hard to get out, emotionally and spiritually." When he tries to get out, he's at risk of tipping over. The youth have to rise to help him out.

John talks to them about God—how merciful he is. Using portable technology, he shows the camp a video, "The Power of One," that starts with an image of a human hand and shifts in increments of ten to the power of one more, starting with ten square yards, then ten to the second power, and so forth each second until the human's place is just a spot on the planet, then all is lost in solar system, the galaxy, and beyond. John talks about how hard God is to comprehend, and that's why he sent his son to live among us. He reminds the campers that God loves them unconditionally and that they can pass that love on to the families. They will give grace. And grace will be given to them.

Neil Flowers once started a camp with a *Gilligan's Island* analogy. He observed that the folks on *Gilligan's Island* set out, encountered a storm, ended up lost, and then proceeded to do amazing things with the resources they were given, like making radios from coconuts. But they never could fix the boat. At Salkehatchie, we fix lots of things, but sometimes we forget to focus on fixing the boat—our own boat, our life—and the lives of the families we serve.

Fairfield Camp director Bill Brown announces, "You will sweat. You may bleed. Remember, millions of people have suffered in service to Christ. Many have even died."

And so it begins. Food for thought as the body starts the work.

Matching volunteers to homes

On the first day, the entire camp population tours all the homes that will be served by the camp. The tour allows for direct experiences at a variety of homes. A few camps have chosen to show video images of the homes so that the site teams can form early and spend more time at their chosen family's home. The camps serve from two to fourteen homes. The tour can take from less than an hour (when homes are clustered in urban neighborhoods) to more than six hours (when homes are scattered across an entire county). It's an impressive sight to see scores of people standing in the middle of a cotton field, surrounding a house.

For the families, the arrival of the tour can be an overwhelming experience. Imagine seventy-five to one hundred seventy-five people arriving at your house, looking around, walking through, holding hands, and saying a prayer. Some family members clap their hands and shout for joy. Some smile shyly and stay in the background. One told us, "I was scared. I don't know why. All those people!" Another lady hugged each and every member of the tour—all seventy-five of them. Wary but open, the families begin to reveal their homes to the volunteers.

For many first-time volunteers, the tour of homes on Saturday is a sobering experience. As one said:

> We drive down a hard, white sand road embedded with crushed oyster shells. We approach a cluster of dwellings—one old four-room, wood frame house, another falling wooden structure that seems to have been a barn or garage, two rusty trailers (one looks occupied, the other abandoned). The yard is sand, with occasional tufts of grass or weeds, and is strewn with hundreds of crushed beer cans, cigarette butts, and other trash. Chickens peck around in the yard. Rusted yard furniture, about ten old car carcasses, and a rusty tractor shell are tossed about the yard. A tiny picket fence frames a plot in front of the house where gladiolas and other flowers are up and about to bloom. This entire area, about two acres, sits under splendid live oak trees. The view beyond the lot is an incredible vista of tidal marsh and coastal estuaries.

Many volunteers have never seen an outhouse, a house with collapsed floors, or children piled on a single mattress on the floor for a bed. Volunteers see physical conditions radically different from those in their own sanitized, insulated homes. During a tour, one veteran volunteer observed, "From one year to the next, you forget things. Like today, when I walked in that last house—I had forgotten the smell. As soon as I walked in, I smelled the poverty. Man, it just blows your mind, the kind of conditions people live in." A youth commented, "The house has no electricity. Never had electricity. That blows my mind. We're putting up a pole and the county is coming to make sure it fits the standards."

We find comfort in the awareness that Jesus always gets there before we do. More often than not, his picture hangs on a wall as visible proof.

A young adult who served as a youth volunteer reflected:

> When you're young, you're afraid. Simply because your world is safe. And everything foreign represents a change to that safety zone. So, to have an eye-opening experience that is truly positive, controlled, and safe allows the young mind to explore other possibilities. Because you can keep that interaction in the safe zone.

When Salkehatchie volunteers first met their brother Reuben, they were immediately humbled. Art told this story:

> Old houses die slowly. In time, the unpainted wood is subject to selective decay and the house leans precariously. The ridge pole breaks and the roof gradually caves in. The floor boards and joists, now exposed to the rain, quickly disintegrate and vanish. We drove up to a small roofless ruin of this kind, near Beaufort, in January. Only the walls, which leaned at a forty-five-degree angle, remained. A local resident guided us there when John told him we were looking for poor people who could benefit from our Salkehatchie Summer Service program.
>
> We sat looking and thought to ourselves, "He's got to be kidding. No one lives there!" But as though to refute our thoughts, he [the local resident] got out of the car, walked to the "door" and called, "Reuben! You there?" A muffled voice answered from within. I wiped my hand across my eyes and got out of the car. The canted door swung on its hinges and an elderly man came forth, like Lazarus emerging from the tomb. We were no strangers to poverty but we knew we were in the presence of "one of the least of these."
>
> He invited us in and from a pile of rags he produced a cast net that he had woven and which he proudly held aloft for us to see. My eyes went to the sky overhead, to the tree limbs burning in the corner (it had been eight degrees Fahrenheit in nearby Aiken the night before), to the few rags, and little else, that constituted his belongings. He had lived there for four years, we learned. When we left, it was with the promise that we would come back and build him a small, one-room house this summer. As we drove away, I

looked back at the small ruin sitting in the open field, still not quite willing to accept the reality of what we'd seen.

At home, I would weep in telling my wife about our experience. On cold days and rainy ones I would think of Reuben. Later, John, David, and I would visit him again and take him a tarpaulin, a sleeping bag, and a few simple items. No big deal. It wouldn't do to insult a proud person. But how do you say "I care" to your brother?

Last week on Good Friday, at Edisto Beach, I found a net-weaving shuttle that had been washed up on the beach and which was encrusted with some kind of coral-like growth. I cleaned it up and Maxine and I took it and a small canned ham to Reuben on Easter morning. He was cooking breakfast over an open fire in the corner of his "home." Because of this he couldn't accept our invitation to worship with us at Brick Baptist Church in Frogmore. I was pleased when he smiled at the shuttle we'd brought.

Someone said that you can tell how close you are to God by counting your possessions. If they are small in number, you are probably very close to him. Jesus must be very close to Reuben.

The majestic individuality of each person in the families living at the homes doesn't become obvious to the volunteers until they tour the homes and respond to the inner urge to connect with particular individuals. Some are inspired by the adrenaline-pumping physical challenges, such as replacing steep roofs, rebuilding a foundation, or adding on an entire bathroom. Others are moved by the smile of a grandmother or the presence of little children. Litters of puppies or kittens enhance site appeal. Lots of shade or the picturesque setting of a rural home can also be enticing. Whatever the initial draw, the richness of the connection does not emerge until the work begins and the relationships build.

Different camps use various procedures to attach volunteers to homes. Adults tend to be matched based on their own preferences and skills for the needs of the house and family. They are assigned before camp begins, so that they can anticipate their supply needs. Some camp directors ask youth volunteers to pray and choose their homes after the tour. After initial choices, the leader then coaxes people to rearrange their assignments so that the crews are balanced by age, gender, and experience. The crews must be neither too large (Joe Long limits crews to twelve members so they can truly get to know one another) nor too small for the tasks at hand. Some camps are more systematic and use a rating system, tallying preferences expressed by the youth and making assignments based on responses. Others have a lottery. Somehow the teams that form between volunteers and families seem meant to be.

For example, at one site, an elderly lady lived in her home, still grieving the death of her son in a car accident the previous year. On her team a young volunteer had just given birth to a baby and placed her for adoption; she was still grieving her loss. Another youth volunteer on the site was being raised by adoptive parents and was brooding about why her birth parents released her for adoption. These three women bonded through their grief and, together, experienced incredible healing and growth. Over and over, the families and volunteers share a part of themselves, becoming connected.

Immersion

After the preliminaries, the camps prepare participants for the intense week ahead.

Building a site family

Once the site crew is formed, they become a family. They spend the rest of the week together so that Salkehatchie becomes a small group experience. At first, no one knows just what skills and tools the group members have with them. Somehow, collectively, the group of adult leaders and youth, preferably with a young adult and/or college student as well, must perform or arrange for carpentry, plumbing, teamwork facilitation, roofing, electricity, site management, first aid, spiritual guidance, home design and décor, waste disposal, family and community relations, and a host of other tasks. And it works, over and over again.

Some camps conduct team-building exercises for the site teams. For example, at Marty Gunter and Matt Yon's Summerville Camp, each team wrote its goals for the week on poster board. The images included individual and collective prayers:

> This week I want ...
> > ... to be a human-being, not a human-doing. To realize that I'm

here for more than work.
  ... to build a handicapped ramp.
  ... to help build the roof, tear up walls, come closer to God, get to know my site people, have fun!
  ... to make Ms. Ida happy with the work we do and how we do it.

Dear heavenly Father, please help us to
  ... be patient with everyone,
  ... become closer to the people on our site,
  ... be strong and wise,
  ... be a blessing to others and be safe,
  ... listen to what you tell me to do,
  ... approach this mission with a humble attitude,
  ... NOT COMPLAIN.

Throughout this week, please be with the Salkehatchie families at sites throughout the Carolinas. Be with our families at home. Be with our brothers and sisters in Christ throughout the world. Thank you for the privilege to serve you. In all of this, let your will be done. Amen.

At Camp Pee Dee, each site team comes forward to the altar, where the site leaders carefully wash the hands of each person on the team in a solemn service reminiscent of the servant Christ washing the feet of his disciples.

Spiritual preparation

The campers do not work on Sunday. In the morning they worship at local churches. In some areas, they attend services that are culturally different from those in their home churches. A White urban dweller gave this account of attending a service at an African American church in a small town:

> What moved me most was how everyone in the congregation seemed to have a leadership role in the worship service, even the children. We sang energetic gospel songs. The adult choir had four members. The children's choir had ten. Even the preschoolers had a choir. The pastor called all the children to the front and prayed over

them, asking God to seal them in his blood and protect them from alcohol, drugs, and Satan. A young deacon who seemed to be no older than fourteen delivered a polished and enthusiastic message, extolling us to release ourselves to make way for the Lord. This young man became a member of one of our site crews.

On Sunday afternoon, the site crews often visit with their families. They do a preliminary assessment:

> The family of six has only two bedrooms, but if we close in the porch and add a new porch, the boys will have a place to sleep. The family has no place to eat a meal together but if we take out a wall, they could fit in a table. The interior walls are coated in black oil from the heaters. The roof leaks in two places and ceilings are falling. The bathroom sink is about to fall from the wall. The floor caved in at two places. There are only four outlets in the entire house and extension cords are all around, overloading the circuits. Several windows are broken and others are loosely held in place by tiny nails. Some of the sashes are rotted through. The back door is rotten and about to fall off. There are no storm windows, no insulation. We ask about the winter. It freezes here.

Gathering to worship on Sunday.

Safe. Dry. Warm. These are the Salkehatchie priorities. Make the place safe—eliminate fire and health hazards, including barriers for people with mobility limitations. Fix the brokenness, make it secure from intruders. Make it dry—fix the roof and plumbing. And make it warm—so people can be healthy and have low heating bills in winter. If the place can look prettier, that would be great, too. Fairfield Camp Director Bill Brown tells participants that they cannot buy paint until there is insulation in the attic. On Sunday, the site crew makes preliminary plans for how to accomplish these goals during the week.

Later, on Sunday, before recreation, camp leaders go over safety basics. "Don't do stupid stuff" is rule number one. They add a few others, like proper use of power tools and ladders, the importance of drinking water, basic first aid, dealing with site hazards, and so on. The youngest and newest volunteers need extra attention as the work begins. Jay Gore, now in his thirties, reports, "We were fourteen years old. The first hammer swipe Ward made at Salkehatchie was in glass and the glass fell down and cut my arm." They learned. Ward has since become a twenty-year Salkehatchie veteran, having served as site leader and assistant camp director many times. They all learn.

The work begins

On Monday at five o'clock in the morning, the wake-up calls begin: pounding a spoon on a pot, yelling in a bull horn, ringing a bell, singing (off key, of course) a song like, "Joy to the World." Everyone pops up, gobbles some breakfast, and heads with their site team to the home where they hold a devotional and start work, sometimes by six-thirty. At the Penn Center, we could take no pride in how noble we were to arise so early, because when we awoke at five o'clock, a bus was already passing by the camp, filled with migrant workers on their way to the fields. We realized they do this every day, not just for a sacrificial week.

After the devotional, there is likely to be a moment when everyone sort of takes a deep breath. As one youth said, "When you get to the worksite on Monday morning you just … it's overwhelming because you look around and where do you even start?" The site leaders typically suggest what to do, and the project begins. The first day's work always feels like the most productive, because it's mostly about demolition. Out come the sledge hammers, crowbars, Wonder Bars, and shovels. Shingles come pouring down, walls and stairs get knocked over, floors are ripped up, and useless things hauled away.

A mountain of debris begins to form by the roadside. Sometimes we're so enthusiastic we forget to plan ahead. Like we throw all the shingles down on the ground without laying out an old tarp first. So when it's time to pick up the shingles, it's a hassle. "Think before you toss" is a lesson that applies to many site jobs.

Demolition and clearing look like amazing progress. Reality usually sets in by lunchtime, though. One site leader observed:

> My own survey on Monday morning revealed that none of my assigned teenagers could make a saw cut or pound a nail without bending it, but their enthusiasm made up for their inefficiencies. By the end of the week they had acquired many basic skills. Two of our best workers were tenth graders, Meredith and Michele, who ultimately performed every job that our assignment required. I was extremely proud of them and I'll always remember the day that they mixed fourteen 80-pound sacks of concrete mix all by themselves—a job that would have exhausted me—while singing hymns in their sweet voices!

And from the youth's perspective:

> The hardest thing is that you're willing but you don't have the know-how to do things. You have to be patient. You have to really sit down and learn. We gain knowledge and grow spiritually as well.

As the old is torn away, new jobs reveal themselves. When you touch one need in the house, it is related to another, and another. As you tear away the shingles, you realize the roofing boards are rotten. When they are torn away, the damage in the rafters shows. Then someone steps through what had been a perfectly good ceiling. Plumbing is always like dominoes. Fix one part and the next one needs repair. Soon the list of jobs to be done in the week grows long. On Monday, the go-fer who trucks back and forth to the builders' supply and hardware stores stays busy. The supply lists are long. The inexperienced volunteers need considerable coaching and supervision on the first day. By day's end, everyone typically feels enthusiastic and the place looks so radically different (mostly demolished), they feel they have accomplished much.

The families stand back, amazed, on the first day and often seem worried. The tearing open of the house is a major invasion of their privacy. As one youth observed, "We are moving her life around." The families had no idea how badly deteriorated the place was until they saw it laid bare. Volunteers work with family members to tenderly move and protect the family Bible, old pictures, or official papers. They find plaques like the one at the home of a dear ninety-two-year-old woman:

> Ms. Hattie has never received the Order of the Palmetto or a presidential citation. What she has received is something far more precious. Twenty years ago her children and grandchildren gave her a personalized engraved plaque that cited her patience, ability to hug away tears, constant love, and other qualities that made her the "Best Mother and Grandmother Ever."

Oh, that any of our volunteers could earn such honor from their own families!

The families start talking to the youth and are typically amazed to discover that the youth are working without getting paid. Some of the families have no church experience and, initially, wonder why anyone would work so hard without pay. By week's end, they have an entirely different understanding and express awe at the love that has been shown. Most families have long practiced a faith and have been praying for help. One camper notes:

> Every house I've been in, there's always a picture of Christ or a religious photograph or a cross or something. And these people are living in poverty but they still have faith. I don't know if I'm the Christian that they are, sometimes, and it's very humbling.

Volunteers discover signs of a family's faith in wondrous ways. Jay Gore recalls:

> We found out about his passing. ... We went back to the house we had worked on the year prior. Of course it was vacant, abandoned.

There were a bunch of cats living in the house and a bunch of dead cats. It was totally nasty. I climbed through a window because I saw his Bible on the floor. It was one of the real thick, King James versions, the thick guy, one of the old school ones. And he had it together. He had driven three sixteen-penny nails in it, like you would punch holes in a piece of paper and bent them over to hold the pages together. That Bible is now in the Penn Center.

At another home, Mr. Harper had a massive framed picture of The Last Supper. It, like the walls around it, had turned black from the kerosene heater emissions. A little piece of the frame, about four inches long, had broken off. The youth took the picture down to clean it and paint the walls. Mr. Harper watched them to be sure they took care and asked them to save the piece so he could glue it back together. They cleaned it (as best they could), glued the frame, and on the last day, when they hung the picture, it hit them: "We're not here for us, we're not here for him, we're here for God."

Initially the families seem hesitant to get involved, but by day's end, and certainly by late in the week, they join along in the hard labor. Young family members get on the roof or crawl under the house. Older people pick up trash or wield a paintbrush. Children wear nail aprons and kerchiefs and carry buckets around to put stuff in. Curious neighbors watch from a distance at first, then stop by, then offer to bring ice or something useful, then jump in and help work.

The relationships between the youth volunteers and youth who live in the homes can be awkward. Seventeen-year-old Anna Harrison wrote this:

> There is a sixteen-year-old girl named Samantha and she seems to be really nice. Ms. Woods isn't real friendly but she seems pretty nice. She has a boyfriend that sleeps there and they both do a lot of drinking. There's a ton of trash to be hauled. There are two other teenagers—boys—neither was around much today. I imagine it is kind of intimidating to see us come in there and try to fix their house. Samantha is very shy but seems to need friends.

More often than not, the young people are sensitive to the dynamics of how they relate to the young residents. As the volunteers and residents do jobs together or just hang out during breaks, chances are they will begin to relate and soon feel as though they are friends.

The crews do a safety check before they leave on Monday. They make sure no ladders are upright, so that neighborhood children are not tempted to climb them. They take valuables, like tools, and lock them up. They cover everything with tarps in case of rain.

When the volunteers leave for the night, the families are left with a raw, exposed house and silence. They do what they can to secure the place. Ms. Thomas told us how she was nervous all night and could not sleep with her back wall off, because a year ago, her sister and brother-in-law were shot to death down the street. At another home, Ms. Irby arranged for her nephew to sleep over because she doesn't trust her neighbors. Many elderly people in small towns tell us, "You gotta watch out around here. There's so much dope."

Reflections

Each site crew and family devote time each morning and sometimes at day's end to devotionals that form a basis for their day's preparation or closure. One crew started and ended each day with this call:

> Leader: The cross ...
> People: We shall take it.
> Leader: The bread ...
> People: We shall break it.
> Leader: The pain ...
> People: We shall bear it.
> Leader: The joy ...
> People: We shall share it.
> Leader: The Gospel ...
> People: We shall live it.
> Leader: The love ...
> People: We shall give it.
> Leader: The light ...
> People: We shall cherish it.
> Leader: The darkness ...
> People: God shall perish it.

Leader: Go in peace.
People: Amen.

Some volunteers keep personal journals each day. Many site crews keep a group journal at hand so that crew members can write their thoughts periodically throughout the week, while they take breaks.

Starting early in the week, youth are given the opportunity to reflect on their experiences with the whole camp. Camp directors encourage adults to let the youth take the lead in expressing themselves. Adults are careful not to deliver sermons or tell the youth what they should be thinking or what they should be learning. Salkehatchie is about letting young people discover and share, in their own words and their own ways, the meaning and glory of God as well as the facts of life on earth. They need encouragement and freedom from judgment so they do not fear they will get it wrong. Most often their expressions are brief, perhaps in slang. They speak to each other, in the language of youth. The Holy Spirit gets revealed in fresh ways through the eyes and hearts of young people.

Early in the week, the young people tend to talk about the house and the physical tasks to be done. For example, a youth at Swamp Fox camp said, "Before today, I didn't know anything about plumbing, and I never would have thought I would be under a house, in the mud, with a million bugs." Another reported, "At our house, there are at least six varieties of roaches: albino white, bright red, and various shades of brown and black."

By midweek, they are gaining familiarity with the family and the neighborhood, and their focus shifts to their concerns about people who live in or near the home. Later in the week, they begin to discover new self-awareness, and they reflect about themselves and what they are learning.

Chris "Christy" Culp McIntire, John's daughter, says it like this: "I always say, 'guttin' the house, but it's really gutting yourself more than anything. A lot of people don't like to do that. It takes a lot of courage to come down here and open yourself up like that."

The Christian theme of redemption is symbolized in the physical work. Fixing an old house is like redeeming it, making it clean and whole again. In various ways, camp directors and spiritual leaders encourage volunteers to reflect personally and in community with the others at the camp. For example, at Black Swamp, Mimbee Baker and Rev. Caroline Matthews lead a service on Monday evening to help the campers focus their energy. They acknowledge how hard it is to give burdens to Christ, even though he asked us to do so. They ask each camper to write the particular burdens they brought to camp on a piece of paper. Then, with quiet music in the background, one by one the campers give their burdens to Christ by nailing them to a cross. They carry the cross outside where each camper takes someone else's burden off the cross, signifying their community of support for one another. They then place the burdens in a pan, where they are burned and offered up to Christ. The campers are then sent forth to help carry the burdens of the families they serve.

At Fairfield Camp, the site crews sit in groups and the director asks them to share with one another the scrapes, bruises, and "boo-boos" they acquired that day. He encourages them to think about the scars they brought with them. Then the groups discuss the signs of injury they saw in their site house and the family. The director asks, "What are you doing about the injuries?" They talk about what they can do to promote healing.

At Pee Dee Camp, a representative from each site crew lights a candle on the altar, then, in a circle with the other reps, shares something about the day's work. After all site family reps have shared, others may tap their shoulders and take their places, sharing their own reflections.

Amazingly, after ten or eleven nonstop hours of labor in the blazing heat, an evening meal, and reflections or a program, the youth still have energy to play soccer or basketball. They hang out, making music, talking with one another, building friendships, and often continuing their reflections about the day's events in more personal ways. Over and over, young people have told us that this is one of the best parts of Salkehatchie—when they reflect with one another, in pairs and small groups, informally. They are reluctant to turn out the lights at 11:00 p.m.

Grueling routine

At each house the crew works in small teams across various simultaneous tasks. For example, at one house, there are teams working on the roof, building a ramp, and fixing the plumbing under the house. As work gets done, these teams evolve into others that are painting, laying floors, and fixing the front door. A crew tackles the black walls, covered in residue from the emissions of the oil heater. Someone needs to check the windows, many of which are broken.

An adult reflects:

> So much to do! So little time. Can we afford this? We only have $1,500 and a few extra donations. Lines from Dr. Seuss's *Cat in the Hat* float through my mind:
>
>> This mess is too big and so deep and so tall!
>> There is no way to clean it—no way at all!

We do jobs we would like to avoid, because crews are small and someone has to do it. So we find ourselves on the roof even when we thought we were afraid of heights or under the house even though it disgusts us. And, lo and behold, it's not so bad after all! One volunteer observes, "Your sense of self dissolves. You have new appreciation for the passage, 'Whoever loses their life for my sake will find it' (Matthew 10:39)." Everybody does clean up, though no one wants to do it. We take breaks. Angels (church volunteers) bring ice and, sometimes, popsicles or watermelon. The youth goof around and make the chores fun. They paint each other along with the walls.

We learn about hydraulic jacks, cement block foundations, sawzalls, Skil saws, and things we've never heard of before, like Kool Seal, which gets applied to metal roofs to seal leaks. Fifteen-year-old Fuller says:

> It's like thick white paint that looks metallic when it dries. You apply it with a mop pole and big roller. You have to be careful—the trailer roof is thin metal that sits on two-by-twos—I have to step on them. If you step between, it will dent the roof. And the roof is slick.

We talk about being "up to your waist in waste" as we work on sewage problems. We help family members sort through mounds of old stuff. We patiently install Sheetrock. We haul thirty tons of junk or more (we know how much it weighs because it gets recorded at the landfill).

We make mistakes. No matter how many times the site leader says, "Measure twice, cut once," we will inevitably cut some pieces wrong. Young people are, after all, young. They're inexperienced. Some are prone to distraction, like the young man who, when asked to remove a rotted window, removed the perfectly good one right next to it instead. Accidents happen—mostly minor ones—but each week most camps typically have at least one volunteer at the emergency room, most often for a nail in the foot.

The go-fer for the site family drives the truck back and forth to the builders' supply or hardware store, sometimes thirty miles away, one-way. She learns about TSP, drywall, sink hangers, and the differences between spackling compound and mud, a window sash and sill, and 16-penny and 8-penny nails. As soon as one list of supplies gets filled, another begins: tube cutter, plumbing tape, five gallons of glue, two dozen two-by-fours, ten-pound 12-penny nails, fifteen sheets OSB (a type of plywood), door knob, glass panes three @ eight-by-eight, points, caulk, Roach Prufe, seven-foot one-by-four, one gallon Kilz paint, fire ant killer, one sack Quikrete (brand of concrete), and so on.

The crews sort through donated stuff back at the camp—this carpet, that toilet, those cabinets. "Oh, no, the sofa is already marked for another site! And how will we find some bunk beds for the kids?"

We pass on the craft of window replacement from old volunteers to new. Replacing a pane seems simple enough, but consider that a window doctor needs all this equipment: nail apron to hold the stuff while you stand at the window, safety glasses, mallet or muffled hammer to bash out the rest of the

People, as well as houses, get covered in paint.

broken window, leather gloves so your hand won't get cut when you remove the broken glass, measuring tape, paper and pencil to record the exact size of the frame, hard scraper with point to clear out the bits of glass, old paintbrush to sweep the bits of glass and paint, wide scraper to serve as dustpan, old paint bucket for the broken glass, glass panes that were ordered to fit exactly, points and a film container with lid to keep them in, caulk, caulk gun, nail to close the gun, latex gloves to use while applying the caulk, and flat razor to smooth the edges of the caulk. Whew.

By Wednesday morning, no one pops up at five o'clock. The youth lie motionless after the wake-up call. They slowly drag themselves from bed. At midweek, tempers are short. Everybody realizes we cannot finish all we would like to do. We have only one week and we've gotta get it done. We are at the mercy of the weather. Some years it rains so much, it's scary. At times we make big mistakes, like when the delivery truck with roofing shingles drove over the septic tank. It collapsed. We rely on prayers like this one, composed by Art's group at Frogmore:

> Dear Lord,
>
> It's Wednesday. It's hot. There is fatigue. The children at our site wear on us.
>
> Help me to remember why I'm here. Remind me of your gospel message of love and service. For you said: "I give you this new commandment to love one another as I have loved you." And you also said: "I was hungry … homeless and you took me in" … and other things. We know you also meant: my roof leaked and you repaired it; I had no water and you repaired my well; my house was falling down and you rebuilt it; I was down and you reached out a hand and lifted me up.
>
> You said, too: "Feed my sheep … tend my lambs." There is a line in our communion service that says: "Blessed is he who comes in the name of the Lord." We have come in your name and we find our blessing in the work.
>
> I know I mustn't note the speck in my neighbor's eye because of the log in mine, but sometimes his speck irritates my eye. Sometimes we get mad at the poor, forgetting that we're getting mad at the very victims with whom you stand. Channel my anger instead

> against the system that creates these victims.
>
> Help me to remember, too, that you call us to be faithful, not successful.
>
> See us safely through this week. Replenish our love and fellowship so that our words and deeds may be pleasing to you.
>
> Let this week's work be an offering to you whom we love.
>
> Amen.

Humans have a remarkable capacity for resilience in the face of stress. Under pressure, we cope. We take deep breaths to calm down, cry a few tears, ask for help from one another, say a prayer, take a little break, or use appropriate language to simply say, "I'm frustrated!" When stressors keep coming, and pressure increases anyway, everyone reaches the limits of their adaptive coping skills. We resort to maladaptive coping to get rid of the stress.

Uh-oh. That's when we see how people behave when pushed to their limits. Some shut down, sitting in a forlorn heap, moaning, "I can't do this anymore." Some get snarly, snapping irritable remarks at coworkers. Silently we wonder, "What am I doing here? How could I ever think this is fun?" An adult might yell at a youth, "I'm not putting up with this anymore!" and threaten to send him home. We've seen a couple of male youth let go their tempers and start to fight. A worrywart might become a mass of quivering anxiety, wandering around muttering, "We're never going to finish. Get to work." Some crew members pout, others bicker. We might blame each other for our misery, whining and complaining, pointing out the faults in others. Sometime during midweek, almost everyone is maladaptively coping in his or her own way, so we must be careful.

We're human Christians, not angels. Getting pushed to our limits is part of the experience. In these moments of desperation and vulnerability, we realize acutely our dependence on God and our Christian fellowship. Before Salkehatchie, we tend to be aware of God. During Salkehatchie, we learn we really need God. We want God. We reach out to one another, offering a listening ear and advice. Sometimes we just quit for a while and pray. Inevitably, we recall this assurance from Isaiah:

> The Lord is the everlasting God, the Creator of the ends of the earth. He will not grow tired or weary, and his understanding no

one can fathom. He gives strength to the weary and increases the power of the weak. Even youths grow tired and weary, and young men stumble and fall; but those who hope in the Lord will renew their strength. They will soar on wings like eagles; they will run and not grow weary, they will walk and not be faint (Isaiah 40:28-31).

Humbly, we accept that God is handling the problems of the families we have come to love. We are there only to do our share. And he will give us the strength to do that as best we can. With a good meal, group reflections, and some sleep, our tension passes. We're back to coping adaptively. By Friday, we're believing again that we can do anything. Our joy is even greater because we made it through our suffering.

Programs

In addition to the reflections on two or three evenings, the camps sponsor various programs. Often a musical group will perform. An inspirational speaker may come. The adult counselors share insights. For example, an adult who worked many years as a youth volunteer recalls a vivid memory he cannot forget:

> David Stewart, a professional potter and artist, brought his wheel and, as John Culp spoke, David sculpted a beautiful pot. When David was done, John held up the pot and threw it to the floor, where it collapsed. He said to the stunned onlookers, "This is what happened to the families we serve. Their dreams, their ideas, their hopes for their children were crushed. Think of what is precious to you. You can lose it all, too."

One year, after John shattered a beautiful ceramic pot, volunteers picked up the pieces, formed a cross with paint stirrers, and glued pieces onto the cross, creating a beautiful mosaic, signifying the broken made whole in Christ.

At Union Camp one summer, John Culp and Fred Reese got a burial casket and told the campers to write all their bad feelings and sins on papers and put them in the casket. They loaded the casket onto a dump truck and drove it from site to site, yelling "You are forgiven." Then they buried the casket at the dump.

Worship at Salkehatchie Native American camp.

In 2004, the Native American Salkehatchie camp traveled to Rocky Swamp United Methodist Church in Neeses, South Carolina, where the beautiful old church has been commissioned for worship by area Native American Christians. Keith Hiott taught the campers about the sweat lodge. They knew from their experience with their site families that pouring sweat, while physically releasing toxins, can also make you feel spiritually open and purer. So they understood how such a ritual can have meaning. Keith also told them about how, through the sweat lodge ritual, the Creator speaks to us through fire, as through the burning bush, and in the darkness. Sharing the experience as a group is an important part of the worship. He also described the medicine circle. They were advised to "Be still and know that God is God" as they participated in worship that involved smudging (purifying the air with burning herbs), storytelling, songs, drums, and dancing. The participative worship style fit perfectly with the Salkehatchie experience.

Many camps have a talent show. This involves a blend of performances by campers with real gifts and brazen skits by those with none, except a knack for demonstrating that you can be foolish among the people who love you. So we enjoy a cappella songs that sound like angels, rock bands, acoustical guitarists, piano concertos, praise bands, rap and rhythm, meaningful skits, dancers, amateur magicians and comedians, and more.

The art and humor give us respite from the fatigue and obsessive anxiety that is building about all the work to be done. We are reminded, "Therefore do not worry about tomorrow, for tomorrow will worry about itself" (Matthew 6:34).

Midweek perspectives from the families

The families are working with the crew if they can, watching and supporting if they cannot. In some cases, they must be away during the day, for reasons of health or work. Here are some observations from and about families during midweek:

Ms. Betty told us, "It rained that week. ... the boys' pants, the water would be pouring out. And I wanted them to come in so bad. I stood at the door and got some towels and told them they could come and put a towel around them or something for their clothes to get dry. But they went ahead and worked right through the rain."

Mr. Roberts, still amazed, said, "They jacked the whole house up! Once they jacked the house up, everything fell back in place.... That's some old lumber. See them real two-by-fours, they are not those fake two-by-fours like you buy now."

Mr. Moultrie said, "I try helping them when I can. ... Well, I try but I'm in their way because they work so hard. ... I'm enjoying it. The kids that are doing it are enjoying doing it. That's why I'm over here [at the picnic table] and they're over there [at the house] because I don't want to be around them because I'll stop them from working."

Ms. Quick confessed, "They are very friendly people. Like Nancy said, 'I see you trust us.' What can I do, but trust a person? They in my house working and I can be here. ... I left them here yesterday, day before, and went to the doctor. ... If you in here working, I should trust you."

Christy, a volunteer, remembers she was working on Miss Lula's porch and she kept messing up and having to pull boards up. She was getting frustrated—it was midweek. Ms. Lula would say, "Okay, Christy, count down. ... ten, nine, eight ..." and she would calm her down. Christy says, "She was such an angel. I have the pictures of before and after, and it's just amazing. I just cannot believe I was a part of that."

Ms. Hampton needed to go to a store a few blocks away to use the bathroom because the crew had turned off her water. The site leader offered her a ride, but she declined because she didn't want to waste his gas money.

Throughout the week, Ms. Etta gave her site team cantaloupe, grapes, and watermelon. It's the little things that count.

Ms. Jeffers had never had a new refrigerator before. She always got one from the secondhand store and they never lasted too long. She was thrilled when the crew delivered a new one to her.

Ms. Irene Holmes told her Salkehatchie site crew about how God had healed her after she had a stroke. For a while, she was completely paralyzed on one side, but she never lost faith or hope. She said the doctor asked her, "How can you smile when your leg is dead like that?" She answered, "Because this side ain't dead yet. I thanked God for this side. I still had one side that had life and knowing that this side still had life, the Lord provided for this one. So that is what I said to the young people. Just be encouraged. Be encouraged, no matter what happens to you in life, it is not over until you hear the voice of the Lord say it is over." Later, she recovered full use of both sides. She says, "We never understand the mystery of God, but I know that God did it. He is the only one."

At midweek, the families are less anxious than at the beginning of the week. They try to be helpful, give what they can, chat and joke with the "children" and stand back in awe of what they are seeing.

Excerpts from the volunteers' journal entries during midweek illustrate their moods and activities:

> ... Today I was the mom of three kittens.

> ... I jacked a house today.

> ... How can we ever make such filth right? It is so frustrating! Damn poverty, prejudice, ignorance, and double damn vodka bottles.

> ... It rained every day. We roofed in the drenching rain. We had roofed in one hundred five-degree weather, but the rain was scary. It was slippery. We had leaks. It was frustrating.

… Last night I got a chance to tutor Henry, a little boy from my site. I helped him do his homework by showing him one problem and supervising the rest. This morning at school, his teacher said that he didn't do the work on his own, which made me angry. It hit me that I am not just here to fix Ms. Barbara's home and love her family. I am here to help this family become so much more. Children need to be appreciated and told they're smart so that they can one day believe in themselves enough to know that they can accomplish anything if they put their minds to it. Henry's face beamed with joy when I told him he is a smart kid. I don't know how often he hears it, but it's not often enough. So, future readers, please realize that Salkehatchie is not just about houses, that's just a detail. It's about love and helping people feel better about their lives, surroundings, and most of all, themselves. You are here for a reason, the same as me—to do God's will. Never forget that people come first.

… This is my first year at Salkehatchie. I've had great friends before but nothing like the ones I met here (I love y'all!). It's been three days and we have almost finished. My spiritual growth in these past few days has amazed me. I never thought so many people who are completely different in so many ways could forget that and work so hard together.

By midweek the volunteers have learned new skills while developing insights about themselves and the people around them. They are beginning to cope with the frustrations of the physical tasks and the emotional relationships.

> We are blessed.
> People like that, who see a need, show Jesus's face.
>
> *—Rosa Byars, homeowner served in 2003*

Midweek reflections: Revealing God

Steve Brown, Penn Camp director, observes, "God uses you to work on someone else's life, and God also uses the experience to work on you. You never know where it's going to come from whether it's frustration, a personality thing, a problem at the site, or maybe the people there."

Salkehatchie is a personal experience. For many, as they sweat, scratch bug bites, push their aching muscles to do more, and feel sorry for themselves, scripture enters their hearts. They have heard these messages all their lives, now they feel them: in giving you receive; when you are weary—strength comes; everything is possible with God; we need not worry about what we eat, drink, or wear; we are the body of Christ; our faith is manifest in our works. The messages pour over us like a soothing cool shower. When you're at your wit's end, it's easy to release yourself and make way for the Lord.

During midweek reflections, the youth share with one another their moments of discovery. Some do so with great confidence though most do so with nervousness, quaking like the Quakers say they do when touched by the Holy Spirit. Many campers are hesitant to share their reflections before the whole camp, but they do so with each other and adult counselors. Some are silent, pondering the meaning in their hearts.

A sample of shared comments illustrates common themes in what the volunteers say:

Humility

> I had a big fight with my parents before I left for Salkehatchie. I want them to build a walk-in closet for my room. At our site home, there is a girl about my age who shares a bedroom with three sisters. When I asked, "Where's your closet?" she pointed to a hook on the wall and said, "There's my other dress."

•••

> Betty and Joe, high school juniors, worked on a site with younger crew members who seemed to sit around a lot and do nothing. One day, one of the younger teens, Susie, asked if she could help. Betty and Joe sarcastically replied, "No, stay away. There's nothing

you can do now." On Friday, at reflections, Susie shared how much it hurt to be rejected, though it wasn't new for her. She had just been adopted after living in foster homes for several years. She said that Betty and Joe's behavior helped her understand how her little brother feels when she pushes him away. Betty and Joe, in tears, realized their arrogance and cruelty, and asked Susie to forgive them. She did.

•••

We work in the homes of people who don't do physical labor as an act of service. They do it day in and day out, to survive. They manage other people's waste—our waste—all the time. They work as janitors and housekeepers, haul our garbage, and run our sewage plants. They work construction and pick our crops. No one thanks them or celebrates the end of their work week.

•••

Many jobs at the site are sheer drudgery—they bring no glory or even sense of accomplishment. They are true servant work. I saw humble, selfless love when I watched two girls washing Ms. Wilma's glasses in a tub of soapy water under a tree in the yard. They could have been Mary, washing the feet of our Lord.

•••

I realized my braces cost more than our site family lives on in a year.

Prejudice and Judgment

A father who came with his son as a volunteer became resentful when they arrived at the family site on Monday morning and he saw a shiny new motorcycle parked in front of the house. "They've got money!" he said. The lady who lived in the house later explained that the motorcycle belonged to her nephew, who had just been laid off from his job as a New York City police officer. He had a wife and two kids, and was desperate for a job, so he rode the bike all night down the East Coast for an interview as a security guard at a facility near her home. He helped the site crew work on her house. And he got the job.

•••

One year we worked on a house with a satellite dish, a big-screen TV, and a computer. We thought this family must be wasting their money. It turns out that a man who lived there was bedridden. He couldn't go anywhere or do anything. His wife said he was stuck in the house and didn't have anything to live for. That was the reason behind the big-screen TV. It wasn't so that they could have a Super Bowl party and invite friends from all over. It was for the simple reason that it gave him something, in a sense, to live for.

•••

An African American volunteer, the only one at this camp filled with White people, shared that an African American store clerk had asked him, "Where are our people?" He responded, "I don't know what you are talking about. These are my people. They are my family." He affirmed to the camp that racism is alive and he experiences it back home, but that at Salkehatchie he is accepted for who he is.

•••

A light-skinned resident who looks Caucasian discusses skin color with the White youth. "I'm supposed to be Black but I'm not sure I am ... I don't know where I came from." The youth realize what it means to have had slave ancestry and unknown roots.

Justice

Salkehatchie puts you into touch with things you've been shielded from your whole life. You see these people at school, in stores, or walking around town, but you don't go into their homes, you don't use their bathrooms, you don't drink from the faucet in their house. When you go in and meet them on a one-to-one basis, you realize they should be treated with the same respect and given the same opportunities you have.

•••

The lady at our house has multiple sclerosis and goes to an adult day program. She was ready for a bus to come pick her up at seven o'clock in the morning. She sat in her wheelchair, waiting. The bus didn't come until nine o'clock. That's not fair. She just waited.

•••

It's very easy to ignore all the poverty and need in the world and to turn away from those that you could help, but now that I've been close to those in need, I realize that sometimes they need help to help themselves.

•••

Mr. Bubba worked for a man for fifty years. He plowed with a mule, earning a dollar an hour. We figured that he made $36,000 in his whole life.

Compassion

The neighbor's four-year-old boy came over to help. As the youth get to know him, they learn he believes his mother left him because she hates him. He still remembers the fight his parents had before she left. Sometimes his dad watches the crew from across the street while he smokes marijuana. The boy's pants wouldn't stay up. One of the guys took off his belt to help tie up the pants. The little boy said, "Don't hurt my legs." The youth showed him how to use a belt the way it was intended as a clothing tool, not a weapon.

Tough choices

The site crew pondered this dilemma: Ms. Jaco's light bill is $25 per month. She has no regular income. Her water has been off for two years because she couldn't afford the bill. She catches rainwater in a barrel. The crew paid to have the water turned on. But how would she pay her water bill? They ask her to choose between lights or water: she chooses lights. Ms. J has no refrigerator. Should the crew buy her one? It would increase her light bill.

•••

Ms. Bradley has no water because her water bill from the town system is $300 in arrears. Should the site crew take part of their money and pay it? Or should they try to get the old well working, maybe put in a new pump? If she cannot pay her water bill, should the crew just leave her with no water except what she can get in jugs from her daughter down the road?

•••

We're weatherizing her house but what can we do to weatherize her life? She lives in a rough neighborhood.

Sacrifice

You don't come down here to fix up a house and have a homeowner say, "Oh, thank you very much. I appreciate it.' You come down here to serve God. Whether you get a thank-you—it doesn't matter.

•••

I sliced my hand on the tin (roofing). It hurt, but I realized it didn't hurt as much as Ms. Lucy's pain.

Faith

> I came to Salkehatchie this year feeling distant and not as close to God as I would like. Because of Salkehatchie, I feel much closer to him.

• • •

> This week I'm learning that a lot of my problems are because I don't listen to God. I don't listen to my heart.

• • •

> Trailers are so dark on the inside. I learned we can bring light, physically and in spirit.

Life's Fragility

> When our site crew arrived on Sunday, we spent more than an hour talking with the family about repairs we could do. We walked around the house. Suddenly, we realized that in a back bedroom, the family's twenty-something disabled daughter lay dead! The family was preparing for her wake and burial and, as is the custom, she was laid out at home. In deference to the grieving family, we offered to call off the work. But a council of family members headed by Ms. Hamrick, a white-haired matriarch who had lost both her legs to "sugar" (diabetes), decided the work could proceed along with the funeral rites.

• • •

> This year we saw three small wooden crosses that mark the spot where a drunken driver collided with a huge live-oak tree near Penn Center. The driver and his family lived in a home that we repaired last year. [This experience motivated the youth to share the exposure to drinking and driving they had in their own lives.]

Self-Discovery

Todd has lived a charmed life. His parents love to hike and have taken their children to beautiful places all over the country. He's close to his grandparents and cousins. He loves school, has great friends, and has just about everything he wants. He's never really thought about poor people. Every minute at Salkehatchie has been a revelation for him.

•••

An adult who went to Salkehatchie as a youth observes, "I definitely remember more about Salkehatchie than I remember about basketball camp, Boys State, or other camps I went to. There's a more intense feeling because you're in something totally foreign to you."

•••

Jefferson, an only child, has never had to share personal space with another kid before. Things are crowded at camp. He spent much of the week badgering other participants, telling them to move their stuff and acting immature, from their perspective. A nice long talk with an adult counselor about his feeling that no one liked him helped him see the light.

•••

Jay discusses the awareness of privilege. He says: When you're there, you're working hard, and you're hanging out hard, you're socializing … . I think it hit me hardest when I got home and threw all my dirty laundry into my washing machine. I was able to wash it, pull it out clean, and go on with my life.

Courage

My first year, when I was fourteen, I spent the entire week painting the outside of the house and playing with the children. Outside, there were fewer cockroaches and the stench was bearable. I enjoyed the week immensely. The next year, I was braver. I single-handedly repaired a bathroom and helped build a new bedroom. I killed two rats and stepped on a thousand cockroaches. I loved it!

•••

A boy on our site had a roach phobia. We were moving a heavy object, and one crawled on his arm. He did not make a scene. He finished his task. Then he went outside, around a corner, and quietly threw up. Then he got back to work.

Limits

Our lady's water system is rusty. There's so much we I cannot do. I want to fix it all, this brokenness.

•••

There's no job that's too small for someone to do.

Cleansing

Back home, a couple of months ago, Allen and a friend spent a night in jail after getting picked up for possession of marijuana. Allen knows he should spend less time around his friends who are into drinking and pot. His parents are talking about sending him to military school. Hanging out with Salkehatchie people helps him feel better about himself.

Resilience

It's been a rough year for James, a young volunteer. His mom left his dad for another man. She moved out and his dad is an emotional wreck. James wasn't sure if he should leave town for a whole week. He's glad to know his site leader is someone who has been divorced and is now happily remarried. It happens.

•••

One volunteer said that when he looked down at his hands and saw the scratches and cuts, he was thinking that when we are trying to do God's work, it is tough on us.

•••

This year, Donald had to do the unthinkable: He was a pall-bearer at the funeral of his best friend, who committed suicide. Donald is a quiet guy, but this is his fourth year at Salkehatchie, and it feels like a family reunion.

Inclusion

So much of life is exclusive. But Salkehatchie people are inclusive. They want people to be a part of them. They want to be a part of their lives. People will share with you experiences they won't share with others.

•••

At Salkehatchie no one is excluded—we all treat each other as equals, and by the end of the week we are like one big family, full of love and Jesus Christ.

Community

The kind of people you meet are incredible. I wouldn't change that for anything. Everybody's kind of humbled, and we're all here for one reason. You just meet the coolest people here. They just have more of a desire in life, a desire to find out more, they're curious and they're artistic. They're down-to-earth. You just can't find that in many places today.

•••

John Culp's son, Wes, illustrates how being a Salkehatchie veteran builds friendships back home: "When we moved while I was in high school, I was like the total new kid and I didn't have anyone to eat lunch with. I saw a guy wearing a Salkehatchie T-shirt and he became my first friend."

Relationships

You don't know somebody until you sweat with 'em. I met my first love, first date, first kiss at Salkehatchie and thought he was just a dreamy guy.

•••

You make lifelong friends.

•••

Coming every year is like a family reunion.

•••

When Dave Dillon, camp director, suffered a serious accident during the winter in his home community and he was in the hospital, "Salkehatchie people showed up right and left."

•••

I should have started coming here sooner. I really enjoy being around friends that you can trust and talk to about anything. It's amazing what people can do when they work together in Christ.

•••

At Salkehatchie, I can cry. At home, I never cry. Sometimes at night I just go out for a walk and cry. I'm not even sure why. I don't want to leave the friends I have here.

> People are looking at us.
> We are making a statement.

—John Culp

Honor

Too often, Salkehatchie volunteers work to honor the memory of a volunteer who has died. In 1996, Katherine wrote:

> This year has a special meaning for me. For three out of four years, I worked on a Salkehatchie site with Karin, but this year I work with her in a different fashion. This year she is in my heart. It's enough to keep me going when I think nothing can push me on. It is hot. It is hard. But we do this for a special reason that each worker has for himself. That is what will build a home and many friendships by Friday. This is for you, Karin.

•••

The volunteers share their tender memories of Robert, Karin, Rachel, Brad, Gus, Steve … and the many other Salkehatchie volunteers who have passed away. No words can describe the blessed images of time spent together with departed loved ones on sites and at camp. We try. Our tears are our futile expression.

•••

I just lost my grandfather last month. Ms. Quick is a grandmother. Working on her house means so much to me.

And the discovery goes on as the week evolves. The reflections reveal the participants' growth in Christian character. As they gain insight, they ask, "What are you trying to tell me, God?" At first, our lives seem so different from those we came to serve. That's superficial. Clearly, their struggles are similar to the ones we have back home. As we confront our site families' issues, we confront our own. As John Culp says, "We are the broken going to help the broken. So often, back home, we don't have anyone to cry with. This week, if you haven't cried, you haven't come to Salkehatchie."

Neil Flowers says, "The soul grows up."

Lauren Jackson sums it up this way: "You sweat together and get rained on together. You learn to do things you'd probably never do otherwise. You work harder than you ever have before. And you're changed by the time you leave."

Teamwork is a necessity on every Salkehatchie site.

The neighborhood

At first, people in the neighborhood walk or drive by slowly, staring. In rural communities, many people cannot afford cars, so they ride bicycles. They circle around, watching. They "come by here." Kum bah ya, as the Gullah people would say. Teens from the neighborhood stop and ask, "How can I learn to do this? I want a job." In the evening, at one camp, site families are invited to share, "Who came to visit today?"

At first, they just watch. And wonder. One by one, they join in.

At a site one year, Monday was the Fourth of July, and the neighbors sat outside all day, tending a grill and drinking beer. They just stared and never said anything directly to the crew. On Tuesday, one came and offered use of a ladder. By Wednesday, they brought ice and spare lumber. By Thursday, a couple were up on the roof, helping to finish.

> Give as much as you can.
>
> —*John Wesley*

The site crew invites others to join, if they are able and willing to serve responsibly. Even little children get to work. In Bennettsville, a drunken man approached David, a site leader, at grocery store on Saturday. He said, "I'm coming to help you next week." And sure enough, he showed up sober at his aunt's house on Monday morning. He worked from sunup 'til sundown each day. He shared that he was an unemployed father of two and that he knew he had a drinking problem. He confessed, "I needed this." He obviously relished the support of the team and the opportunity to labor hard during the week. David worried that he would return to old habits. We prayed that he would find steady work and a healthy lifeline.

More often than not, everybody in the neighborhood seems to be related. Cousins, aunts, uncles, in-laws, they all come by. Teens from the family may join in, learning alongside the youth volunteers. Or they may keep their distance, unsure of how to relate to these strangers who have come to their home. Extended family members may come from far or near to lend a hand. Some bring baked goods or prepare meals for the workers. Some come in the evenings, after work, to pick up shingles, mow the lawn, or do other tasks that help complete the work.

A neighbor of a site family walked over and handed the site leader two hundred dollars. He said, "We took up a collection at my church and want you to have this."

Wrapping up

The week seems to be over before it's even started. By Thursday, the crew realizes what it can and cannot do. They prioritize. "Nothing gets torn out after Wednesday" is the golden rule, but everyone violates it and starts at least one more job. The crews often stay late on Thursday. Every minute counts.

By Thursday, the crews have learned a lot. They've encountered numerous problems, explored numerous solutions, and are doing what they can. At one site, the toilet had been clogged for months. After a couple days' effort with umpteen devices, digging around the sewer line, and great work with a plumber's snake, a pair of little boys' underpants was extracted from the sewage line. ("That little Stefon! Where did he go?") That cleared the way for water drainage in general. When the crew arrived, the tub had looked like it was filled with old, dirty water left from Noah's flood. Now the water receded easily. A little Clorox and a lot of elbow grease and, voila!—a functional bathroom.

Brian Rollins illustrates how the devil is in the details during the last-minute countdown to quittin' time. Late on a Friday morning, he and his girlfriend, Lesley, tore out plumbing and a wall and tried to put in new ones with only a few hours to go:

> July 4, 2003
>
> If I have learned one thing in my previous years at Salkehatchie, it is that Fridays are miracle days. God is in every movement we make!
>
> About mid-morning, John Fooshe, our site leader, led us to the bathroom and handed Lesley a box. "I need y'all to replace this drywall." He pointed to the small cracks and bubbles on the rotting wall. "Also, if y'all would replace the knobs of the faucet, that would be fantastic. Thanks guys, y'all are awesome!" John gave us a sweaty, shiny smile as he lumbered off to go finish other jobs.
>
> "Oh, great ... plumbing. We'll have it done in two hours," I said to Lesley, still feeling the urgency that comes with Fridays. The tub was cluttered with an old shower curtain, pieces of wood, and other tools. I stepped in and began removing the faucet handles and spigot.

The noontime sun shone through the window on Lesley's sweaty brow as she wiped a drop off her face. She nodded in interest as I handed her the old faucet equipment. She kissed my cheek and smiled. A few minutes later, I finished cutting the old drywall out. The inner wall and pipes were exposed and a smell of old wood lingered from the opening. A large brown spider fled from the light back into the dark space.

At least there aren't any snakes, I thought. Lesley and I took measurements so we could install the new drywall. I noticed its shape was irregular, and it would be especially hard to hang because of its position in the corner.

Oh well, I'm good with my hands—I can craft it to fit, I thought confidently. Little did I know the trouble to come. The holes for the faucet weren't in the right places in the first piece of drywall we cut. The next piece wasn't shaped correctly, and the third and final piece was a little too big. I began to lose patience in the humid and stuffy bathroom.

Lesley began shaving one corner of the drywall while I shaved the opposite side. As we placed it once again, the top corner was still too long. "I'll make it fit!" I said with sarcastic ambition.

I pounded the corner, expecting it to make the small squeeze. "C'mon you—." At that moment the corner cracked; not much at all, but enough for my annoyance to grow.

"Calm down," Lesley said softly as we held it in place. I looked at her, took a few breaths, and noticed we both smelled of hard work.

"Less than three hours to get everything finished," she said, checking her watch. I looked again at the corner of the drywall. I observed that the water barrier wasn't even damaged. It was still functional. We screwed it in place after a few more minutes.

"Finally!" I yelled. After we collected other tools we installed the new faucet knobs.

"There's still a showerhead left in here," Lesley noted, examining the box. "I think we should go ahead and install it," she continued.

I sensed her spirit of desire to bless Ms. Legare abundantly. I asked, "Are you sure we should? I'm not familiar with this type of stuff. John didn't ask us to do the showerhead, but I guess we should."

After a short break, Lesley and I returned to the small bathroom and admired our work so far. The urgency of the afternoon squeezed every moment of free thought. I observed the old showerhead and attempted to unscrew it with my hands. That didn't work. Lesley handed me a wrench. I applied the wrench and turned it hard. Nothing happened. I turned it harder. Nothing, not a budge.

> Thank you for friends beside me, friends behind me, friends in front of me.
>
> —*John Culp*

Lesley and I worked at unscrewing the old showerhead for the next forty-five minutes. My frustration rose. I yanked the wrench from the pipe and threw it onto the floor. Exhaling a deep breath, I said a small prayer. We didn't have much time left before everything had to be finished.

"We'll get it done. We have to keep trying," Lesley said as she touched my shoulder. We then tried twisting it with two wrenches going opposite directions.

"This wrench is too long to twist where I want it," I told her with clenched teeth. The frustration kept building in the heat. I thought about how plumbers must feel sometimes. We went back to using only one wrench, only this time we twisted a little too hard. The pipe bent downward and snapped off. We gaped in disbelief. I was so mad that I screamed.

"I HATE PLUMBING!" I dropped the wrench and piece of pipe and slumped down beside the tub. Lesley sat down beside me.

"What are we gonna do now?" she asked.

I stared at the wall in front of me in silence. Sweat trickled into my eyes, stinging as I wiped my face in my filthy shirt. The thick heat of the hours clung to my skin, and the pressure of the day clung to my conscience. A buzzing fly brushed my ear, and I heard the distant noise of the rest of our team. In my mind, terrible doubt seemed to smile back at me as it tightened its grip around the situation. I worried for Ms. Legare, and closed my eyes in defeat—yet I felt that nothing was hopeless.

Not knowing what to do next, I opened my eyes. It was like God spoke to me saying, "You have shown your love to Ms. Legare. It will be fixed.

At once peace came over me. "It will be fixed," I told Lesley. "It has to be."

We showed John our broken copper pipe. He was so surprised; I thought he would be enraged. "Oh no," he said with disbelief. "Y'all didn't have to do that!"

After a few minutes of stressing and assessing, he had some patching material and knew what to do. He fixed the pipe within the hour and we replaced the showerhead. It looked much better than the old one. And it worked! After three hours of toil, Lesley and I emerged, satisfied that we had done our best on that bathroom.

"It must have been God's will that the showerhead be replaced, because I never asked Ms. Legare whether or not she I wanted a new one," John said with a laugh. Then it hit me: God wants the most for his people; this was all part of answering Ms. Legare's prayers!

"All that for a showerhead," I told Lesley, reflecting back on the long afternoon. I knew a lesson was to be found in our experience. I guess God showed me that it didn't matter if it was a new showerhead or a whole new house. Even if Ms. Legare never uses the showerhead, it is our love for her that matters. Giving all of our energy for the betterment of this woman's life and for the glory of God gives us something supremely divine in return.

Jobs like Brian and Lesley's are repeated a thousand times over at the various sites across the camps each summer.

By week's end, the site crew has created a symbol for the family, most often a cross placed somewhere near the house, signed with the crew members' names. Once a crew carved the Salkehatchie hammer and cross symbol into the door of an outhouse they built, right where the half-moon usually goes. Another imprinted the symbol into a concrete step they poured at the front door threshold.

The priority is making the house safe, dry, and warm in winter, but there seems to always be time for "frou-frou." In most homes, crews decorate the house with fresh kitchen curtains, towels, bedspreads, or other cheerful household items. This may be nonessential, but goes a long way toward bringing good cheer and order to the household. Frou-frou knows no bounds, ranging from baseboards to mitered corners, curtains to easy chairs, linens to linoleum. It takes only minutes to paste up a roll of wallpaper border. Barely longer to feather paint a bedroom (try this: white base paint, powder blue feather paint topped by lime green feather paint. Precious!).

One family included five boys, ages four to nine, who had been sleeping on the floor or in one of two broken beds. Their new room included two sets of bunk beds covered in Spiderman sheets. They were bouncing around saying, "It's so pretty!" As we left at four o'clock that afternoon, we heard one little boy say to another, "Do you want to go to bed now?"

The crew also tries to leave small tools, cleaning supplies, and food for the family's immediate needs. Many leave a new Bible signed by the crew. Rocking chairs are a great parting gift for elderly people. If they have time, the crew may build a basketball goal for the children or even a doghouse for the pet. Youth volunteer Jennifer Savitz reported:

> The teenagers built a swing and tied it in a tree early one morning. When the children woke up, they rushed to the swing. As the youth pushed Carla, the five-year-old, her face glowed radiantly with appreciation. The swing is Carla's first. She always thought that swings were only for playgrounds. Her joy overwhelms the youth as they reflect on their own material goods.

Salkehatchie is like reading a book or painting a picture. During the week, you get to know the characters and the events. At the end, it all comes together.

On Friday, at some predetermined time, everyone must stop what they're doing, clean up the site, and pack up their tools. They make sure the house has working smoke alarms. On Friday afternoon or Saturday morning, the closing tour begins. The entire camp visits each home. At Summerville, the entire camp encircles each house, joins hands, and offers a prayer. The crews say farewell to their families, although many slip by the next day, before they go home, for a final parting.

Our work is done only for this week. As we tour the homes completed by various crews, celebrating the accomplishments, we pass house after house in need of repair. Someone says, "God, please tell me no one actually lives there," as we pass a shack that looks occupied. It will be a whole year before we return.

Communion

Friday night is a sacred time. The camp shares final reflections, and each person brings a material symbol from their family's home representing something meaningful about the week for them.

Many share their symbols and their reflections about what the symbol means to them or insight about something that has been revealed or discovered during the week.

Some people bring objects that symbolize their week:

Window—"At Salkehatchie, it's easy to see God. Most times, I prefer to leave God out of everything. At home, every day, it's hard to see God. Here, I see more clearly."

Pink marble—"I actually had energy and time to play. At home I would be exhausted."

Benadryl—"I got poison ivy all over me in 100 degree heat. I learned that God may let a hard road get even harder. It brings you closer to him."

Roofing nail—"I was afraid of heights. I went on the roof anyway. Ms. L was afraid of us - we could have damaged her house."

Safety glasses—"We know we need them. We often don't use them. That's how we treat God."

Cord chopped off by power saw—"This was just one of the frustrating experiences I had this week. I realized my limits. I need God."

Penny found at the site—"Can't do much with it. Put a bunch together, and you can do a lot. Like us and the body of Christ."

Screw—"Something little can bind things that are large."

Box cutter—"Before 9/11, I only knew of this as a tool for good, to open boxes or cut things so people's houses can get fixed. I know now that a tool meant for good can do great evil if the user makes it do so."

Wood—"I learned I love the smell of wood. It reminds me of Jesus."

Other people bring no tangible objects, but themes they have reflected upon:

> ... Poverty is boring. People get trapped in the monotony. Salkehatchie breaks that cycle.

> ... Ms. Darby is dying. I learned that you have to learn to die, to make peace with life.

> God is great and God is good.
>
> —*John Culp*

> ... I learned you can be almost dead and not know it.

> ... It took me a whole week to hang a door. I never knew what patience was.

> ... We have dealt with this mess for a week. We do it for love. They do it for LIFE.

… When did I stop singing, dancing, telling stories, enjoying silence? I didn't even know what I was missing until I came here.

… We worked on James T.'s house. He is probably an angel. It doesn't make sense.

… This week I have cried tears of anger, joy, sadness, compassion.

… I hate painting. But I would paint every ceiling in this town just to stay with these people.

… How many times do you get to be an answer to someone's prayer?

… I sprained my ankle before I came. I came anyway. Now my whole body hurts, so the ankle doesn't seem so bad.

… I've had a rough year. I made some really bad choices. I spent this whole week filthy and sweaty. For some reason, I feel really clean and fresh now. I hope I can stay this way.

… If we ran a military war the way we run our war on poverty, we'd all be dead. I'm trying to figure out where all the other Christians are.

… They taught me that God is already present and at work ahead of me. God is already with the suffering. I don't take God anywhere. I run to catch up.

… If you can't see Jesus on the rooftop or in the eyes of someone at your site, then all the preaching in the world won't help.

John Culp once raked all the symbols into a trash can to symbolize that in a moment, everything you value can be taken from you.

The evening ends with communion. Christ's sacrifice has deep meaning as, exhausted, we partake of the bread and the wine, the body and the blood.

Sometimes, Friday reflections do not end until one o'clock in the morning. Many young people never go to sleep—they spend the night visiting with friends. On Saturday, the volunteers are up early and ready to return to civilian life.

The youth seem to remember most how they shared the meaning of the week. Eighteen-year-old Les talked about the spirit at the camp:

> Especially at night when you have devotions and stuff like that where people go to the front altar and talk. ... It's just overwhelming how much work they got done and they are just coming together and working for God. It's awesome. Everybody's smiling. I don't think I've ever seen one person be discouraged. Even when they don't think they're ever going to get done, they are still like, "We got done what we could and we did a great job."

Homeowner family reflections

The families who live in the homes express themselves in countless ways when the work is done. They cry with joy, clap their often than not, they give credit where credit is due: to God. Here, we share a sample of their reactions:

> ... Mr. Powers, a blind man with no legs who lived in an old school bus with no water or electricity, said he was so pleased with the

Site family takes a break.

renovations to his bus home that he was just going to drive it to heaven when he died. The crew also built a porch, where he sat after they left, strumming his guitar for the neighborhood children.

… At the end of the week, when the whole camp came to see his home, Mr. Goins played "When the Saints Go Marching In" on his guitar as more than a hundred volunteers marched across his new porch and through his home.

… Mr. Rhett, who received running water to his house for the first time through Salkehatchie, for years afterwards left cans of beans and corn on his kitchen shelf where he could see them, because they were a gift from the children who worked on his house and he wanted to save, rather than use, them.

… Ms. Kinlaw, age eighty-eight, was so delighted with her new porch, renovated house, and running water that she clapped her hands and said, "Now I can die!" The youth were confused by her comment and wondered what she meant. The adult counselors encouraged them to ask her. She had been so ashamed of her house before, she was concerned about what people would think when she was "laid out." The youth learned that "laying out" is an old funeral custom where the deceased person's body is prepared for burial and presented in her own home for final viewing by loved ones and neighbors. Ms. Kinlaw was pleased that now her passing would be in dignity.

… Ms. Langdon's husband had died thirty years before, and her roof had not been replaced in all that time. Different groups had patched it. In some places she had eighteen layers of shingles. She said she had not prayed since her husband died because she thought that God had taken him away from her. She had given up on God. On Thursday night of Salkehatchie week, she got down on her knees, prayed to God, and thanked him for sending the little angels to help her out.

… Ms. Dixon wishes more young people would do service like Salkehatchie. She says, "I kind of feel like so much is going on with the young people and I just wonder what happened that some of them gets in so many things. They know they are going to get caught, but they go and do it anyway. And I'm always trying to teach them and tell them these things. … And, too, they don't have to work like they did back then. They got plenty of time to do these things."

… A young volunteer says, "We built a shower for one family. They had all these little kids. Before, they just had a ladle and a bucket, and they would just kind of shower off with that. So when we put this running shower in there, this little kid was afraid he was going to drown when he got in the shower. We were all trying to get him into the shower and he just wouldn't do it. So finally we got him in there and when he realized he wouldn't drown, he wouldn't get out of the shower after that.

… A veteran of the first Gulf War, still suffering ten years later from a post-war mental illness, whose two-room cinder block house was transformed, exclaimed, "You've inspired me! These young people work with such happiness. I work hard, but I never laugh about it."

And in their own words, family members told us:

… They gave me a Bible. It had everyone's name on it. The names of everyone that worked here. I was very touched by that.

… They were the nicest children. I never heard one bad word. And there was no smoking cigarettes.

… What truly blessed me was the devotion they'd have each morning. One morning, the thought of the day was Jesus. He was a carpenter by trade. He used his hands to do work, to hammer and nail and do work like others. That was the thought. That was what they were bringing out, what Jesus did in his day.

… I had a girl from church come up the other day, she brought me some tomatoes. We were talking about it, I showed her what all the group had done for me, and she started crying.

… I just go from room to room and cry. It looks so nice. I am so grateful.

> But go and learn what this means: "I desire mercy, not sacrifice."
>
> —Matthew 9:13

… You see, I'm sixty-six years old, names I can't remember. I know every one of [the volunteers] though, and they know me. Names, I can't remember names. Names aren't that important, but a face of a friend is always important to me. I can live with that. They respect me and I respect them, so I like that.

… I like to sit out there on the porch, especially in the late evening and early morning when the breeze is cool and everything is quiet. The air is very fresh. Believe it or not, the best air you want is early in the morning. Three, four, five o'clock in the morning.

… And it's more than I expected. Because I expect for them to do the carpenter work. You know, the porches and that's it. I didn't expect for them to do the inside, too. What needed to be done. [They fixed the bathroom, floors, painted.]

… Cindy give me a chair, that wasn't 'spected. Cindy left me a rocking chair. So I was good to them, and they was good to me.

… I am proud of what they accomplished. We are blessed. People like that, who see a need, show Jesus' face. He told his disciples about helping people that have needs and that is what they are doing. Regardless of what religion you are in, you can help. The Bible has got all different translations. The New World Testament, the

King James, and they are all diverse. It is different, but it means the same, and people use those Bibles just like he created people of different nationalities and races. You cannot take from a person what their religion stands for.

… When you see them carrying on, it is just exciting to me because you don't see so many young people carrying on. It is just exciting to me because you don't see many young people really want to get involved with the Lord and carry on for the Lord. That is a beautiful thing and that's what I look at. Before they start, they always put the Lord first. Have their little prayer and devotion and I be looking forward to that. And when they got through, I said I will miss my devotion with the young people this morning.

… It was wonderful and I was surprised and I was happy. I kept pinching myself, "Is this me?" And everyone was so nice and protective of me. And one thing about it, I was so happy that I just had to cry.

… If it had not been for them, I would not have a home.

Sometimes, the family writes a letter. Ward and Betsy Bradley received this one:

Dear Mr. and Mrs. Bradley,
Thank God for people like you. You don't know what you did for me. I am still crying and thanking God. You don't know what you did for me. The Lord know I tried, but I couldn't with $6.25 an hour, so he sent you to fight my battle. Next year I be with you for a day to show you how much I love you, and anything I can do for you just let me know. I love you from my heart. I never see people like you. When I finish, I will take a picture inside and send it to you. Have a good day and I will be writing more soon.
—T. C.

The comments reflect awe, gratitude, and relief. They are moved, perhaps mystified, that people so young can give so much. Like the volunteers, they focus on the warmth of the relationships, not just the work on the house. They acknowledge the hand of God in everything that happened.

Sometimes the families give tangible gifts in return. For years after Salkehatchie served them, Gertie and John Mills, owners of a supervised home for people with mental disabilities, prepared a cook-out feast for all one hundred sixty campers at Penn Camp.

Ms. McColl, a sixty-three-year-old grandmother raising her eight grandchildren in a three-bedroom home, joined with her sister to prepare two hundred "Thinking of You Care Kits," which they passed out to the entire camp during the final tour of homes. Each kit was in a little plastic bag and contained the following:

> *Rubber band*—To remind you to hug others and that we are all banded together through Jesus Christ. (Romans 12:10)
>
> *Toothpick*—To remind you to pick out the good qualities of everyone, including yourself. (Philippians 4:8)
>
> *Band-Aid*—To remind you of hurt feelings, whether yours or someone else's. (Hosea 11:4)
>
> *Tissue*—To remind you to dry someone's tears, or perhaps your own, so you can see the tears of others. (Revelation 7:17)
>
> *Candy Kiss*—To remind you that everyone occasionally needs a treat. (Romans 16:16)
>
> *LifeSavers Candy*—To remind you to think of Jesus Christ as your lifesaver. Whenever you need to talk, He's willing to listen. (John 14:6)

In almost all cases, when volunteers return to visit a year after their work at a home, the family bursts with happiness at their reunion. The house is typically in order and all parts are working well. The family got the boost it needed to manage things on their own, with continuing help from God and their immediate neighbors.

Uppers and downers

Most volunteers leave their site family with a feeling of elation. As one young volunteer said, "I am glad I experienced the pain and suffering ... I have had the most religious, educational, and 'funnest' week in my life!"

Not always. Sometimes, the family doesn't respond positively. For example, one crew worked at the home of a single man with a mental disability, perhaps paranoid schizophrenia. He lived alone. Most of the week, he quietly watched from a distance. On the last day, he accused the youth of stealing his DVDs and cursed them. The site leader convinced him nothing was missing. But he never apologized.

> You gotta have love in your heart.
> God put this love in their hearts.
>
> *—Mrs. Goins, home renovated in 2003*

At another site, Mr. Manigault was going to have his house condemned by the city and be forced to move because the yard was covered with filthy junk. He agreed to let the crew come and clear his yard and paint the outside of his house. He never let them inside and he stared at them all day, with a frown on his face. He never warmed up.

One day while the volunteers were working, someone broke into the school where they stayed and stole money, cell phones, CDs, and a lot of other things. The youth were crushed because they had developed a love of the community and did not want to believe that any one of the community could harm them in such a way.

And in the Lowcountry, a crew worked hard all week. The young man whose house they were repairing had nothing to say all week except criticism. Every board was too long or too short (which may have been the truth). Everything was painted incorrectly. They just couldn't satisfy him. He was always aloof. This story has a better ending, however: on Friday, before they left, he gave one volunteer a wooden cross made from a dogwood tree. And he emotionally told the group his thanks for all they had done. He seemed to have been transformed by the week.

Carpenter training grounds.

Often, first-time youth and adult campers focus on whether the family seems grateful or not. More experienced campers share previous experiences and their understanding of how dependence on charity can be humiliating. Some families are embarrassed that they must ask for help. Rather than focus on what the family may be thinking, the volunteers redirect their thoughts to why they care about gratitude.

Stuart observes, "In ten years, I've never been on a Salkehatchie site where folks haven't had their feelings hurt at some point during the week. Pride is a powerful force in our lives. It yields to little. We all feel it. Even when we give ourselves in love, pride wants credit for the accomplishment." God does not call us to be heroes. He calls us to simply serve.

Art pondered for years about a family who never said a word of thanks the whole time they were there, even when he returned to do some finishing work after Salkehatchie week. Then he discovered through other sources that each year on the anniversary of the Salkehatchie week, the family holds a celebration to thank God for their help.

As we say, "It's not what you do. It's what God does through you." Sometimes, we don't know how the seeds we have planted come to fruition.

The broader community

While a core group of volunteers work on the houses, another extended network provides support. Teenagers, of course, have ravenous appetites. Teams of people from various churches make meals. At Blythewood Camp, Gayle Bell enlists various individuals and groups to sponsor meals through the week. Using a different approach, Kathy Robinson regards food service as her volunteer commitment. She goes to Black Swamp and Penn Camps each summer and cooks three meals a day, seven days a week. Before she goes, she and the other kitchen volunteers beg, borrow, and all but steal food supplies. They cook biscuits from scratch, bake cookies, and prepare meals from menus preferred by youth. Hoards of supporters from the volunteers' home churches and the communities where they work contribute in similar ways.

Salkehatchie brings out the ecumenical spirit of diverse Christian perspectives. Baptists, Presbyterians, AMEs, Episcopalians, and a host of others all chip in. Calls to contacts in various churches yield a dump truck for a day, a backhoe to dig a sewer line, donated furniture, waiver of fees for the county landfill, consultation from an electrician, and countless other blessings. Mayors and other local officials bend over backwards to help.

The *Marion Star and Mullins Enterprise*, a local newspaper, published a letter from the Russell Freeman, director of the Marion Camp. Russell highlighted the outpouring of support for Salkehatchie Summer Service from the community. He named the school principals and superintendent who provided facilities, the county recreation department that provided respite activities, the various churches that provided food and entertainment, the mayor and county administrators, the Department of Social Services, the Rotary Club, the specific banks, grocery stores, and builders' supply stores. Russell wrote:

> This article may seem to be nothing more than a long thank you letter, and I am certain to have inadvertently left out someone or some organization. But I feel that it is much more. This is a testament to the strength of your community, a community that truly cares and puts that caring into action. I don't know how you act the other fifty-one weeks of the year, but I would find it hard to believe that you acted much differently.

In 2006, this process of gratitude and recognition was repeated forty-one times, in all the communities that hosted Salkehatchie camps. Before the camp week was over, the work for next year's camps began. Camp leaders made plans with local people about how to find the site families for next year, where to store materials, and so on. The cycle goes on.

After the week—transformative love

We love to tell the story to anyone who will listen. Each in her or his own way, the youth pass on what they have learned during their week at Salkehatchie.

All churches that send volunteers to Salkehatchie sponsor a service for them to share their experiences. At Trenholm Road UMC in Columbia, fourteen-year-old Luke Reynolds gave this testimony during a Sunday morning worship service in 1993:

> Salkehatchie has been the most important week of my life. It was my first time this year and it meant a lot to me in different ways. I learned more in that week than I have in all my years of school. I was taught about roofing and plumbing, paint and tools, and love and compassion. I also learned about reality.
>
> I worked on a house owned by a woman named Ms. Lester. It was in really bad shape, barely livable. I had seen houses like it before, of course, everyone has. But after I met Ms. Lester and got to know her, it hit me that this house isn't just a building; it's a home. A person lives, sleeps, and eats there. A person just like me.
>
> Ms. Lester's neighbor was Paul Jones. He is about seventeen, and he would come over every day and help us out. He is a really classy guy; he writes poetry and sings in his church. He lost his mother as a child, and his grandmother, who was his best friend, died a couple of years ago. His family is slightly better off than Ms. Lester. Anyway, I think about him all the time and I love getting letters from him. I hope he makes it out of Yemassee and goes to college. He told me that it meant a lot to him that people would come and help Ms. Lester. I guess it makes him feel loved. I've only been one year, but I think that's what Salkehatchie is all about, loving people who need love.

> No matter what happens, I know there will always be someone that loves me at Salkehatchie.
>
> —*Luke, age fourteen*

Paul has the sense, intelligence, and spiritual roots to go far in this world. All he needs now is people who care about him.

I can remember when my older brother came back from his first year. He seemed to be in seclusion constantly for the following weeks, angry at what he had, compared to the poverty he had seen at Salkehatchie. I was about eight or nine, and I didn't understand. I thought he would be happy after helping those people. But Salkehatchie didn't give me an altogether happiness, either. It made me feel good that there were so many people who cared and wanted to help, but I also had to answer to some saddening questions, including the predominant one: Why do I have so much when others have so little? I think it's an important question to ask, for everyone. This aspect of Salkehatchie really can weigh heavy on the conscience. After reflecting upon my life so far, I will never be able to forgive myself for being so ignorant and unaware of the troubles of rural South Carolina. I ignored it for fourteen years, but after my week in Yemassee, that awareness will never leave me. Deep in my heart, I know now that I have an obligation to all my brothers and sisters in this world who need help, and I'm going to try to be there for them whenever they need me.

Another great thing about Salkehatchie is the special friendships you make. There were about one hundred eighty people at Penn Center. I'm sorry to say I only got to know about twenty of them. But even between the people that don't know each other, there is a bond, a sort of respect. Everyone has come down there for the same reason, to help, and we all respect each other for that. It's actually a step beyond that; it's a love that joins us all. No matter what happens, I know there will always be someone that loves me at Salkehatchie.

My week in Yemassee has affected me so deeply that it's impossible for me to put in words what it meant to me. If you are not only physically able but willing to get up at five o'clock and work all day, I suggest you enroll for a week. I don't know if all your years or the rest of mine will be as strong as this one, but it has already touched me in a way that will never be forgotten and will always show in whatever I do. To me, Salkehatchie is sacred and I will love it for as long as I live.

The voice of a youth's witness generally has more credibility than the word of adult laity and clergy. When young people speak, other people listen intently, with their hearts as well as their minds. Young people mature by leaps and bounds in the time they spend at Salkehatchie. Each young person does so at his or her own developmental pace. Some, like Luke, are more expressive than others and comfortable speaking in public. Most share their awareness in other ways.

Sixteen-year-olds Emily and Rob formed a team to make a presentation to their church. Emily, the writer, made notes and Rob, the speaker, presented them. They told their church that their memories of Salkehatchie were the most fun and Spirit-filled days of their lives.

> The first two days fly by ... greeting, tour of homes, choosing a site family, attending church, large meals in the gym, your last time to relax. Choosing a site to work on is the most critical part of the week, because for the next six days you will do everything in this group of ten to twelve people, young and old.
>
> Monday morning, work starts, and by no stretch of the imagination could you predict the kind of work that gets done: roofing, plumbing, painting, siding, insulation, flooring, wall repairs, porches, and finally cleaning—all done by inexperienced teenagers, old men, and the occasional professional, and all within a budget of less than $2,000.
>
> But the Salkehatchie experience has little to do with the workload. As soon as you enter the camp on Day One, there is a spirit that fills the air. This spirit is of joy, the gift of service. It's amazing to look around at a group of one hundred forty plus people and realize that every one of them paid $180 to be there, only to spend a week waking up at five a.m. to serve another family, with no

tangible reward.

Salkehatchie is not about the work. It's the Salkehatchie Spirit that gathers once a year and knocks you off your feet.

It's about new friends, old friends, your site family, overcoming struggles as a team, and making bonds that will last a lifetime.

It's about stars that shine in the eyes of the family you just helped.

It's about the spirit that follows you to the neighborhood where you work and brings the neighbors, without a request, to help out.

I look forward to my favorite week of the year for 357 days, until it finally arrives. I encourage all of you, ages fourteen to whatever, to experience it.

It's all about the spirit.

Twelfth-grader Whitney Simons spoke to her church congregation after her first year at Salkehatchie:

> Ms. Liza lived in her hundred-year-old house for fifty years. Widowed twenty-five years ago, she raised twelve children and still watches over many grandchildren. She lived in this two-bedroom, one-bathroom house without one complaint. Although the roof leaked, the floors sank, and the house was barely standing, Ms. Liza was content. The mere company of her family and our presence was gratifying to her. She never once asked us to do anything. So many times I have wanted more, thought I needed more, when I already have so much. I might have helped fix Ms. Liza's house, but she really fixed me. She taught me to be content with who I love and what I have.

Some young people disclose the revelations they received while at camp. An adult counselor reported that one young woman changed her life: "When she spoke at church, she revealed that at Salkehatchie, she discovered God. She said that before, she was faking. She came to church to socialize. She made fun of kids who listened to Christian music. She partied. She said that now, knowing God is awesome."

The youth also share privately, with their friends and family. One mother reported, "He told us the whole thing. Then he told us the whole thing over again the next day. He kept talking about it. He kept saying the same things."

And a father said, "We went to dinner last night, after Robert got back from camp. He was in the middle of eating a piece of prime rib when he started to cry. He said it was hard to eat when he didn't know what Mr. Kneece was having for dinner."

Youth minister Lee Porter summarized it as "daring discipleship" in 1989:

> I wish you could see them as I have seen them this summer.
>
> I wish your eyes were filling with tears of joy and pride as mine are. ...
>
> Look there, on the tattered roof of a rotting weathered shack, working anxiously in a race with an approaching storm.
>
> Look again, and see the human bridge built by a hug shared with a dirty, unkempt child too young to know the size of the obstacles before her.
>
> Yes, behind you, the palsied face of an old man, bound in a chair which will hold him till death, fed by gentle, caring hands.
>
> Listen ... to the depth of insight pouring from young hearts and minds grappling with the immensity of human need and the timid response of a culture blinded by superficiality and greed.
>
> Watch them commune, embrace, laugh, weep; yearning for life's substance, they seek and meet the living Christ in people and places that outwardly seem poor candidates for his habitation.
>
> These are a few of the divine/human portraits I observed during this summer's Salkehatchie Service projects.

Occasionally, youth attend Salkehatchie and go home discouraged. Some have hurt feelings or are confused by an inexperienced site leader. Some choose not to come again. Some seem to be unprepared for what Salkehatchie has to offer. Each person is on his or her own spiritual journey, and we can only pray that a seed was planted and that each person grows in some way, even if the experience was negative.

Sara and Richard Hagins encourage the youth to write at least briefly about what Salkehatchie means to them. Over the years, the reflections have been written by different young people, but the themes are consistent:

… I would not trade this week for anything!

… When I hear the word "Salkehatchie," I think love, friendliness, and the feeling of God in your presence.

… The best thing about Salkehatchie was the friends I made and the love and respect that everyone had for each other.

… AWESOME! That is how I think I would describe this past week. I made a lot of great new friends, and the Spirit of the Lord is always present. The atmosphere is full of love and sharing.

… I found it increasingly amazing as the week wore on how these individuals from all walks of life and different places around the state come together and form, in a matter of minutes, a close-knit team. I think this is one of the main things that showed God's presence this week.

… Salkehatchie was a time of struggles and a time of growth. The support I received from my site members helped me press on.

… The week that seemed it would never end is over, and I'm looking forward to next year already.

… Money and material objects don't really matter in life. The things that matter are love, family, friends, and one's relationship with God.

… In just this one week, I feel closer to God than I have ever felt.

The youth express awe at their accomplishments and mystery about how they can work so hard and feel so good. They, like the site families, focus on the relationships that they formed with the family and one another. They express a deeper awareness of God. This is the essence of Salkehatchie.

Most volunteers leave their site families with a bittersweet parting and never see them again. Others stay in touch in simple ways, such as through

Christmas greetings or a brief visit when they return for camp the following summer. Some develop long-term relationships and return to visit, most likely bearing gifts such as school supplies, food, or holiday presents. When we talk to volunteers and site families about their Salkehatchie experiences from years ago, they express tender affection and excitement about their relationships, even when they have had no contact. The memories seem to last forever and the emotions stay strong.

Salkehatchie volunteer families

For some volunteers, Salkehatchie is a family affair. There are family groups at camps that include mothers, fathers, sons, daughters, foster children, aunts, uncles, nieces, nephews, brothers, sisters, cousins, or godchildren. The McFaddin family of Easley brings three generations each year, led by granddad Larry, who turned seventy in 2005. Some adult volunteers bring their young children to help out or watch what they are doing. Many camp directors and site leaders today started attending Salkehatchie with their parents when they were teenagers.

For most youth volunteers, their parents stay at home. Some parents provide behind-the-scenes support by preparing meals, providing transportation, or gathering donations. Some just don't do manual labor. As one volunteer said, "Dad's exercise entails taking off the tie and maybe

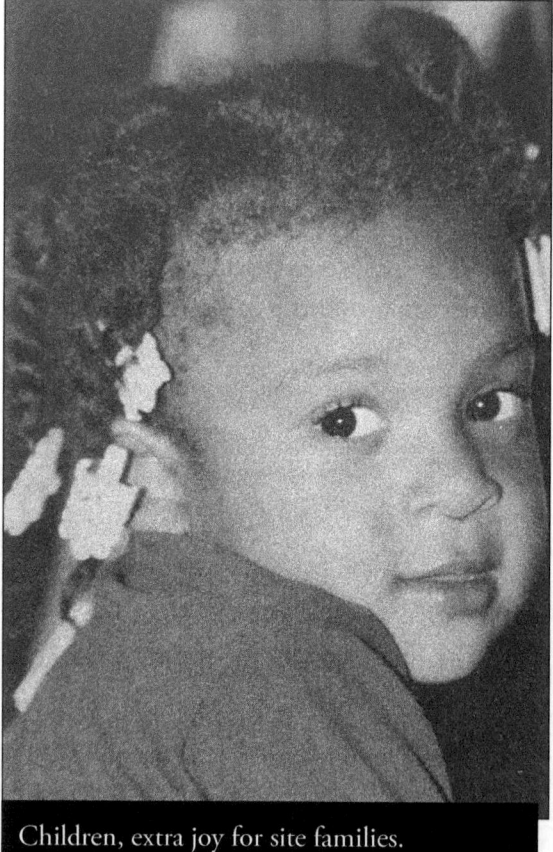
Children, extra joy for site families.

walking around the block." Others cannot get off work, or they have caregiving responsibilities for younger children or older family members. Some are not inclined to living in cramped quarters with rowdy youngsters. Some have health problems and cannot tolerate the heat.

Many parents want their children to have the mission experience on their own, for personal growth, free from parental influence. Many drop in during the week, to witness what their children are doing. Some want their children to be occupied for a week and have confidence that a church camp will be a good thing. Some youth volunteers share, sadly, "My parents just don't get what I do at Salkehatchie." Another observed, "My parents like that I come here. My mom said that she can't wait for me to come home so I can tell her the stories. 'Cause I go home and I tell her everything, and she just sits there and she soaks up what I tell her."

In most cases, what their child experiences comes home with the child, and the family knows a change has occurred. John Culp once said, "One of the proudest moments of a parent is to see a child stand for truth." Salkehatchie is about truth, about revealing the reality of God's world.

Salkehatchie volunteers composed the following message to parents who send their children:

> To the parents of youth participants in SSS,
>
> *Thank you* for your trust in your child that enables him/her to venture out in areas of service that fulfill the discipling role of the servant Jesus in ministering to people in need.
>
> *Thank you* for providing them with security and goodwill and support to make possible their participation.
>
> *When they come home,* encourage them to talk about their experience. Listen carefully and patiently, ask questions, and identify with some of their new understanding and determination to be more involved.
>
> *Don't be surprised* if they are more sensitive to the needs of people who are poor and who fall between the cracks in social service delivery systems.
>
> *Don't be surprised* if they want to organize some local project to help improve housing of poor people in the neighborhood.
>
> *Don't be surprised* if your child comes home with some more ma-

turity, self-confidence, ability to work with others and deeper sense of what it means to follow Jesus.

The word is out among parents of teens, because hundreds and hundreds are registering their children for Salkehatchie Summer Service each year.

Families also form at Salkehatchie. No one has kept a list, but over the years, many couples have met at Salkehatchie and later married. Vince and Anna Brawley met as high school students at the first camp in 1978, got to know one another over several summers, and married after college. Other couples include Jeremy and Jennifer Grainger, Melanie and Jason Moore, and Scott and Summer Flowers. They and many other married couples worked on site homes together, spent the evenings reflecting and getting to know one another, and continued their relationships long after camp was over.

When young adult volunteers marry someone who has never served at Salkehatchie, sooner or later, they tend to bring their spouses to see what it's all about. Baker Ratliff takes the cake, though. He and his bride, Jennifer, married on Saturday and he brought her to Huntersville Salkehatchie Camp on Sunday. They stayed for the week. He and Jennifer, like many young adults, have limited vacation time. A volunteer for many consecutive years, he just did not want to miss a summer of service. And Jennifer wanted to share the experience he loved so dearly. What a way to start a life together!

Go back home and live it

Yes, it's more than a week of hard work. Salkehatchie is about trying to find meaning in life. Salkehatchie volunteers go through highs and lows and feel stress and peace, chaos and clarity, confusion and enlightenment. They exhibit what psychologists call "helper's high," feelings of elation and increased energy that come from helping others. Research has shown that people who give of themselves report positive feelings long after they have helped others.[1] They feel calm and less vulnerable to stress.

Similarly, the families express elation that comes not only from the relief that their houses got fixed, but also from having witnessed the love and joy of the volunteers. People feel a warm, uplifting feeling when they witness

---

1. Allan Luks and Peggy Payne, *The Healing Power of Doing Good: The Health and Spiritual Benefits of Helping Others* (New York: iUniverse.com, 2001).

acts of moral beauty.[2] They become inspired to help others themselves.

For youth, it's about bridging life at home with life in that vast world out there. In an atmosphere of faith, hope, and love, young people have an opportunity to learn about themselves, the world, and God. What they do with their opportunity varies from one person to another. Many share that they yearn to believe with blind faith, to accept grace, to reach for their physical and emotional limits, and to give up their selves.

Salkehatchie appears to be about building family homes, but it's also about building church—that is, promoting faith, community, and outreach to the world. The experience brings together people who look and act differently from one another. They discover they are much more alike than different. They are together. When they leave the week behind them, the volunteers, families, and communities know the power of unity through faith.

Come With Me
Ben Lincoln Barnett, July 4, 2002

Come with me on Saturday … as friends and strangers trace with curious eye the face of poverty, deeply furrowed and badly worn but lined with grace and shrouded by nobility.

Come with me on Sunday … and sit in cushioned pew and sing with sainted sinners the songs of Zion, while angels all around attend and look with expectant gaze and listen with turned ear.

Come with me on Monday … as an army of would-be carpenters descend the slopes of human need to humble homes, with hammer in hand as club, with saw as saber, and with nail as spear.

Come with me on Tuesday … as new boards of friendship are laid side by side like tongue and groove, and by common labor are pushed together and joined to span the gap of loneliness and alienation.

Come with me on Wednesday … as a seemingly immovable mountain strikes a proud and indignant pose and thumbs its nose at those who, by faith and sweat and blood, intend to move it and cast it into the sea.

Come with me on Thursday … as weary soldiers fraught with frustration

---

2. Jonathan Haidt, "The Positive Emotion of Elevation," *Prevention & Treatment* 3, no. 1 (March 2000).

glimpse the first, telltale signs of a dream taking shape and form and begin to slowly rise on the wings of hope and promise.

Come with me on Friday … as the tools are laid to rest in their boxes and the buzz of the saw is stilled, and behold with wonder the homes that love built and listen in awe to tales of miracles and stories of lives transformed.

Come with me full circle to Saturday … and watch through blurry eyes as the triumphant band of soldiers return in happy exhaustion to land and home and kin that will never again, for them, seem quite the same.

Chapter 4

How Salkehatchie Summer Service Came to Be

Maybe Salkehatchie Summer Service could have started anywhere and anytime, but clearly, several forces converged in a particular time and place to shape what it is today. The forces—a blend of history, culture, geography, politics, economics, and social relations—touched the life of Salkehatchie's founder, Rev. John Wesley Culp. The spiritual forces in his life inspired his vision and kindled his passion for this mission. His mentors, family, friends, and the connectional church nurtured his vision and helped make it real. The youth and adult volunteers embraced the spirit, made it happen, and passed it on.

Once begun, Salkehatchie played a role in shaping the evolution of its own context by being a catalyst for change in one community after another. Today, Salkehatchie Summer Service covers the state of South Carolina and has spread into other states, touching the lives of people from all walks of life.

Salkehatchie Summer Service acquired its name from a pristine river in the lower part of the state. One day in the mid-1970s, John drove around the county where he worked, thinking about creating a youth mission. He crossed a bridge over the Salkehatchie River. As he was telling his wife, Peggy, about his day, she suggested the name for the service, and it clicked. If John had been driving a few miles to the south, where the Coosawatchie River flows, the service could have been known as "Coosawatchie."

River enthusiasts extol the beauty of the Salkehatchie River with its magnificent cypress, tupelo, and oak trees; frolicking wildlife; and mystical silence.[1] The name of the river comes from ancient times. "Hatchie" is a Muskogee (Creek) Native American word that means "creek." "Salakla" means "goose" or "swan" (the two are not differentiated in many North American languages), so a probable translation of the term is "Goose Creek."[2]

When people of European descent hear the word "goose," they often think of a domestic goose, the kind on a farm that might lay a golden egg if they're lucky. Native Americans think of the noble wild goose, a bird honored for its dependability, persistence, and good teamwork.[3] Geese fly long distances as a flock in a V-formation. When the pacesetter at the front becomes tired, it drops back and another quickly moves into the leadership role. Such cooperative rhythm is a fitting image for the service done in the name of Salkehatchie.

> While I breathe, I hope.
>
> —*South Carolina State Motto*

The Salkehatchie River wanders through an entirely rural coastal plain of farmland, forest, and swamp until it merges with the Combahee River and flows through St. Helena Sound into the Atlantic Ocean. Known as the Carolina Lowcountry, the summer heat, heavy humidity, lush vegetation, and swampy fields create an aura of mystery. The air feels thick and time seems to move slowly. People who live there seem more open to mystical experiences than those who live in crisp urban centers.

The river flows through historical colonial Barnwell and Beaufort districts, once populated by plantations with large slave workforces. The plantation cultures survived on cotton in the inland areas and a mixture of rice, cotton, and indigo closer to the coast. In 1860, the population of the Salkehatchie River basin counties was approximately 66 percent Negro

---

1. Tom Blagden and Barry Beasley, *Rivers of South Carolina* (Englewood, Colo.: Westcliffe, 1999).
2. Thanks to Dr. Bruce Pearson, professor of linguistics at the University of South Carolina. I suppose this means that in English, "Salkehatchie River" is a redundancy, i.e., "Goose Creek River" or "Swan River River." Dr. Pearson's interpretation contradicts rumors among Salkies that "Salkehatchie" is an Indian word for "salt catcher" or "love."
3. Thanks to Cathy Nelson, lay leader for the Rocky Swamp American Indian Ministries.

(55,613) and 34 percent White (28,671). Of the Negro population prior to emancipation, 97.6 percent was enslaved. Almost all the Native Americans had disappeared; they were vanquished by disease, assaults, assimilation, and removal to the West. By 2000, the population of the basin area was 38 percent African American (85,412) and 62 percent White (137,968), with almost 7 percent also claiming a Hispanic background. For more than a hundred years after slavery, the area remained predominantly rural and agricultural. Spanish-speaking seasonal farm workers from Mexico and other parts of Central America, along with occasional Creole-speaking Haitians, have long lived in this area. For most of the past four hundred years, until the past two decades, the racial and ethnic groups of the Lowcountry lived strictly segregated lives. (For an overview of Salkehatchie's geographic and historic background, see Appendix A.)

Building cultural bridges by rebuilding houses

Salkehatchie Summer Service started in 1978, when racial integration was still new in South Carolina. Southern states did not begin to seriously desegregate until after the Civil Rights Act was passed in 1964. When the first White volunteers left their suburban homes and came to the South Carolina Lowcountry, they began building a bridge across a divide that was about far more than race. The people lived in worlds that also differed by economic status, social class, and culture. As we examine Salkehatchie's history, we realize the service is also bridging past and future. Today we look at the societal conditions that inspired Salkehatchie's founders through the lens of the twenty-first century.

The 1970 Census statistics for the Lowcountry, used as part of the justification for creating a summer mission, indicated severe poverty in the area.[4] Segregation and other forms of racial discrimination contributed to deplorable disparities between African Americans and Whites with regard to financial well-being, health, education, housing, and political participation.

Although Salkehatchie started in the Lowcountry, where a substantial portion of the population in poverty is African American, the service has spread throughout the state, where many poor people are White or identify themselves as Native American or Hispanic/Latino. Each community has a

---

4. As reported in the Work Camp Project proposal submitted by John Culp to the South Carolina Conference of The United Methodist Church. Columbia, SC. 1977.

unique culture.

In the hills of Appalachia in the northwest corner of South Carolina, Salkehatchie volunteers work on steep terrain in areas of persistent poverty. For centuries, staunchly independent families have lived along highways, up dirt roads, and in hollers. The little subsistence farms they once maintained now can barely be sustained. In the red hills of the Piedmont, that area between the Appalachians and the Sandhills, textile manufacturing was the backbone of the economy for almost a century. In the last quarter of the twentieth century, half of the textile manufacturing jobs in South Carolina were lost.[5] In communities like Union, South Carolina, and Huntersville, North Carolina, Salkehatchie workers repair dilapidated homes that were once part of thriving mill villages with close bonds among neighbors. The villages are now run down or abandoned, like the empty factories near them. Many people have moved away in search of work, and those left behind have lost their sense of community.

Many areas of South Carolina have become home to new immigrants from Central America. They come to work in construction, landscaping, poultry, and domestic services. They often live desperately crowded together in abandoned mobile homes. The 2000 Census for South Carolina reported a 208 percent increase in people of Hispanic origin between 1990 and 2000, though population updates in some areas indicate that the number has tripled since 2000. Newly immigrated local people as well as the remnants of South Carolina's Native American nations often struggle to keep their homes in decent condition.

In the Sandhills and other areas of the state that were historically part of the agricultural backbone of America, independent family farms died as mechanized agriculture emerged. In places like Clio and Scotia, people struggle to make ends meet in minimum wage jobs at scattered industries owned by companies based far away, in distant states or countries. These industries come and go; jobs can disappear at any moment. People often feel insecure about their future and the economic solidarity of their communities.

In the Lowcountry, where tourism thrives on the shores, breadwinners who live inland leave their families before sunup and return after sundown, driving long distances to work service jobs at minimum wage. Even if they

---

5. Palmetto Institute, "The South Carolina Challenge: Regional Economic Analysis," September 16, 2002. http://www.palmettoinstitute.org.

U.S. Census, 1970 Socio-Economic Characteristics of the S. C. Lowcountry Region

Compared with all United States

Characteristic	Lowcountry	U.S.
Median family income	$3,952	$7,699
% of families in poverty (income below $3,800)	28.7%	10.7%
% of persons over 65 who are in poverty	52.4%	19.2%
% of children under 18 who are in poverty	40.0%	15.1%
% of housing units classified as standard (with all plumbing and kitchen facilities)	71.3%	93.4%
% total housing units that are overcrowded	14.0%	8.2%
% households that are Black	45.6%	11.1%
% households with six or more persons and income less than $7,000	61.8%	27.0%
% of households that are female-headed with own children	13.4%	10.7%

had the money—which most do not—they barely have the time to work on their houses. In most of the communities where Salkehatchie workers go, people who are old or have disabilities are left behind, while those who are able go elsewhere to make a living.

The economy at the local and state levels clearly affects families' well-being and places them at risk of becoming or staying poor. Economic trends are both promising and discouraging. The good news about poverty is that overall, compared with past decades, rates are declining, especially in urban and developed areas. In general, people are more educated and thus more employable than in the past. Discrimination has declined. US citizens generally have supported public policies that help provide medical care and food supplements to the poor, especially those who are very old or very young. But the middle generation, their caregivers, are less fortunate and often ineligible for assistance. They are expected to work but often have no access to jobs and no benefits such as health insurance; this puts the whole family at risk of losing everything in case of a medical crisis.

One sign of significant gain in poverty reduction since 1978, when Salkehatchie started, is the change in housing conditions. In 1970, 149,300 occupied housing units in South Carolina lacked complete plumbing facilities; twenty years later, in 1990, 20,177 housing units lacked plumbing; and in 2000, 9,521 still lacked plumbing (these numbers do not include homes with plumbing that fails to work).[6] The numbers are still too high, particularly given that 8,398 occupied homes lacked complete kitchen facilities in 2000 (which means they had no sink or refrigerator). And the 2000 Census estimates that 75,000 housing units in South Carolina are "unsuitable;" 60,000 of these are in rural areas.

> Our children must never lose their zeal for building a better world. They must not be discouraged from aspiring toward greatness, for they are the leaders of tomorrow. We have a powerful potential in our youth, and we must have the courage to change old ideas and practices so that we may direct their power toward good ends.
>
> —*Mary McLeod Bethune, legendary South Carolina educator*

So there is good news and bad news. Many poor Americans are better off than their ancestors and need not fear falling through their floors or freezing from the bitter cold inside their own homes. Nowadays the families served by Salkehatchie may be less likely to need basic structural work, but their

---

6. US Bureau of the Census, Historic Census of Housing Tables. (Washington, D.C.: n.d.). Complete plumbing is defined as: 1) hot and cold piped water; 2) a flush toilet; and 3) a bathtub or shower, all located in the housing unit

houses are still desperately fragile. More people live in trailers and manufactured homes made of flimsy materials and hard to restore. They may have plumbing, but it often does not work and it is made of inferior materials that quickly deteriorate or fall apart. Families struggle with preventable diseases, chronic disabilities, and members lost to prison or alcohol and drugs. Men are increasingly missing in action; more homes than ever are fatherless. The working poor, those employed full-time, sometimes from two-parent homes, find it harder to make ends meet as costs rise and wages stay the same. Families are smaller and social networks are eroding, as families have fewer kinfolk or neighbors they can call on for help. Many old people have no relatives living nearby. Average educational levels are up, but the living wage jobs are in industries that require more than a basic education, so pursuit of a comfortable lifestyle requires advanced education. Many indigenous South Carolinians are simply under-qualified and cut out of the contemporary job market. So poverty prevails, along with its evil brothers and sisters—addictions, violence, preventable illness, and hopelessness. There's much work to be done.

Poverty also continues to be unjustly distributed. According to the 2000 Census, South Carolina's overall poverty rate is 14.1 percent—that means one in eight persons is poor. This figure is misleading, because the probability that an African American or Hispanic person is poor is still much higher—one in four—as compared to fewer than one in ten for White people. And the absolute differences between the economic status of Whites and other ethnic groups are growing rather than shrinking. For example, the average African American per capita income in 1970 was $7,893 less than the average White per capita income; in 2000, the difference was $10,761.[7]

Poverty hits rural communities the hardest. A close look at the statistics about poverty reveals geographic pockets of persistent poverty where things have not changed much in the last few decades. For example, the poverty rate in Allendale County in 1980 was 46 percent; in 2000, it was 41.2 percent.

In the twenty-eight years since Salkehatchie began, poverty has persisted, among certain groups in particular. At the same time, many families have prospered, including those from groups who could only have dreamed of af-

---

7. D. H. Swinton, "The Economic Impact on African Americans after Brown," in *And Miles to Go Before I Sleep: Fifty Years in South Carolina Since Brown v. Board of Education*, ed. F. R. Sheheen (Columbia, S.C.: University of South Carolina Institute for Public Service and Policy Research, 2004).

fluence in past centuries. This phenomenon of growing prosperity coexisting with abject poverty is known as economic disparity, or the income gap, and it is growing rapidly.

One way to look at the gap is to compare people with high incomes to people with low incomes. In South Carolina in the year 2000, the average income for families in the bottom fifth of the rankings by income was $13,390, while those in the top fifth had an average income of $116,223—a difference of $102,833.[8] Families in the top fifth have 8.7 times as much annual income as families in the lower bottom fifth. If societal resources were more equitably distributed, the lower figure would be much higher, the difference from the average for the top fifth would be less, and those who are more wealthy might have only two or three times more than those with fewer resources. Some would argue that in a Christian culture, the distribution would be even more equitable.

Nowhere is the great divide of disparity more visually apparent than on Hilton Head Island, adjacent to St. Helena's Island, host to the early Salkehatchie camps. Families still live in abject poverty, huddled in trailers and dilapidated shacks, just a few hundred yards or a few miles from mansions that serve as vacation homes for some of the richest people—Black and White—in the world. The traditional, environmentally friendly ways of the African American small farmer, who grew vine-ripened tomatoes and other fresh produce, is being replaced by chemically induced turf farms and golf courses. Many of the oyster beds are polluted, leading to the demise of the local fishing industry. The wildlife is changing. The future is uncertain.

When people live together in a society, interdependent with one another, issues of adequacy and equity regarding material resources significantly affect their quality of life and sense of cohesion as a society. Adequacy of material resources refers to the minimum amount necessary to sustain a productive life in the society. Levels of adequacy vary from one society to another. In the United States, an adequate standard of living includes basic food, clothing, shelter, transportation, and health care that helps the person fit into his or her community. For example, adequate resources may require a car or access to public transportation (otherwise the person cannot sustain employment) and dental care (because the societal standards are such that

---

[8]. J. Bernstein, et al., "Pulling Apart: A State-by-State Analysis of Income Trends" (Washington, D.C.: Center on Budget and Policy Priorities, 2000).

people with rotten teeth are shunned in the workplace). At a house, plumbing (to facilitate daily hygiene) and electricity (to facilitate doing homework in the evenings) would be included in adequacy standards.

Equity refers to the fair distribution of resources. If some people have five bathrooms in their houses and others have none, that is unfair. If some groups, such as Whites, have safer and more well-equipped houses than other groups, such as Native Americans, that is unfair. If some groups can get home improvement loans or grants and others cannot, that's unfair.

In a just society, resources are distributed equitably and everyone has adequate material supports. But in the US, the pursuit of prosperity has caused many people to lose sight of the call to justice and they leave poor people behind. Many people—rich, poor, and in between—have even succumbed to what is known as "affluenza."[9] The symptoms of this crippling affliction include ridiculous Christmas indulgences, never-ending wish lists, excessive waste, and debt. Affluenza is an extreme form of materialism caused by the unfulfilled desire for more money and wealth. On a personal level it leads to chronic fatigue, serious mental disabilities, stress disorders, and addiction.

Collectively, people can lose sight of real value, such as the worth of a simple cotton shirt. As an example of the culture in which Christians live, according to the April 15, 2004 New York Times, at Neiman Marcus you can buy a simple T-shirt for $150, or a cheaper one, at Bloomingdale's, for only $59. On a societal level, affluenza creates an extraordinary imbalance of resources in the world between those who "have not" and those who "have more." Coupled with the worship of technology, particularly in the form of personal electronics and communication devices, affluenza has contributed to millions of people feeling disconnected and yearning for meaning. Those afflicted are unlikely to ever see places like the pristine Salkehatchie River basin or even to gaze at a star-filled night sky. They yearn to know the Spirit that moves across the waters and the spiritual power that extends beyond themselves and beyond the electric power grid and the satellite system. As one Salkehatchie youth said, "Life interferes with God."

As Salkehatchie moves into the future, the gaps between those who have material resources and those who have less are growing. Where is God in a

---

9. John de Graaf, David Wann, and Thomas H. Naylor, *Affluenza: The All-Consuming Epidemic* (San Fransisco: Berrett-Keohler Publishers, 2001); *Affluenza: the Epidemic of Overconsumption*, DVD (Seattle, Wash.: KCTS-Seattle and Oregon Public Broadcasting, 1997).

world so polarized? Why would anyone in the richest country in the world live in a house with no plumbing? Why does one neighbor, though crippled, have to struggle to use a plastic slop bucket as a toilet while another neighbor spends $150 (OK, only $59) on a T-shirt? Of course these questions are not just about plumbing or housing or clothing indulgences. The core issues are substantially deeper, reaching the very essence of what our relationship to God and our neighbors should be.

So while some people prosper excessively, others are left behind in abject poverty. As disparities between groups that are Black-White, rural-urban, old-young, and poor-rich grow, society feels more divided and less cohesive. People may also feel less positive about their state and community. For example, a 2003 survey of South Carolinians revealed that Black and White citizens tend to give different ratings when asked to describe race relations in South Carolina today.[10] Among Whites, 52.1 percent say race relations are good or excellent while only 31.3 percent of Blacks say good or excellent. Most Blacks say race relations are only fair and 18.7 percent say they are poor. If Blacks and Whites are living together in the same communities and yet many see their relations so differently, work must still be done to promote harmony and wholeness. The sunshine of God's love is blocked somewhere.

Church transformation

Salkehatchie has always been about more than building relational bridges. It is also about a new way of doing service missions. In the 1960s and 1970s, federal, state, and local governments initiated extensive programs to try to remedy historic disparities and improve conditions. Some policies and programs succeeded; but others failed, bogged down by politics, compromise, and fiscal constraints. Something was missing in the way the government service and programs were done; people talked about the "broken system." By the 1970s, reformers were tired of working through the federal government. People needed inspiration to have faith in the power of community participation for positive change.

The churches took on the challenge. The faith and nonprofit sectors were sorely needed to lead the moral and spiritual healing. In 1970, the United

---

10. R. W. Oldendick, "Racial Attitudes of Blacks and Whites in South Carolina," in *And Miles to Go Before I Sleep: Fifty Years in South Carolina Since Brown v. Board of Education*, ed. F. R. Sheheen (Columbia, S.C.: University of South Carolina Institute for Public Service and Policy Research, 2004).

Methodist Church General Conference, through its Board of Missions, called for a new spirit of volunteerism. The board reminded members that the church is about giving ourselves, not just our resources (2 Corinthians 8:5).[11] The board expressed concern that volunteers sometimes were imperialistic, paternalistic, condescending, and inclined to emphasize how different they were from those they served. The church called for a radical change in the minds, hearts, and attitudes of its members toward people who may not look like themselves. Observing that a rift often grew between US volunteers serving in developing countries and the local people, and that indigenous volunteers didn't encounter the same problem, the board suggested that Methodists send volunteers to work closer to home, where they would feel less different. This would be a new model of service.

Salkehatchie Summer Service emerged as an initiative based close to the homes of its volunteers, at a time when Christians were seeking to break down barriers of race and class and embrace new ways of living together. In the 1970s in South Carolina, clergy and laity were still inventing ways to promote racial harmony, encourage peacemaking, protect the environment, and encourage community participation. There were few models for effective change. There, in the mystical Lowcountry atmosphere, Methodists and Gullah people came together to create this form of action that would bring healing to hearts and homes while teaching young people and encouraging their moral leadership.

At the beginning of the twenty-first century, South Carolina Christians are still chipping away at the unfinished business of Black-White relations. Meanwhile, churches have formed Hispanic ministries to embrace the new immigrants. Remnants of East Coast Native American groups and Native Americans from around the country have organized for mutual support. In 2001 they succeeded in convincing the South Carolina Conference of The United Methodist Church to commission the beautiful Rocky Swamp Church in Neeses as a home for Native American ministry. The pool of volunteers has changed, at least superficially. Many of the youngest Salkehatchie volunteers spend their first week ever unplugged while at camp. Since birth, they have been constantly surrounded by electronic media of some sort: baby monitors, television, music, video games, computers,

---

11. Randle B. Dew, "Forward Motion in Mission: Some Thoughts on Voluntary Service." Board of Missions, United Methodist Church, Los Angeles, October 28, 1970.

Evening reflections.

telephones, digital this, digital that. Few have ever known the beauty of true silence. They think of private time as when you sit alone, with headphones on, or at the computer, surfing the net. They barely know how to listen to themselves think without distraction, much less listen for the still, quiet voice of God.

Youth, and others, hardly notice the invisible walls they have around themselves—walls that barricade them from warm, personal interaction with other human beings. Walls that keep their minds and hearts busy, focused inward. Walls that limit God's access to their hearts. What separates us from one another also separates us from God. As Paul Leob says in Soul of a Citizen, "When we shrink from the world, our souls shrink, too."[12] Loeb also reminds us that the ancient Greeks used the word "idiot" for people who could not involve themselves in civic or community life.

Most Salkehatchie camps disallow personal CD players or other electronic devices (except perhaps a shared source of music at the worksite). The young people must learn how to live without electronic stimulation.

---

12. Paul Rogat Loeb, *Soul of a Citizen* (New York: St. Martin's Press, 1999).

Without the distractions that tug at their minds and hearts, they actually run the risk of feeling whole—unified humans with heart, mind, body, and soul in harmony.

In some ways, Salkehatchie Summer Service is a product of its time and place. In other ways, its origins are timeless and without geography. The call to love our neighbors, to build bridges with people who are different from ourselves, is as old as the history recorded in the ancient Old Testament scriptures. To find one another and build relations is to reveal the kingdom of God. When Jesus was asked, "When is the kingdom of God coming?" He answered, "The kingdom of God is not coming with things that can be observed; nor will they say, 'Look, here it is!' or 'There it is!' For, in fact, the kingdom of God is among you." (Luke 17:20-21, NRSV). We need only to open our eyes and hearts to this reality by casting aside the burdens of daily life and realizing what is right in our midst.

The Christian tradition includes many references to rivers. In our hymns, we gather by the river; we cross over the River Jordan; we sing of a God, irritated by our complacency, who is going to trouble the water; and so on. The Salkehatchie River environment offers revealing physical, cultural, and socioeconomic qualities that help us discover the reality of the kingdom around us. Few people actually ever see the beauty of the river, but it exerts subtle, yet powerful, influences on its surroundings. There, in the Salkehatchie River valley—home to "never forget" Confederates and proud Gullah people, in a gorgeous resource-rich section of the planet Earth, at a time when Christians were discovering new ways to serve and Americans were rediscovering how to build community from the ground up—something mystical happened.

John and friends

Along came John. Big John.

The Salkehatchie story is also the story of the Reverend John Wesley Culp, a White boy born in 1945 and raised in segregated Union County, South Carolina. John is an uncommon man, a most uncommon man. It isn't just his appearance, although at six-feet-four-inches tall and 235 pounds, he does stand out in a crowd. Neither is it his southern drawl nor the loose-jointed gait with which he strides across the intervening space to shake your hand. His uncommoness is expressed in the warmth of his smile and the feeling you have that John has probably never met a stranger in his life. When you meet him, you know that you're in the presence of a very loving and caring person. Each year, John convinces thousands of youth and adults to pay money to spend a week exhausting their physical and emotional limits serving others. On any given day, you may find him moving from a visit in the home of a poor person with mental retardation to a meeting with a university president or corporate executive; his tone and presence remain the same in any environment. He is, indeed, a most uncommon man.

John is not the type of minister to carefully craft his sermons so that people will like what he says. When he feels a prophetic message from God, he says it whether people like it or not. As some would say, John is the type of minister who comforts the afflicted and afflicts the comfortable. He worries that Christians want to be comfortable and content, and overlook the revolutionary conflict that Christ started and expects us to continue. John knows little fear; he says he is confident that wherever he goes, God is there ahead of him. John is full of courage, compassion, and love. Yet his heart is humble.

John, a highly educated man of action with a sharp and keen mind, is a man of short words and profound truths. His speech is peppered with terms like love, grace, and good.

> "John, tell us what Salkehatchie is all about."
> —"It's about grace. God's amazing grace."
> "John, tell us about (name someone)."
> —"He was a good man. He had a good heart."
> "John, what should we do when they tell us to go away?"
> —"Just love them. Show your love. Tell them you love them."

The youth adore him. At age eighteen, after four years of participation in Salkehatchie, Nora Freeman wrote:

> My hero is not in history books. He has never been talked about on national news, and he does not have a lot of money. He is a simple man. He works as a Methodist minister in a very small church next to a highway. Though he may never be a national figure, to a grow-

ing number of South Carolinians, he is the most important man in the world.

… John Culp is a miracle worker. He realized that all it takes to build a bridge—between the young and old, Black and White, rich and poor—is commitment, hard work, screws, nails, and a tremendous amount of love. He has dedicated his life to breaking down walls of poverty and misunderstanding and replacing them with new roofs, porches, electricity, kindness, and trust. John had the inspiration to start the program, the gumption to make it work, and the leadership ability to help it grow. He is an engineer of bridges and an architect of love. He is a hero indeed.

Known to some as "Reverend Bubba," John is the youngest son of a pharmacist and a schoolteacher. He grew up in the 1940s and 1950s in Union, South Carolina, a mill town that was the county seat. His family worshiped at Grace United Methodist Church, founded by his great-grandparents and their neighbors in 1873. The granite cornerstone for the church came from his great-grandfather's quarry. John's ancestors chose the name for the church "so that she may never fall from grace." He can wander the cemetery in the backyard to ponder the lessons he learned from his many ancestors interred there. Many of the grave markers are remnants of marble columns from the old disassembled Union County Courthouse, which had been designed by Robert Mills, architect of the Washington monument and many other public buildings throughout the United States.

John attributes his grandmother with instilling in him the value of caring for others. She lived in a little wooden house where she took in people who needed a temporary place to stay. She helped Black people in the area when they needed food, clothing, or other assistance. She would gather things from people who had them and give them to people who needed them. She didn't talk much about what she did. She just did it, because it was the Christian thing to do. But most of the other people in the town called themselves Christian, and they didn't give the way she did. She dared to be different.

God apparently had great expectations of the little boy John, who also learned to do kindness by receiving kindness. As a child, John had a serious speech impediment; he could hardly talk. Many people in Union thought he was slow; other children ridiculed him. John's father developed a mental illness and had to be hospitalized, creating serious family hardship. A neighboring family reached out to him, helped him get involved in Boy Scouts, and, over time, his confidence emerged and he overcame his speech problem. His neighbor's kindness inspired John, who in turn has inspired thousands, affirming again and again that one small act can lead to much greater acts.[13]

John graduated from the University of South Carolina Business School in 1967 with a degree in marketing. "I can sell anything," he says, "And what I market most are values. Values like, every life has worth—my grandmother taught me that." He met his wife, Peggy, when they were counselors at the Asbury Hills United Methodist youth camp. They married after college, and John worked as an accountant, but not for long. He entered seminary at Emory University's Candler School of Theology in Atlanta. There, after a life spent in strict racial segregation, John encountered African Americans as a pastoral intern at Grady Hospital from 1968-1970. His clinical training required that he reflect on the visits he made with patients. His eyes and heart were opened. He was exposed to people and life conditions that he never realized existed. He had barely begun to process the emotions induced by the experience when he began his ministry.

During seminary, John and Peggy ministered in the summer at Lake Santee in south central South Carolina. There, John preached from a dock while people gathered 'round in their boats. His first church assignment, from 1971-1974, was at a small church in the small community of Liberty, near Easley and Clemson in Pickens County. From the start, John's ministry broke with tradition. His church was small and out of the way, so to stay there all day would yield little action. Itching to do the Lord's work to the fullest, John opened a church storefront office in a town building at the intersection of a youth recreation facility, the commercial district, and two residential districts—one a historic White mill village and the other a Black community. From this office, John and his summer volunteer intern could walk the streets and minister to all. He began a clothes bank, talked with folks from all walks of life, and became a visible and active participant in the community.

The idea for Salkehatchie came together through the combination of

---

13. From a sermon by Rev. Russell Smith, former Salkehatchie youth volunteer; pastor, Covenant First Presbyterian Church, Cincinnati, Ohio. Russell's maternal grandfather was the neighbor who reached out to John.

earthly events in John's life. Sister Colie Stokes said years later, "Nothing is coincidental. Everything is providential." As John's ministry grew, he experienced his own transformation. He knew the struggle of South Carolina Christians to build bridges across racial divides. In 1974, the bishop assigned John to serve Hampton and Varnville in the heart of the Lowcountry in Hampton County. There, he met Roman Catholic nuns who lived in the tiny town of Gifford.[14] The nuns had come from "nowhere" (John's word) to do hands-on work with the poor. Their faith community, the Sisters of St. Mary, had charged all its members to create centers of prayer and presence among poor people. Of the initial group, one had served in Africa, another in New York City slums, and another in the Chicago city schools. All were White. For a year, some practiced living in deprived circumstances in the woods of upstate New York. After careful research about where to go next, they arrived at Gifford, a town with a near 100 percent African American population.

> It blows my mind that my dad was the one who started Salkehatchie. I honestly believe that one of the reasons God put my dad on earth was to do just that.
>
> —*Chris "Christy" Culp McIntire*

The mayor, the first Black mayor of Gifford, invited them to stay. The sisters bought a sharecropper's house and worked in the fields with the sharecroppers. They felt particularly called to work with the Hispanic and Haitian migrant workers, the native Gullah people, and pregnant young girls, who were being denied an education. When they arrived, White children in the county attended private academies and Black children attended the public school. Waiting rooms at public facilities were still segregated. The African American townspeople treated the sisters with suspicion and wondered if they were from the FBI. The sisters created tutoring programs and crafts classes to build community. They knew that prejudice was beginning

---

14. The nuns served in teams of three at a time. Between March 1976 and June 1994, these sisters lived, prayed, and ministered in Gifford: Sr. Margaret Donner, Sr. Maureen Quinn, Sr. Rita Claire Davis, Sr. Mary Margaret Joyce, Sr. Anne Elisabeth DeVuyst, Sr. Rose Ann Cappola, Sr. Helen Ann Wolf, Sr. Rosemary Riggie, and Sr. Colie Stokes.

to crumble when the Masons gave them the key to their lodge so that they could conduct their tutoring programs. The sisters saw daily the deplorable houses that their neighbors called home.

The nuns showed John the homes in the area and said, "What are you going to do, John?" They inspired him. He thought about a youth work camp. Still, he hesitated. He was afraid the kids might get hurt.

"What are you going to do, John?"

John knew about the call of the United Methodist Church toward volunteerism. He wanted everyone to feel the call for mission near their own homes. He wanted every young person to have someone teach him or her values, like his grandmother taught him. He yearned for a way to teach the biblical principles of peace and justice. He felt called to minister to those church members who, in the eyes of God, lived in affluence and thought being poor meant you had to buy an economy car when you wanted the deluxe version. John loved working with youth. He understood middle class youth and family life. "Some of the worst poverty is in suburban America," he observed, "The poverty of loneliness, lack of communication, emotional, and spiritual poverty. ... These kids are dealing with divorce, estrangement, drugs."

"What are you going to do, John?"

In 1975, John was contemplating the idea as he drove across a bridge over the Salkehatchie River. He envisioned young Christians, full of energy, reaching out to the desperate poor whose homes were crumbling around them. He envisioned the self-indulgent youth being humbled before the great dignity and faith of people whose lives were bare of materials and full of spirit. He saw an opportunity for God to touch the hearts of the privileged and the vulnerable.

"What are you going to do, John?"

John knew the idea of a youth work camp was not new. He was familiar with reports from the US Society of Friends (Quakers), which had been operating work camps for periods ranging from a weekend to a week to a summer to multiple years.[15] Originally, Quaker work camps operated in war-torn areas and were run by pacifists who wanted to show the power of constructive work relative to the destructive work of war. They were

---

15. David S. Richie, *Memories and Meditations of a Work Camper* (Lebanon, Penn.: Pendle Hill, 1973).

designed to place high school and college students in the midst of poverty, exploitation, and physical destruction, so that they might understand the economic and social injustices that contribute to violence. The workers were taught to be "love made visible" through social justice and community. The Quakers began the camps after World War I and then started operating camps in the US on Native American reservations, in the rural south, in mining districts, at migrant camps, and near urban centers.

As they brought youth from middle-class homes into the work camps, and required them to pay their own way, the Quakers discovered the transforming power of physical labor, community, and exposure to people who have suffered injustice and inequality. The youth found great meaning and joy in what they were doing. Earlier in the century, many adults had been raised on farms and knew what it was like to toil and sweat from sunup until sundown. Increasingly, however, young people from urban and suburban areas had no idea what physical labor was. The integration of physical, mental, and spiritual well-being helped young people understand themselves, each other, and the people they came to serve. One leader of the work camp movement observed that this growing understanding was not achieved by intellectual arguments—there were no formal lessons. Rather, "It was a transformation which gradually took place as these young people of different persuasions and experience united to rebuild what had been destroyed, and at the end of the day, contemplated the meaning."[16]

The United Methodist Church had begun to embrace the work camp mission. Appalachia was particularly the place to be. The General Board of Global Ministries of The United Methodist Church (the national conference) supported Red Bird Mission in Kentucky, which was founded in 1925 to promote multiple aspects of community development in the impoverished areas of the state. In 1969, their work camps took off exponentially under the leadership of United Methodist minister Rev. Glenn "Tex" Evans, who started a spin-off mission, the Appalachian Service Project (ASP). Within five years, after fifty volunteers came to Union College in Barbourville, Kentucky, and repaired four homes, ASP was sponsoring multiple work camps and serving hundreds of homes each year. The Hinton Rural Life Center in the mountains of North Carolina began about this time, in the 1960s, though its work camps came later. In Tennessee, in the summer

---

16. Clarence E. Pickett, *For More Than Bread* (Boston: Little Brown, 1953), 359.

of 1974, several youth from a UMC in Nashville returned from a mission retreat wanting to take their experience into their own backyard, the Cumberland Mountains. They prayed for guidance and the Mountain T.O.P. (Tennessee Outreach Project) dream was born. By the summer of 1975, Mountain T.O.P. had involved more than two hundred volunteers representing twelve churches in community service work.

In South Carolina, Rural Mission, an ecumenical nonprofit organization providing human services to low-income Sea Island families and migrant farmworker families, was founded in 1969. Rural Mission aimed to foster, promote, and minister to the spiritual, economic, social, educational, medical, and housing needs of five Charleston County islands: Johns, James, Wadmalaw, Yonges, and Edisto. Since its inception, addressing the housing needs of the sea island families was a priority.

John knew he was not alone. Many Christians were feeling a similar call to serve God by guiding youth to the Spirit while addressing poverty. His call, though, was not to draw from resources far and wide to create a mission. His call was to reach the hearts and minds of the rank and file parishioners who were prone to think of missions as work done elsewhere, rather than in their own backyards, in partnership with their own neighbors. He was moved to influence not just the poor, but the very nature of the church and how it functions. He struggled with how to create a mission fully supported by people within their own state and communities, close to home. And his heart told him that young people would lead the way, if only the church could help them channel their energy and passion.

"What are you waiting for, John?" his nun friends asked.

He walked the fields and he prayed.

The nuns in Gifford often fed him. One cold winter day, John went to visit them. He finally knew what he was to do. Still, it took him three years to gain the approval of the South Carolina Conference of the United Methodist Church. In 1974-1975, the South Carolina Youth Council of the United Methodist Conference determined that a need existed for youth to be involved in service. John agreed to serve as state coordinator for "Come and Help Us" week, a project designed to help church youth move beyond the walls of their comfort zones and experience a real world.

He led a 1976 youth mission to clean and perform construction work at the Killingsworth Home for women in Columbia. The following year, he took a group of mostly White youth into an African American community to do renovations for the Bluff Road UMC in Columbia. While successful, these mission projects inadequately challenged the youth. The buildings they repaired were part of institutions, and although the youth came to know people served by the institutions, they could easily regard the experience as separate from their own lives. John realized that each youth had a home, and that to really stimulate their awareness, the youth needed to enter the homes of people whose lives, on the surface, looked different from their own but were substantially similar. The personal arena of the home would provide the setting for more intense interpersonal relations.

John continued to work with staff and volunteers from the state conference of The United Methodist Church, including Marian Jones (and later June Willson), youth ministry coordinator; Oscar Smith, conference missional secretary; and Morris Thompson and Mike Watson of Volunteers in Mission.

John crafted the idea of a youth work camp focused on rehabilitation of the homes of poor people. Through John's influence, they particularly targeted the Lowcountry and rural areas of the state, with a focus on senior citizens.

Pooling their collective experience and wisdom, the committee developed a proposal for a United Methodist-sponsored camp that would involve youth from across the state.

The original 1977 proposal for a "Work Camp Project" indicates the goals and objectives to be:

> The youth work camp stands at the crossroads of church and community. The youth and adults of the UMC, desiring like Christ to serve others, can realize their discipleship. Through it, senior citizens who often feel that they have been cast aside by a youthful society can receive both a tangible impact on their lives through the repair of their homes and they can also experience the warmth of Christian love reaching out to someone in need.

The proposal stipulated typical activities, adult-youth team ratios, expectations that the youth would study in preparation for the experience, and included this statement:

> It is vital for each participating youth to understand that the pri-

Salkehatchie site multi-tasking.

mary purpose of the youth work camp is to bear witness to the love of Christ by helping improve the living conditions of the poor. We do not condemn or degrade or demean the people with whom we work. We simply extend our hands in Christian love; and we accept the people right where they are and just the way they are.

The committee issued a call for volunteers to come to the Lowcountry for a week in the summer under John's supervision. The committee sketched a game plan, but the players brought the spirit and gifts that made the magic happen. John named the camp Salkehatchie Summer Service, in tribute to the area's wonderful river and its surrounding basin. For those not from the area, the term "Salkehatchie" was an enigma—hard to say and hard to spell. From the beginning, it set the tone of mystery and discovery that is inherent in the Salkehatchie experience. As it turns out, Salkehatchie is a perfect metaphor for this sheltered, nurturing experience that winds through life, attracting volunteers who come for sustenance, stay a while, and fly forth to distant places to share the fruits of that sustenance and tell the tales of its beauty.

Early Salkehatchie

On June 17-24, 1978, the first Salkehatchie camp began with base camp at Gifford-Luray Elementary School[17] in Hampton County, a few miles from John's church and a few miles from where the Catholic nuns ministered to poor and migrant people in the area. The Gifford camp was an experiment for the conference. Forty male and female adults and youth came from ten churches in seven communities. The early camps included volunteers from Mechanicsville UMC; New Market UMC, Hartsville; St. John's UMC, Aiken; Lee Road, Berea Friendship, and Aldersgate UMCs, Greenville; Clemson UMC; Washington Street, Shandon, and Francis Burns UMCs, Columbia; Cayce UMC; and Norway UMC.[18] At first, members of the churches in Hampton County were reluctant to come. John speculates that perhaps working so close to home would require participants to confront themselves, and that may have been frightening. Thinking of mission as far away was easier. In later years, the churches of Hampton County embraced Salkehatchie. The Black Swamp Camp is held annually just a few miles from the church John pastored when the service started. The Black Swamp Camp directors live just a few miles from the camp headquarters. They are truly serving their neighbors.

The 1978 Gifford Camp worked on four homes in the communities of Scotia, Gifford, Red Root, and Allendale, and on a community building in Ruffin. In the Scotia community, Salkehatchie campers went to the home of an elderly African American lady who lived in a sharecropper's cabin. Her rooster ran into the woods when the youth arrived; the kids laughed, but John observed that the lady had lost her friend, the only living companion she had on the premises. She had no bathroom and no running water. The youth were naive to rural living and were challenged to repair the home quickly so the rooster could return home to roost. The crews had few tools and inexperienced leadership—they did what they could. Some homesites

---

17. Thanks to Principal John Dodge.
18. The insurance list for the first Salkehatchie Summer Service included the following individuals: Dale Albred, Mike Alexander, Vince Brawley, Manning Brown, Ashley Brunson, Foye Covington, Sallie Covington, Alice Craly, Joe Craly, John Culp, Clarence Gass, Ginny Gentry, Wally Harris, Anna Harrison, Tom Hayden, Ronald Jeffcoat, Nathan Jones, Dana Lemons, John Liebenrood, Tine McCormac, Billy McDowell, Sharon McMillan, Dick Miller, Malcolm Moses, Fred Murry, Harry Perry, Becky Redfern, Frank Ruth, Jeff Salka, Brian Segars, Virginia Smart, Mike Smith, Edward Stiltz, Brenda Walters, Austin Watson, Ruthie Mae Williams, June Willson, Denise Wil-son, Ruth Ann Wilson, and Amy Yarborough.

had no source of electricity so the crews used no power tools at all, only hand saws and other primitive equipment.

The participants, who paid $40 each, slept on mats and cots in the school and showered outside, using hoses with cold water. The mosquitoes were so thick the volunteers had to spray pesticide.

The camp directors had planned no recreation, so the exuberant youth made their own, which included sending John's bedding up the school flagpole. The camp experience was not scripted. From the beginning, the approach was to bring out the unique strengths of the youth and to facilitate their discovery of solutions to problems. They worked during the day and they shared reflections in the evening. The local newspaper came, took pictures, and ran stories.

The participants loved it. The youth's reflections were like dynamite—although when at play, they seemed to be undisciplined disciples. John observed:

> They were so sharp. This was like heaven on earth—the youth were filled with unconditional love. They were aware that no one else was helping these families, and that if they didn't do it, no one would. This gave them a feeling of immense empowerment. The value of the mission was immediately apparent. By the end of the week, they became like a perfect church, the body of Christ.

In his report about the experiment to the conference (Salkehatchie Summer Service was accountable to Volunteers in Mission, the Board of Missions, and the Conference Council on Ministries), John wrote:

> In a parish setting the Salkehatchie Summer Service gave structures for youth and adults with different needs and aspirations to come together in ways that were redemptive and meaningful. The stereotypes of poverty were broken down and the participants were able to discover new persons in themselves and others.
>
> Local churches were able to bless and support these missionaries who became witnesses and servants of the living Christ in ways they could understand and become involved with. This was an outreach of the local church that was refreshing and challenging. It

was an event that caused attention, investment, and celebrations in the congregations from which these youth came and to which they returned.

These youths were able to span over their culture or "the bubble of their plastic world" to learn new truths and feelings about themselves and others. The youth and the occupants of the homes shared so beautifully the gift of themselves. Each workday gave the participants an opportunity to use skills and talents they had never used before. It was fulfilling to see constructive change taking place even if it was just hammering a nail, painting a tin roof or just simple conversation. They were able to see the simplicity of living of others and the value of this lifestyle compared to their lifestyles.

The Salkehatchie Summer Service was able to repair a few homes, but the lives that were involved experienced much more. We all wanted to give more of ourselves, to repair and work harder, to stay longer and to continue to share our lives. We have witnessed a truth that is holy and eternal and this will go with us.

There will be another Salkehatchie Summer Service this coming summer because the participants want to continue and so does the Spirit.

The youth sensed that their world did not have, couldn't understand, the new truths and feelings they had discovered as they grieved the last day. It was an experience that only grace could give.

From the beginning, participants found Salkehatchie hard to describe with words. It was physically and emotionally draining and yet uplifting. Participants felt transformed, as if their lives were changed forever. Yet it was hard to say what was happening—it was mysterious. "You have to be there" was how many finished their efforts to talk about it.

On Labor Day 1978, John's vision for Salkehatchie Summer Service was affirmed after he responded, as the volunteer fire department's chaplain, to a house fire caused by faulty wiring. The fire killed three young children, ages two, one, and three weeks. Their home was a little wooden house, what some would call a shack, that sat in a field along a highway. Even today, affluent people pass these houses with barely a glance as they travel in their air-conditioned cars to the beautiful beaches. John's compassionate heart was wrenched by the grief of the parents, who were barely literate but filled with expressive love for their lost children. The family had no church and no means to provide a funeral, so John ministered to them and led the funeral service. They buried the three little children together in a thin cardboard coffin. John's passion was fueled by the awareness that with just a little know-how and minor materials, the house could have been safe and the family would still be together. The people with the know-how and the materials were disconnected from the people with the need, and John was inspired to change that.

From the beginning, Salkehatchie Summer Service was contagious. The second year, almost every person who participated the first year came again, along with others, and the camp doubled in size. Twenty-one United Methodist congregations sent adults or youth to the camp. This time, they paid $50 and received T-shirts with the small hammer and cross symbol designed by Charlotte White. In later years, a larger drawing of hands holding the hammer and cross (designed by John Liebenrood, a veteran of the first camp) was imprinted on the back of each shirt.

The Gifford sisters shared the story of the first Salkehatchie week with their friend, Sister Ellen Robertson, at Camp St. Mary, a Roman Catholic mission in rural Jasper County. In 1972, Sister Ellen had started the St. Mary's Human Development Center, now known as the Lowcountry Human Development Center, in Ridgeland, South Carolina. Since its inception, the family-focused center has provided education for parents of young children and developmental child care for the children. Sister Ellen and her staff had always operated a flexible program that tried to do whatever was necessary to help the mothers finish their education and job training, which required counseling, emergency aid, and a host of other interventions, including housing rehabilitation. Sister Ellen invited John to bring the campers to St. Mary's for Salkehatchie week during the second year and he jumped at the chance for them to stay amongst the holy work that was underway for the community. For three years—1979, 1980, and 1981—the campers slept in the classrooms and porches of the rural community center on cots contributed by the National Guard Armory. Claflin College donated one hundred old mattresses from dorm rooms. Campers swam in the swimming pool, which was the only pool within seven counties where Blacks could swim.

In 1980, John's report about the camp noted that participants developed culture identification, strong relationships among themselves and with home occupants, and construction skills. He observed that third-year youth assumed leadership. A lesson learned was that holding an adult volunteer retreat in May, prior to the camp, helped to assure that the needs of the whole camp community were met and that each site team did not become over-identified with their site to the neglect of the whole community. John emphasized the need to structure the week to provide time for reflection, interaction of experiences, expression of feelings, teachable moments, and nurturing growth. He noted the need for the priest to be present in us as we encounter our personal limits. And he closed with these words:

> Salkehatchie Summer Service is an evangelistic call to break down the noncommitment and apathetic wall. The participants become pioneers of the faith as they structure new molds of ministry and service to a foreign land. They respond with a yes or no and discover new worth and meanings to life. Redemption and rebirth has never been comfortable, but the freshness and freedom is worth the price.

A pattern was beginning to emerge. Participants formed site families, teams dedicated to the family and work at their site. They shared with one another back at the community camp by revealing their feelings, discoveries, and frustrations. Inevitably, the difficulty of the work, the enormity of the poverty, the challenge of communal life, and the absence of the resources each participant relied on in her or his regular life precipitated a new awareness, a vulnerability, a perception of human limitations. In this humiliated, uncomfortable, even miserable state, amazing spiritual revelations occurred.

Around 1980, Sister Ellen invited Emory Campbell, native of Hilton Head Island (before it was developed into a resort), to speak to the Salkehatchie campers at Camp St. Mary's. Sister Ellen and Mr. Campbell knew one another through their work on the islands. Once a month, they traveled by boat to Daufuskie Island, occupied almost entirely by Gullah people and made famous by Pat Conroy's book, *The Water is Wide*, and the subsequent movie, *Conrack*. Sister Ellen advised island residents about child care, and Mr. Campbell inspected the water quality in his role as an environmental health specialist with the Beaufort-Jasper Comprehensive Health Center.

At the Salkehatchie meeting, the Harvard-educated Mr. Campbell began with, "I'm a Gullah nigger." The youth dropped their eyes and heads—they were obviously shocked.

"What's the matter—you never heard the word 'nigger' before?"

And so the dialogue began.

In 1980, Mr. Campbell became director of Penn Center, and in 1982 the center became host and founding partner to the Salkehatchie Summer Service. From a White perspective in the early 1970s, the independence of the Gullah people added to the mystical nature of the Lowcountry. From the Penn Center perspective, the idea of helping White young people discover and understand African American culture while helping them overcome their historic disparities was not new. Penn Center had hosted weekend youth work camps for various groups in the 1950s. Workers had trained Summer Freedom School volunteers and Peace Corps volunteers headed for Africa. They knew what it was like for middle- and upper-class highly educated White people to tremble with anxiety as they entered the home of a poor African American family. And the Penn Center community had already detected the severe cost of development to the native islanders as they began to lose their land, one family at a time. Mr. Campbell observed, "We saw immediately what Salkehatchie could do. We were trying to keep people on their land."[19]

John, who was in love with the Lowcountry, felt an immediate affinity for, and support from, the dynamic minds of the Penn Center people, although a Methodist clergyman in Beaufort County warned John to stay away from Penn Center. He said, "I wouldn't be caught dead there at night. They're Communists!"

Mr. Campbell also realized that Salkehatchie was teaching young people—future leaders—about solutions, not just problems. They were seeing poverty and housing needs firsthand and learning how people cope with their challenges, learning to respect their strengths and understand their unfulfilled potential. As the camp evolved, he also noticed how the camp was helping race relations, from Black as well as White perspectives. In the Lowcountry, poor Black people had often received assistance from White people, but they did so with an element of suspicion and distance. They

---

19. Interview with Mr. Emory Campbell, March 21, 2003.

always trusted the church and Penn Center, though, so they embraced the Salkehatchie missioners with enthusiasm.

And so Penn Center became home to the original Salkehatchie camp. Still today, during Salkehatchie week, you can stand on a porch and look out over the live oaks dripping in Spanish moss, the historic wooden buildings, and the cabin where the Reverend Dr. Martin Luther King contemplated his "I have a dream" speech. Parked beneath those trees, in front of the old buildings, you will see a long row of church buses and vans, each bearing the name of a United Methodist church from somewhere in South Carolina.

John and the other founders did not just initiate Salkehatchie; they stayed with it and nurtured it. John was sent to Trinity United Methodist Church in Aiken and served there as its pastor from 1980-1987. He returned each spring to drive the back roads of Beaufort and Hampton counties with Emory Campbell and the nuns, in search of Salkehatchie homes. Each June, he led the Penn Center camp. By this time, John's family—his wife, Peggy, and children Wes and Christy—had come to know Salkehatchie as a way of life. Wes and Christy were active youth volunteers and took it upon themselves to keep their father honest and humble as John's following of Salkehatchie missioners grew.

In Aiken, the meaning of Salkehatchie became even clearer to John. Salkehatchie is essentially about the transforming power of love as a nonviolent means to justice. In 1984, John started a series of community seminars in Aiken to create dialogue about the significance of nuclear weapons. The United Methodist bishops had recently released a report called, "In Defense of Creation: The Nuclear Crisis and a Just Peace." The topic had particular relevance in Aiken County because it is home to major nuclear industries. The livelihood of many residents depended on them, and many members of John's congregation were employed by the Savannah River Plant, a nuclear weapons manufacturer. A local newspaper ran an article that criticized John's actions. A few days later, a letter to the editor in defense of John appeared, written by Art Dexter, a retired nuclear physicist and research supervisor who had given his career to the manufacture of nuclear bombs at the Savannah River Site. One day, Art put his hand on the casing of a bomb. He felt its demonic power and immediately converted to the idea that the production of the weapons was placing the world in critical danger. He retired and devoted himself to helping others understand the risks of nuclear war. John didn't know Art before the letter appeared, but he sought him out, and a lifelong friendship blossomed.

> If John Culp sees something that needs to be done, he does it—no matter the cost to him.
>
> —*Emory Campbell, former director of Penn Center*

John has a gift for connecting people so that action follows. Fred Reese likened him to the disciple Andrew, who introduced Peter to Christ. "I want you to meet somebody," John says to folks, and then he arranges for the meeting. Inevitably, some collaborative action follows.

John took Art to the Lowcountry and introduced him to Sister Mary Morrissey, Penn Center, and Salkehatchie Summer Service. Art and his wife, Maxine, started going to Camp St. Mary and living there at weeklong intervals, driving through the fields, stopping to ask if people needed help, building ramps, wrapping tar paper around houses to make them warm, delivering produce. Previously, the nuns had never had familiar relations with Protestants, but now Art said, "We loved each other from the start." With the sisters, Art said, "Maxine and I became beggars for Christ. It took courage, but we kept an eye open, and would just ask for stuff—furniture, whatever."

When John moved to Salem UMC in Greenville (1987-1993), he continued his leadership at the Penn Center Camp while other Salkehatchie camps sprang up around the state, under his guidance as statewide program director. While in Greenville, he started Asbury Missioners, a program for inner city, at-risk youth to go to summer camp. In 1993, he was transferred to Bennettsville, in the Pee Dee, pinelands, and tobacco farming area of the state. The next year, he turned over leadership of the Penn Center Camp, and started the Pee Dee Salkehatchie Camp to serve Marlboro County.

After he moved to West Columbia (Mount Hebron UMC, 1997), he passed the Pee Dee Camp directorship to Neil Flowers. He then declared his retirement from Salkehatchie and missed a summer while he went on an exchange ministry to England. Within a year he was back in the saddle, directing the Salkehatchie camp in his hometown of Union for a few years.

In 2002 he started a camp in Bishopville, Lee County.

So, the Salkehatchie story is John's story, too. John's path is sometimes a lonely path. He gets discouraged. He gets tired. He is frustrated with people who will not relent in their punitive attitudes toward others. He gets angry. One summer he was enraged to the point of tears when a pompous building inspector told a site crew they could not give electric power to a home because the workers had no license. The family had been living with a patched network of cords and wires hooked to an ancient breaker box—the house was a fire waiting to happen. The site crew had skillfully created an alternative, safe set of wiring and breakers, and they wanted to turn on the power. But, as is often the case with Salkehatchie homes, they had not obtained a building permit, because all their work was unlikely to meet code standards. The work they did do would radically improve the home's safety and stability, and protect the inhabitants from danger, but might not be quite up to code.

The inspector told John, "Don't you ever come into my county without a permit. I'll shut down your camp." John responded, "You can send me to jail. I'm going to finish the job." The family was in critical danger, and the inspector's cruel "No" was more than John could bear. In the midst of his

Before: Hidden needs.

fury, John seemed to feel wrenching sorrow that the inspector could not see and feel in his heart what was happening at the family's home. Unlike most community members, the inspector seemed to feel no desire to join, to help, to do his part. Strangers had come from afar to help this family, and yet the inspector, a neighbor in the family's own community, a brother in their racial group, would lift no finger to help. The town's mayor prevailed, and the power flowed. Through John's urging, the camp prayed earnestly for the heart of the inspector. Ten years later, John still gets animated when he speaks of the inspector, who has come to represent all those who turn away. He shakes his head sadly and says, "They're mean."

John is still a major guiding earthly force behind Salkehatchie Summer Service. He remains a stubborn visionary who will not compromise the basic values and procedural essentials that guide the various camps. Not everyone agrees with him, but most will at least listen to him. Young people continue to adore him. As Jay Gore observes, "John is probably one of the most wonderful people I've ever met, with his purpose and what he's trying to do. I can't, in words, describe his personal delivery style, but it's extremely unique. He is just so down to earth, and so real, and so simple a lot of times. He just foregoes a lot of the complexities."

John still has his speech problems, which his friends, filled with love and respect, regard as an endearing trait. He mixes up names. For years, he called Arlene Andrews by a blended name: "Andrea." Fred Reese tells of the time John was sharing his understanding about God's call to him to be a prophetic preacher. John said, "I'm a pathetic preacher, Fred." Funny thing is, Fred knew exactly what he meant. Friends tease him about his "Culpisms," such as:

>*Actitist*—Someone willing to take a position
>*Boy*—Male Methodist minister serving a small town
>*Bunk Mailing*—Send-out of Salkehatchie literature for camp registrations
>*Catalina Converter*—For pollution control (on a car)
>*Clumbersome*—Bulky
>*Eudakrist*—What Roman Catholics call Holy Communion
>*Fillins*—Matters of the heart, emotions
>*Floormat*—A procedure

After: Dramatic transformation.

> *Klink*—Small, elite group
> *Pacific*—Not vague
> *Rationize*—How we justify our own budget
> *Vestibles*—Vegetables
> *Wack-A-Ma*—A camp located in the Georgetown coastal area where kids hit their mothers? (the area is Waccamaw, named for an indigenous group)
> *Wallarmelon*—The color of a red T-shirt

Hart Parker, who started as a youth volunteer and is now an emergency room physician, reminisces about how John's son, Wes, would mimic his father's "profound English" on talent night. In a world where the mass media urges people to strive vainly for perfection, John reminds us that we are all imperfect, and that we are lovely and lovable with our imperfections. John's speech difficulties may actually be a gift. His occasional stuttering and search for words causes us to listen carefully when he speaks.

At Salkehatchie, where nothing earthly is perfect, we come to realize that only the will of God is. We deal with houses with no right angles anywhere, families with problems too complex to describe, volunteers with burdens they can hardly bear alone, and communities where cold-hearted people at times try to stifle the efforts of those with compassion. Within all this imperfection, we come together simply to give our bodies and hearts to the will of God, and in doing so, we discover our unity. From the beginning, John Culp has held this as an essential guiding premise of Salkehatchie Summer Service. As the apostle Paul said:

> As a prisoner for the Lord, then, I urge you to live a life worthy of the calling you have received. Be completely humble and gentle; be patient, bearing with one another in love. Make every effort to keep the unity of the Spirit through the bond of peace. There is one body and one Spirit, just as you were called to one hope when you were called; one Lord, one faith, one baptism; one God and Father of all, who is over all and through all and in all.—Ephesians 4:1-6

Contagion

And the contagion continued. In the early years, before each camp, John would say something like, "We will not have more than ninety next year." As time for camp came a little closer, you might ask how many were coming to camp, and John would say, "Well, maybe a hundred, because a couple of people called me and they really need to come. Maybe a hundred and eleven." And then when the week arrived, one hundred and twenty people would be sleeping someplace around Penn Center, waiting for the wake-up call.

The people came. The youth were the sales force. In the tradition of missionaries, the youth and adults from the first camps gave testimonies during worship services at their home churches across the state. Word spread among the United Methodist clergy, youth directors, and young people. The youth and adults who attended the early camps were immediately addicted. They told their friends, "You gotta do this." They arranged their summer jobs and vacations to be available for the next camp.

Salkehatchie outgrew the facilities at Camp St. Mary's quickly, so in 1981 Rev. David Nichols started Santee Camp at Cameron in Clarendon County.

The next year, David was unable to lead Santee Camp. Rev. Joe Long, who had attended Santee Camp the year prior, asked John Culp what would happen. John said, "Well, Joe, if you don't lead it, it won't happen at all." Joe knew very little about home renovations, but his in-laws knew a lot. So Joe and his wife, Kathy Jo, with her parents Charles and Abbie Kneece, led the 1982 Santee Camp, which has run continuously ever since, under Joe and Kathy Jo's direction. They first stayed at a 4-H Camp and later moved to a school.

The Penn Center Salkehatchie Camp outgrew the limits of the Penn Center facilities. Although the camp was built to accommodate eighty people, Emory and John squeezed one hundred and twenty into the spaces. In 1984, John led two separate weeks of Salkehatchie camp at Penn Center. Within the year, plans were underway for the Baker Creek Camp, directed by the Rev. Harry Workman, on the west side of the state with a base at Epworth Camp in Greenwood County.

Leaders began to emerge. Future camp directors heard their calls after they first spent time as site workers and leaders under John's or Joe's tutelage. For example, Neil Flowers met John Culp in Aiken in 1983. Neil was the volunteer youth director at St. John's church, and the youth from John's Trinity UMC came to St. John's for Methodist Youth Fellowship (MYF). After John came and spoke about Salkehatchie, Mike Vandiver, associate pastor at St. John's, and Neil drove down to see what it was like.

Neil had never seen anything like it. There was something about the primitive nature of the experience that was sacred. Neil remembers that he had no idea what to expect when he first took his young people to Salkehatchie. He didn't realize how much they had changed until they returned. He noticed that they actually looked at poor people. They didn't just look past them or through them, they acted as if the people had names and identities and could hug and love. A Salkehatchie veteran for more than twenty years, Neil says, "Something touches me every year." Neil's friends liken him to the disciple Peter. He's a big bear of a man, with faith as firm as a mighty boulder. He was a site leader for nine years before becoming director of the Pee Dee Camp, which he has led for eleven years.

The first camps were led by a core group of about a dozen committed adults who stayed in close contact with one another and intensely discussed and monitored the activities and progress of the camps. As John notes,

"Folks who share a vision find each other." The new camp directors were able to replicate and enrich the characteristics of the first camp that John had led. For the first few pilot years, John, as the state coordinator, submitted evaluative reports expressing lessons learned to the state committee of the South Carolina Conference of the UMC's Mission Outreach. As the interest grew, applications swelled, and more leaders felt the call to reach more places with new camps. John and the original planning committee saw the need for a more formal structure to oversee the growing Salkehatchie mission.

> It was raw. There was no good place to eat or sleep, but it was a great place to worship.
>
> —*Neil Flowers, youth minister and camp director*

Although John has a college degree in business, he is a man of the street and the back roads, more inclined to personal communications than written records. The task of organizing an accountable infrastructure fell to other leaders. The original planning committee evolved into the state steering committee, comprised of camp directors, youth, and representatives of the South Carolina Conference of the UMC.

At first, before other leaders emerged, John kept a close watch over the development of new camps and insisted that new leaders share a common philosophy, values, and vision. He emphasized the art of being a camp director and site leader, with flexibility enough to allow discovery and leadership by youth participants and discipline enough to guide their spiritual development and skills. He fretted that adults might be too controlling or too concerned about the physical restoration work at the expense of ministry to the families and youth. Each community was different. Camp directors and site leaders could learn from one another by sharing lessons learned, but they had to discover their own paths toward lasting change in the places they worked and with the people who lived in the community and came as volunteers to the camp. Thus each camp has its own flavor, reflecting the spirit of its director. Cross-fertilization occurs as adults and youth attend different camps each summer, although most camps have a faithful core group that returns to the same place each year and shepherds the camp experience.

Many of the camp directors and adult site leaders of today were Salkehatchie youth volunteers of yesterday. They grew up learning and discovering. Seeds of leadership were planted in the early years. For example, as a youth, Tommy Wilkes attended Salkehatchie with his family for many years, starting in 1984. Within a few years after college, mission work, seminary, and entry into full-time ministry, Tommy became a camp director and then chair of the Salkehatchie Steering Committee. All around the state, people felt the call to come, they caught the spirit, and they began to lead. This continues to happen again and again as the camps continue to grow.

The ease with which leaders emerge is remarkable considering that simply leading a site requires extraordinary commitment of one's personal resources, as well as at least ten days of direct service including preparation, time at the camp, and organizing when done. Directing a camp requires this, plus extraordinary sacrifice throughout the year. Camp directors have awesome responsibility. They must show compassion and wisdom as they choose families and spiritually guide participants, demonstrate administrative competence as they garner supplies and manage budgets, and use communication skills as they build relationships with and mobilize support from the community. They must impart loving discipline to youth, tackle problem solving in the face of seemingly insurmountable odds, and have the ability to leap tall buildings with a single bound.

Many camp directors say, "I'm crazy. I'm not doing this again next year." But they come. They lead. They are clearly filled with the love of Christ. They love the youth, their fellow adult volunteers, and the families. They shine with it. With help from their friends—the camp community—they do it again and again, with beautiful, fruitful results. Thank God for Salkehatchie camp directors.

Organization

The camp directors coordinate their work through the Salkehatchie Steering Committee. The Conference office provides administrative staff support. Before the days of computers, Ms. Ann Walker would record, by hand, the records of all registration. After she moved on, Tammy Fulmer, Veronica

Williams, and Temeika Green took up the responsibility.

In 1984, the steering committee adopted a formal purpose statement for Salkehatchie:

IN THE NAME OF CHRIST:
- To bring together a community which provides an avenue for significant mission through improving living conditions and developing an increasing circle of fellowship.
- To offer ourselves to persons in need; being sensitive to the needs of all.
- To become more open to learning skills, accepting grace, and being used as an instrument of grace and love.

That year, the brochure inviting participants conveyed a more succinct call. In 1984, minutes of the Salkehatchie Steering Committee reflect concern that the program involve more Black leaders and youth. This concern is recorded repeatedly, almost every year, until the present. In 2004, two of forty-one camp directors were African American. In general, participation by African American United Methodists has been proportionately low but is rising.

By 1985, the program was gaining organization. The February 9, 1985 minutes of the steering committee noted Fred Reese to be liaison to the Conference Board of Missions; John Culp to be program director for all camps; and goals to have a conference-wide focus, establish five camps by 1988, involve ethnic minorities, provide scholarships, recruit adult leaders and carpenters, and share adult experiences through the *Advocate* (the conference newspaper). The committee also took action to promote monitoring and evaluation by developing an expenses ledger for each camp, having each participant complete an evaluation, and following up with families served to obtain feedback.

In 1986, two more camps opened, at Pawley's Island in Georgetown (directed by Steve Taylor) and Horse Creek in Aiken (directed by Mike Vandiver). Mike was another pastor who, like John, was told he wouldn't amount to much. His high school principal told him he wouldn't be able to get into college. God obviously had a different notion—Mike worked, got accepted at University of South Carolina, graduated, and went on to seminary, devoting a period to the US Army as well. Salkehatchie seems full of people who have overcome the odds.

SALKEHATCHIE SUMMER SERVICE

SALKEHATCHIE SUMMER SERVICE is a specialized outreach ministry for Methodist Senior High Youth. The purpose of the service is twofold: (1) to extend a helping hand to our fellow human beings and (2) to provide a work/camping experience for our senior high youth.

The campers work in teams with adult leadership in repairing, fixing, and weatherizing homes of people in need. Specific tasks may include repairing leaking roofs, putting up Sheetrock, painting, glazing windowpanes, cleaning up a yard, hauling trash, building an outhouse, or unloading a truckload of supplies.

But more important, the participants come together for a week of sharing, growing, learning, and loving!

There are 2 SALKEHATCHIE camps; each under the direction of a Methodist minister. Adults with carpentry, electrical, building, and/or "fix-it" skills serve as counselors and instructors.

PENN CENTER—Frogmore, S.C.

Under the direction of Rev. John W. Culp (Aiken), the campers work with those in need on the Sea Islands. In 1984, the camp will take place June 23 through June 30.

SANTEE—Camp Daniel, Elloree, S.C.

Rev. Joe Long (Elloree) and Rev. David Nichols (Branchville) co-lead this camp. People in need in Calhoun and Orangeburg counties are served. July 21 through July 28.

If you are a Methodist youth and have completed the ninth grade, or if you are an adult with special skills to share; and if you are willing to share part of your life helping others, this service needs you.

1984 announcement sent to area churches.

In 1986, at its November meeting, the Salkehatchie Steering Committee adopted a mission statement:

> Salkehatchie Summer Service is a visionary youth servant ministry of the SC Conference of the United Methodist Church. In the

Examining and selecting supplies.

name of Christ, it provides a loving Christian community that allows persons to risk new experiences and growth. We offer our needy selves to others in need. Participants experience discipleship in action as taught by the gospel while physically improving homes of low-income families in South Carolina. We join a broadening circle of fellowship with youth, adult, and resident communities.

We hope that by being open to learning, developing skills, and accepting grace, we can continue to be used as instruments of God's love.

That year, the steering committee affirmed that the strengths of Salkehatchie are:
1. its structure, that allows participants to be servants with their skills and gifts;
2. its community, with friendships that nurture, challenge, and expand participant's horizons;

3. the cross-cultural experience that allows participants to realize we all are one; and
4. the experiential discipleships with youth and adults that develop faith and commitment.

The committee noted the need to formalize the steering committee, to train leaders for the camps and sites, and to pursue smaller camps (seventy to eighty) so that small-group interaction is not lost.

While the formal leaders framed the organization, the fuel that drove the spreading message came from the youth volunteers. Their enthusiastic zest, simple testimonies, innocent discoveries, and obvious growth propelled the adults who were laboring behind the scenes.

In 1986, Rev. Harry Workman submitted this report from the Epworth-Phoenix Camp, based on responses from participants:

> What kind of effect does Salkehatchie have on the participants? Here are some comments from the evaluation session the last day of camp:
>
> • "I will care a little bit more about my family and appreciate what I have and try not to take it for granted."
>
> • "Salkehatchie has made me a more open and better person. It should help me to gain friends and a better understanding of the world around us."
>
> • "I have learned a lot this week, but the thing that I will probably apply most in everyday life is how special friendship can be and not to take things for granted."
>
> • "The high point of this week to me was the way Mrs. W. smiled after we finished her bathroom and kitchen sink."
>
> • "I can use the skills and faith as well as the confidence I have acquired from everyone I have worked with and spent time with."
>
> • "I will try not to be so callous and simply turn away from the hurts of others."
>
> • "Probably every time I use something that our family did not have, I will feel kind of ashamed. I will not take for granted all the luxuries I have."
>
> • "Salkehatchie is not just affecting me from when I leave here. I believe it is a state of mind—caring for your fellow men (and

women). Even though they are poor, they are rich in spirit and love. I hope this feeling of caring and renewal of hope continues on."
- "Salkehatchie serves as a point of reality. Without it, I don't think I could know God, or myself, and love would still be a game played in school."
- "I am not going to be as ungrateful in the things I do or get. I am going to try to be the kind of person God would want me to be."
- "At Salkehatchie you have to deal with prejudices that you don't know you have. You also find the love that makes us all children of God and brothers and sisters of Christ."

From the beginning, the youth revealed who they were. They brought with them hopes and aspirations, their burdens and tragedies. During reflections, they spoke of their realizations about how privileged, though unworthy, they were. They shared their joy at discovering a new sense of church and community while at the camp. They revealed profound pain related to death of loved ones, alcohol and drug use, family violence and divorce, and friends struggling with suicide or teen pregnancy.

In 1987, Salkehatchie participants honored John Culp by presenting him with a green truck at their Penn Center Camp reunion at the Brick Church. In his note of gratitude, John wrote:

> The many times we have shared both tears and joy over these nine years as we developed the ministry of Salkehatchie are dear to me. I am so grateful to each of you for your contributions of love and care. This word "Salkehatchie" means so much to us who have shared the years that I have placed a personalized license plate on the front of the truck which says, "Salkehatchie." We know what this means.

In 1989, minutes of the Salkehatchie Steering Committee record the sharing of lessons learned from various camps: a rule, "no music boxes from home," makes for better camp dynamics; coping with volunteers such as a violent teen and a woman with a history as an "outcast" created challenges; seeing drug deals in the community was difficult but created an opportunity for learning; and government programs through community action agencies can help with resources for weatherizing houses. The committee adopted by-laws and began a series of guiding policies such as the expectation of training for adult counselors, and that anyone who would direct a camp must first serve as an assistant camp director.

In May 1990, after Hurricane Hugo made its devastating sweep through South Carolina in fall 1989, the steering committee initiated a special camp just for college students. Each year, they spend a week at the United Methodist Relief Center in Charleston, renovating houses in three counties under the supervision of licensed building contractors, working to code specifications. Their maturity adds richness to their reflections and sharing as they go through the difficult transition to adulthood. Pat Goss, director of the UMRC, recalls that when she first met John, they drove around the county in his old green truck, looking at houses. She would say, "Forget it, we can't fix that," and those, of course, were the very ones John would choose to fix.

Through the 1990s the steering committee continued to adopt policies and procedures. They decided Salkehatchie could not be a resource for community service for people who are court-ordered to perform service. Salkehatchie volunteers must freely choose to come and cannot be bound to stay by external forces. In 1993 the steering committee expressed concern for liability related to risks on site, and in 1994, admonished leaders to not underestimate the role of women. By 2004, several camps were directed by women. The Black Swamp Camp was led entirely by women, including the director, assistant director, and spiritual leader.

Before 1995, the steering committee had sponsored an annual reunion for participants of all camps to gather at a designated church on a Sunday. That year, they decided the program was becoming too large, and a reunion too difficult. The program was growing so rapidly that by 2001, the committee felt a need to slow down growth, and decided to limit the number of new camps per year to four.

Salkehatchie camps have grown significantly over the years. In the first year, the camp spent $2,940 to renovate four homes. Twenty-five years later, the program spent $519,927 for 216 homes. Since its inception, less than 10 percent of the budget comes from the church conference.

Most funding comes from participant fees and donations. Salkchatchie Summer Service receives no government funding and no allocation from national organizations. It is grounded in the South Carolina connectional church of United Methodists and the communities where Salkehatchie serves.

Twenty-nine years after its inception, there was no formal guidebook about how to conduct a Salkehatchie camp. The work was based on guidance from the Holy Spirit, experiential learning, mutual support among participants, guiding principles, and financial rules. The significance of personal discovery and unscripted learning based in blind faith stimulated the first camp and still permeates the way the camps operate. Without a prescribed formula, curriculum, or checklist, the camp experience must emerge from within the people of the camp. They set schedules, conduct safety lessons, arrange transportation, find meal donors, make plans, and engage in countless spontaneous acts to make the camps run smoothly. The flexible camp structure frustrates some people called to this service, and can induce anxiety, although part of the experience is confronting such feelings.

Almost thirty years of fruitful action attest to the effectiveness of the loosely structured method.

The nuns have gone now. The people of Gifford named the little lane where they lived "Nun Street." Emory Campbell has retired from Penn Center, though he is still a tireless advocate for the Gullah people. John Culp, Joe Long, Neil Flowers, and other early camp leaders continue to direct camps, year after year. And the people come.

The emergence of Salkehatchie Summer Service in South Carolina during the latter part of the twentieth century is no coincidence. The service was birthed along the Salkehatchie River basin, downstream from a place laden with nuclear materials, upstream from a place where historically oppressed people asserted their integrity. For more than twenty-nine years, Salkehatchie Summer Service has given Christians a fresh way to respond to God's call for love of neighbor, peace, mercy, and justice. Inspired by a group of "just do it" nuns and mentored by the wisdom of Penn Center and the Quakers, a visionary pastor from a small town converted his prophetic, righteous outrage about his neighbors' living conditions into a ministry that offers continual discovery and renewal. Salkehatchie teaches Christians to have a heart for the poor while helping Christians realize their own vulnerabilities and need for the Spirit.

A transformed kitchen.

Chapter 5

Making Meaning: Prayers, Poems, Sermons

Salkehatchie Summer Service has inspired thousands of poems, songs, essays, sermons, works of visual art, and reflections that range from a few simple words to major treatises. Here, we offer a few examples.

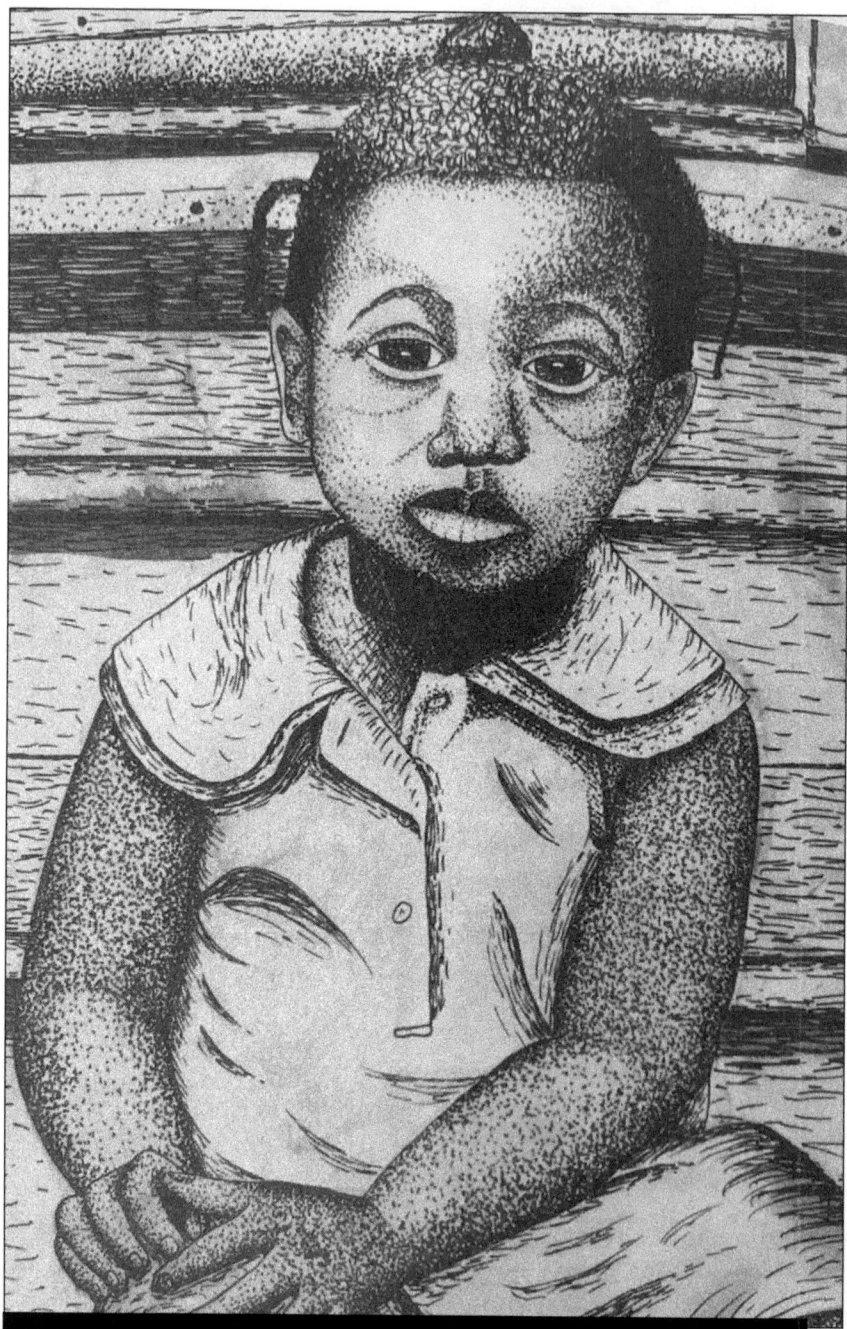

Robert Purcell, son of Kathy Hart and stepson of Ivey Hart, sketched this child at his Salkehatchie site. Robert has since lost his battle with cancer, but his love for the people of Salkehatchie lives on.

Prayers

A Salkehatchie Prayer
Kathy Hart, adult volunteer

Leader:	Praise God from whom all these blessings flow.
All:	Bless the families who opened their homes and hearts to us.
	Bless the families' homes that we didn't get to do this year.
Men:	Praise God for hardware stores,
	two-by-fours,
	a finished roof, and
	new floorboards.
Women:	Praise God for smiling faces,
	white kittens,
	brown cows,
	new puppies, and
	tied shoelaces.
All:	Bless the youth who gave up a week of their summer to do your work.
	Bless their parents, friends, and families who missed them.
Men:	Praise God for new friends,
	free time,
	e-mail, snail mail, and
	IM.
Women:	Praise God for roommates,
	sitemates,
	and the best prom dates.
All:	Bless Reverend Culp, the camp directors, and all the adult leaders.
	Bless their families who listened when they returned home.
Men:	Praise God for first aid kits,
	shrimp and grits, and
	new drill bits.

Women:	Praise God for bug spray,
	Gatorade, and
	brownies, homemade.
All:	Bless the cooks and the bakers.
	Bless their tired skillets, pots, and pans.
Men:	Praise God for sunrises,
	sunscreen,
	sunsets, and
	raining days.
Women:	Praise God for Popsicles,
	Tootsie Rolls,
	Twizzlers, and
	lemonade.
All:	Bless the churches that sent us forth, gave us food, and prayed for our safe return. Bless Camp Christian, Penn Center, and the Brick Baptist Church.
All:	Praise God for Salkehatchie!
	Amen.

The Salkehatchie Hugo Psalm
Robert Hopper

In September 1989, Hurricane Hugo hit the coast of South Carolina with brutal force, destroying houses far inland. By May 1990, Salkehatchie Camp Hugo had been established for college students only. Each year scores of students, mostly veterans of Salkehatchie youth participation, spent a week at the United Methodist Relief Center in Charleston and worked throughout the surrounding counties to repair homes, following strict building codes, under the supervision of licensed contractors.

> The Lord is my team leader, I shall not want;
> for work or wood or paint or partners.
> He makes me to lie down in green tents,

He leads me beside the still waterway,
my body is tired, but my soul is restored.
He leads me to repair places of poverty and prejudice
    for his name's sake.
He prepares a table before me in the presence of
    mosquitoes and gnats.
He anointest my head with sawdust and sewer
    water;
my cup overflows, and spills on my sleeping bag.
Surely good memories shall follow me all the days
    of my life,
as I remember those who dwell in the houses
    built with love.

Prayer for J.E.T. Campers
John and Anna Timmerman, 2001

Blessed are those who share Jesus today.
Blessed are those who teach children to pray.
Blessed are those who love as they give.
Blessed are those who serve as they live.
Blessed are those who bring happiness today.
Blessed are those who show someone the way.
Blessed are those who care about others.
Blessed are those who trust all men as brothers.
You are a blessing.
Until next year—continue to bless!

Early morning site prayer circle.

Morning Prayer
Larry Hedgepath, adult volunteer, 1988

Dear God,

    My crowbar worked its way behind the rotten board in Rebecca Warren's kitchen and as I worked it free from the rusty nails hundreds of cockroaches scurried across the floor and up the walls. We stood there in horror and disgust, but later our disgust would turn to tears as we faced up to the reality that thousands of people in our own state live like this.

But my prayer today is not for Rebecca, because she follows the gospel of Jesus Christ. My prayer is for those who follow the gospel according to Dow Jones. Because Rebecca is merely plagued by the cockroaches that have taken up residence in her home, but the whiz kids of Wall Street have their lives infested by greed and cocaine that has taken residence in their souls.

I beheld the home of Lisa Burns and wondered if the walls would stand another day. Then I beheld the face of Lisa. A victim of cerebral palsy, she sits in a wheelchair, her body writhing with the uncontrolled movements of those so afflicted. I struggled to understand her words. Her condition saddened me but her smile convicted me. It was not the face of poverty or disease but the face of Jesus Christ. Her beautiful spirit caused her disease to shrink into insignificance.

But my prayer today is not for Lisa, but rather for the leaders of this country who still insist on building the implements of war on the backs of the poor and the homeless. And for those who like to say "God helps those who help themselves." God, can you believe that some people who make that ridiculous claim actually believe that they are quoting the Bible? I pray that you will teach us that you sent your son into the world precisely because we are powerless to help ourselves. Empower us to help the helpless as you have helped us.

Finally God, I pray for my new seventeen-year-old friend, Kelly Nolan. I taught her how to saw a board straight and she taught me that the thing young people need most today is adults who care. I taught her to glue together PVC pipe and she taught me that young people respond more to our faithfulness than our self-righteous advice and formulas for a successful life. Through her eyes I was able to see that it is no use for us to preach the gospel to our children if we are not willing to live it with them.

I ask you, Lord, to comfort the afflicted and afflict the comfortable. Help us to exterminate the cockroaches that infest our thinking. Help us to shore up the walls of our sagging faith. Help us adults to leave our children with a world free from the madness we have perpetuated. Convict us right where we live and if we are not faithful may we have the sure knowledge that we will have no place in your kingdom.

In the name of Jesus Christ. Amen.

Poems and lyrics

What Makes Me Happy
Charles E. Stevens Jr.

Salkehatchie workers renovated the home of John and Gertie Mills, where Mr. Stevens resides. This poem was a gift to Salkehatchie volunteers who dropped by for a visit in the fall of 2003.

> I'm happy when the world is not
> When pain is no obstacle, when fear is dissolved
> When people are joined in accord and pleasure
> When the children are in adoration with
>   themselves and God
> When possessions are affordable for the good
>   in the world
> And suffering is denied when we call God
> To receive the gift of love
> From our Father, so divine.

Bridges to the Heart
Emily Andrews and Julie Jones, fifteen years old, 1999

Emily and Julie wrote this late one Wednesday night to prepare for morning devotional at the home of Ms. Bright. She lived in an old sharecropper's wooden cabin in the middle of a huge soybean farm. She had no refrigerator. Late Thursday afternoon, Ms. Bright saw the workers were tired and thirsty and their water supply was running low. She offered them the comfort she had: a single warm can of Coca-Cola. She opened it and they poured it carefully into paper cups, a sip for everyone. It was like communion. The worker's spirits soared.

> As we stand before the house of Alice Bright
> I see a trace of Holy Light.

More than dirty hands and tools scattered on the
   ground
There's something else here, for love is to be
   found.

Giving, helping, aiding, providing,
Opening hearts to someone in need.
Sharing, contributing, teaching, learning
Caring for others by taking the lead.

With every hammered nail and every board we cut,
Our blood, sweat, and tears are shed in the sun.
Sometimes it's hard when your energy's gone,
But it's all worthwhile, working for the one.

The coming together and joining of hands
All striving toward one common goal
Becoming a family and linking our hearts
In the end, discovering our souls.

The joy in her eyes shines brighter each moment,
With a burst of delight in her smiles.
So few possessions, yet so filled with spirit
An impression that can carry you for miles.

With strength and love and loyalty
He is showing us the way.
Answering our prayers by encouraging our spirits
His love is streaming down with every shining ray.

With hope and dedication,
Hard work from the start,
We're building more than just a house,
We're building bridges to the heart.

Ward's Salkehatchie Song
Ward Bradley, youth volunteer

The rain falls through the roof as the children
    start to cry.
Their tears fall through my soul. They tatter me
    inside.
It's a crime against the people played by high
    society.
Mother sighs as the children's eyes grow dull with
    poverty.

An old man lives in a shotgun wreck that lets the
    sunlight in.
It shows the rats and birds and bugs that live in
    there with him.
But, he's got a strong unyielding hope that comes
    from deep within.
He shares his expressions with paintings placed
    on tin.

It's hard to smile when your world is dark, and
    you live from day to day.
You try so hard to stand up, but your world just
    makes you stay.
Well, James, my friend, it's been a while since I
    saw your smiling face.
But I'll remember you until I die. In my heart
    you've burned a place.

It's a group of God's people. They bring his power
    with them.
They want to change the world, but somehow the
    world won't bend.
They cry out for justice, but justice just won't
    come.

They know with hope and loving power, a change
can come to some.

For Karin
Chris "Christy" Culp McIntire

Sweet sounds flowing through the air
The tone of your voice we all love to share
Angels bending low
Spreading great light on your footprints below

Telling you good-bye is something I can't do
I find it so hard for this to be true
Thoughts will progress, days will go by
But I will know that you'll always fly
Songs will be sung, tears will be shed
But we will remember the beautiful life you led

Chorus:
Don't let her spirit go
Don't let your spirit go
You will always be on my mind
Bridge:
The heavens will always shine with your smile
The stars will always shine with your eyes

Salkehatchie Cinquain
Katie Buckingham, youth volunteer

Covered
with dirt and sweat.
It all washes away.

What leaves Salkehatchie with us?
God's love.

Bent
Kathy Jo Long, 2001

Miss Victoria Stockton stood quite tall and
    very straight
Watching the townspeople walk by her front
    yard gate.
She stopped little John Tucker who was bent like
    a "C"
Carrying his younger sister, little Beth Anna Leigh.

"Put that child down, boy. Let her walk on her own!
You're ruining your back. She should walk alone.
Stand up, young man, stand straight and tall
Pull back those shoulders. Put your spine to
    the wall."

"You're a walking old man, tho your years are
    quite few
You're bent almost double—yep, bent right in two.
Just look at me, son, and observe the proper
    stance.
I never carried anything! Why take the chance?"
Little John just shifted sister Beth Anna Leigh
From shoulder to shoulder, her feet swinging free.
"You'll never straighten with a load like that,"
Cried Old Miss Victoria as she straightened her hat.

"I'm fine and straight, as straight as can be.
I walk, and talk, and I take care of me!
Why look at Hattie Lou, crimped over her cane.
For years she pulled weeds down by the

church lane."

"Then there's Mrs. Dorothy with hands gnarled
      and curled.
She sewed year after year for rich Tom's little girls.
Oh, but see how fine my soft hands still look.
I never lifted a thing, not even the Good Book."

"Now here comes Bill Roberts with his
      crooked spine.
He chopped wood for a living, feeding his flock
      of nine.
They're not like me. No, not like me at all.
I learned to take care of myself when I was
      quite small."

"Now stand up, John Tucker. Put down your
      little sister.
Let her stand on her own feet, and you straighten
      up, mister!"
But the children gazed at each other, sharing
      sweet smiles
As John slowly turned, and walked another
      four miles.

With pride he carried her, and walked
      without shame,
For Beth Anna Leigh was a cripple, both legs were
      quite lame.
John knew his back hunched, almost round like
      a hole
But he loved God Almighty and was "straight" in
      his soul.

After Salkehatchie
Art Dexter

Can we participate in Salkehatchie and ever again accept racism in this country, in South Africa, or anywhere?

Can we who have served and loved the crippled, the blind, the cerebral palsied, the mentally handicapped, the "least of these," ever view them again as less than brothers and sisters?

Can we participate in Salkehatchie and not recognize that the neverending arms race deprives the ones we serve of the social programs, the medical care, and support they need?

Can we ever again conceive of using nuclear bombs against defenseless women and children anywhere in the world—gentle women and busy children, with smiling faces, much like those we serve and love?

Can we ever again accept our national neglect of the elderly poor who exist on incomes of only $200 to $300 per month and are condemned to live in hovels, often without benefit of running water or toilets?

Can we ever forget those people we served or those who worked beside us to serve them?

Can we ever again fail to see that we are all one in Christ?

Can our lives ever be the same again?

Now That Summer's Gone
Larry Hedgepath, adult volunteer, 1994

Now that summer's gone
The baseball diamonds are deserted
And a cool rain announces autumn's arrival.
An old woman gazes upward
Staring at the now-drying stains
Which mark the entrance wounds
Inflicted by previous storms.
But that was before
Last summer's invasion,

When a hoard of teenagers
Descended from Heaven
And landed on her roof
With hammers and shingles.
Their aprons sagged
Under the weight of nails
Which they pounded into submission
With youthful enthusiasm,
And their bright smiles
Drove her despair
South for the winter
Now that summer's gone.

Now that summer's gone
And autumn's leaves have all been shed,
Winter's chilling wind howls
Mournful as a distant train whistle.
An old man sits and rocks
Protected from December's cold
By walls which once
Barely separated him
From nature's fickle fury.
But that was before
The teenage wrecking crew
Gutted his porous domicile
One hot July morning
And promised something better
In its stead.
Though he wanted to trust them
He decided to invoke
Divine participation
And discovered one morning
His benefactors
Gathered in a circle
Doing the same.
A curious alliance emerged,

The old Black man,
His young White friends
And of course God,
To whom he still gives thanks
Now that summer's gone.

Now that summer's gone
I think of
The passing seasons
Of my life
And my aching joints
Punctuate my transition
Into the autumn
Of my existence.
I think of summers past
When the same young faces
Made me, for one week,
A better man than I am
The other fifty-one.
With joy and sweat
We came together to do
What we could not do alone
Nor even dare the attempt.

Today I will cherish the memories
And pull out the photographs
And contemplate next summer,
When I will make my way
With loaded pickup
To another site,
For my yearly dose
Of elixir of Salkehatchie,
Which sustains me
Through another winter
Now that summer's gone.

Reflection on Salkehatchie Summer Service
Bill White

We are a community.
We are communities within a community.
We are individuals.

We have accomplished.
We have built.
We are building.

We have had conflict.
We have had disagreements;
We have had frustrations, but
We have opened up to each other.
We have overcome.

We have worshiped in new ways.
We have toured.
We have related to people who once seemed out
      of reach.

We have painted;
We have dug;
We have toured;

We have constructed.
We have blisters.
We have laughed;
We have cried.
We are wondering how to say good-bye.
We are tired;
We are sore;
We are happy;
      and as a community
We are thankful.

What is Salkehatchie?
Jason Jordan, St. Luke UMC, Lancaster, and Stephen Haney, Sardis UMC, Union

June 2001

Jason and Stephen wrote this for the morning devotion at their family site, Wateree Camp.

> S—Spreading of the Christian Faith
> A—Ability God gives us to come together
>   as one
> L—Love that we have for our neighbors
> K—Knowledge we gain from our experiences
> E—Excitement we feel every time we see
>   a smile
> H—Houses that can drive us nuts, but in the long
>   run make us happy
> A—Abundance of love at the worksite
> T—Times of jokes, pranks, and fun
> C—Commitment to help someone
> H—Hope, faith, and love that make a person's soul
>   rich
> I—Integrity we gain from this week
> E—Endurance everyone has even under the worst
>   conditions

Salkehatchie Is
Author Unknown

Salkehatchie is . .
   Sweat
   Action
   Love

Kindness
Exhaustion
Happiness
Adventure
Teenagers
Caring
Helping
Insects
Enthusiasm

Truth in Advertising about Salkehatchie Site Leadership
Arlene Andrews

OK, you're at home, getting ready to go, it's Friday midnight, you're already wiped out, still packing the truck so you can leave at 7 a.m. in the morning.
AND THEN, it's Sunday morning at the camp, the birds sing and the sunrise glows orange. God is beautiful.

OK, you've worked all day, you're in your bed at camp and you're trying to sleep. The screen doors slam, music blares, the youth come and go.
AND THEN, you're listening to the youth as they talk about their site families, their new friends, their anxieties. God is in the community.

OK, at the camp, your cabin has used all its toilet paper. The shower runs hot-cold-hot, never temperate. The toilet clogs.
AND THEN, you think about living the simple life for a week. Only minimal household chores. No dishes to wash. Wearing only comfy clothes. God is the focus.

OK, it's mid-afternoon, and your feet are hot and swollen from standing as your team replaces windows all around the house.

AND THEN, you see a single huge sunflower popping up from a field of kudzu. God is so refreshing.

OK, you cringe when family members kick their skinny dog and say they don't want him.

AND THEN, your site crew hugs the dog, collects money for dog food, and talks to area residents about adopting him. God is merciful.

OK, keeping up with the receipts is driving you nuts.

AND THEN, you look at your balance sheet and watch the loaves and fishes principle work. You find great bargains for supplies, and the budget stays in the black. God is generous.

OK, you've got bug bites on your ankles, neck, arms, wherever. You must live in a slimy coat of bug repellent and blotches of cortisone cream.

AND THEN, I dunno. It's hard to see God in this one. Still working on it. They do heal after days and weeks. God is healing.

OK, you're sitting (again) in the emergency room with a sick or injured young person, worrying about the tasks that are going undone.

AND THEN, you realize how many young people you've gotten to know as you sit in the ER or drive around. God is patient.

OK, (about 3 p.m. Wednesday) This has got to be the laziest crew ever.

AND THEN, (about 11 a.m. Friday) you think the entire crew has hypermania! They won't slow down!! God is strength.

Roofing, a social experience.

OK, Men! What makes them think whatever they are doing is more important than what the women and girls around here are doing?

AND THEN, you notice those guys are staying late at the site again tonight. Yesterday they worked from 6 a.m. until 8 p.m. Where do they get the energy? God is forgiving.

OK, you're drenched in sweat to the point that stinging salt runs into your eyes and your clothes stick to your body when you go inside for lunch.

AND THEN, when you're back home, your skin is soft for days, as if you had been to a spa resort. The impurities and toxins have leaked out. God is cleansing.

OK, bruises appear on your body for days after the trip is over. Your shoulders and back are sore.

AND THEN, you sleep the deepest, most wholesome sleep ever

when you get home. God is peace.

OK, you spend five grueling days working from sunrise till sundown in blistering heat with a crew that plays and bickers in the home of the sweetest person you've ever met who looks at you with fear because she's not sure you know what you're doing.

AND THEN, at the end of the week, the place is beautiful, the crew and family are grinning and crying, and you feel more energetic than you have in months. God is love.

The Salkehatchie Virus
Thomas M. Thompson

Beware of this Virus!

It is very infectious and contagious.

Merely hearing stories concerning the Salkehatchie Virus may result in leakage around tear ducts and/or uncontrollable smiling. It may even lead to reaching for your wallet to spend money for helping people you don't even know.

Occasional association with carriers of this virus, such as providing meals, running errands, or raising money for them, may bring on sudden feelings of well-being as well as knowledge that you have helped someone less fortunate than yourself.

Prolonged exposure to chronically infected Salkehatchie campers—including working, eating, talking, and praying with them for periods of up to one week—may cause an incurable desire to continually pay good money to become hot, sweaty, dirty, and tired by working on roofs or under houses of people of different social, ethnic, or economic backgrounds than your own.

The only antidote for the Salkehatchie Virus is a hug, a thank-you, a prayer, or simply a smile from one who has been drawn from the depths of despair because you succumbed to this virus.

After-effects of exposure to the Salkehatchie Virus include strengthened faith, joy of accomplishment, new friends, gratitude for what God has bestowed upon you, and strong feelings of love for your fellow man.

So protect yourself, or you may find these things happening to you! Oops, too late! I see the symptoms are already starting.

... You Might Be at Salkehatchie
Larry Hawkey

A keen observer of the human condition, Larry has provided the definitive guide for those who aren't sure if they've ever attended a Salkehatchie camp:

If on Monday you go to a house, rip out the kitchen, tear out the bathroom, leave the kitchen sink in the side yard and the toilet in the front; but before you leave, you tell the owners to "Have a nice evening," you might be at Salkehatchie.

If your mother finds pictures of you getting down and dirty on the Internet, and it makes her proud, you might be at Salkehatchie.

If someone tells you, "You really look hot," then hands you a water bottle, you might be at Salkehatchie.

If you throw your pants up against the wall and they stick, you might be at Salkehatchie.

If you think a minivan is just a pickup truck with a top, you might be at Salkehatchie.

If you drink three gallons of water in eight hours and only pee once, you might be at Salkehatchie.

If you spend forty-five minutes looking for a board stretcher only to find out Richard has the only one, you might be at Salkehatchie.

If you say the word "Sawzall" just because you think it sounds cool, you might be at Salkehatchie.

If you have a bag of clothes that could be classified as a biological weapon, you might be at Salkehatchie.

If you think safety goggles make you look cool, you might be at Salkehatchie.

If you decorate your safety goggles, you might be at Salkehatchie.

If you fall asleep in a crawlspace, and wake up thinking someone has dropped a house on you, you might be at Salkehatchie.

If you have been the main course at an all-you-can-eat buffet for a family of fire ants, you might be at Salkehatchie.

If you send a fat man up on the roof to look for rotten spots, you might be at Salkehatchie.

If you spend half a day pulling up carpet from the front yard, you might be at Salkehatchie.

If it is 6:30 a.m. and some crazy man is singing a song about sleeping birds, you might be at Salkehatchie.

If you work your tail off for someone you don't know, and you paid for the privilege, you might be at Salkehatchie.

Essays and sermons

Love
Art Dexter, 1987

I have defined the Salkehatchie Summer Service program in the following way: It is a grueling, bone-wearying week of rising at 5 a.m. and laboring till 5 p.m. in 95-degrees-plus temperatures, in primitive and often filthy conditions while sharing in the misery of others and simultaneously experiencing more love and fellowship than one could hope to realize in a whole lifetime!

Today I want to leave the work part behind and share with you just a little of the love that one experiences.

Adolfo Pérez Esquivel, a Nobel laureate, once said: "If we do not have the capacity to love, we can do nothing. If we do not have the capacity to love, we cannot work for our brothers and sisters. If we do not have the capacity to love, we cannot believe in God."

In the *Tales of the Hasidim*, the question is asked, "How can you tell that night has ended and day has begun?" and the answer is given, "It is when you can look in the face of any man or woman and see that it is your sister or brother. If you cannot see this, it is still night."

Leo Tolstoy once said, "The sole meaning of life is to serve humanity."

St. Francis of Assisi put it more succinctly when he said, "It is in giving that we receive."

As a Salkehatchie participant I can define love in other ways. Love, for me, was the sandbox that Don Andrews built for two little migrant girls named Tina and Maria. It broke my heart when Don related that he had always wanted to build a sandbox for his son, but his son and his wife (a United Methodist minister) were both killed in an auto accident.

Love for me was hearing the plaintive plea of Devin, a fellow worker, who asked me to pray for his son who had ruined his life with drugs.

And I remember the night that our roommate Harold Peel got word that his mother had died. I remember how compassionately Vernon Jones, Keith Parker, John Culp, and I comforted Harold and helped him to pack and load his tools into his pickup. And after we each embraced him with love he departed at midnight for the sad and lonely journey to High Point, North Carolina.

Sometimes love occurs in unexpected places when Christ leads us to those he called "the least of these." At one of our sites lived an elderly grandmother, who was a double amputee, and her mentally deficient 27-year-old grandson who still wore diapers and whom she had to keep in restraints because the grandmother could no longer chase him should he wander off. Behind their trailer is a small hovel in which her granddaughter Francine and Francine's husband, James, live. Francine is severely intellectually disabled, can only communicate in grunts, and salivates continually so that her blouse is always soaking wet. James is also intellectually disabled. Both were living in terrible squalor and had been treated badly by most people all of their lives. Our group turned their hovel into a thing of beauty and furnished it in the same way. In the process, Francine and James became the most-loved people of all our sites. They were very special to us all. On our last day there, Francine and James were brought back to our dorms and treated to the luxury of a shower. They loved it and spent forty-five minutes reveling in the water! Francine was so proud of the perfume she was given to wear and wanted everyone to smell it! All of the children God has created in his image are beautiful, if we view them through the eyes of love.

I have said that the work is physically taxing. But it is also emotionally taxing in many ways. I seriously doubt that many could make it through the week if it were not for the loving support that comes from the members of the group. When someone is reduced to tears (and this happens frequently), there are always others to share the tears, to give an embrace or a touch. Love is never in short supply.

Parting is always hard and yet, even then, there is love. I can still see Tisket Jenkins, a widow with two children, standing in the dust beside the road, waving to us with tears running down her cheeks, as we drove away with tears in our own eyes. She had related earlier that no one had ever helped her or shown her kindness. We had taken her to our hearts, and she had returned our love.

Salkehatchie doesn't fit just into the time frame of a week; it goes on in varying ways throughout the year. Some of us have known and shared a year in advance with the people whose houses we work on. Smaller groups of our people may return after the week to do additional work or to help others in numerous ways. Since our work in July, a UMC group has returned and done further work on John and Gertie's place. Another UMC group from Simpsonville is making plans to return to the coast in September to work on the home of a blind woman and to repair the floor of an old plantation praise house, where an eighty-year-old man tries, on Wednesday evenings, to instill biblical values in young people.

And we maintain our ties in other ways. One night, a few weeks after we had left St. Helena's Island, a phone call informed us that Miguel, the six-year-old brother of Tina and Maria, had drowned in a tragic accident. When we arrived, we found the father, Angelo, in shock; but Lydia, the mother, was endeavoring to be strong for the sake of the other six children. Maxine, my wife, and I marveled at her love when she went to the funeral home and dressed her little dead son by herself. That night at the wake, we shared their tears as their family and we stroked Miguel's cheek and hair and kissed him. The little children asked questions of their mother, and we all tried to understand how someone as small as Miguel could contain something as large as death. The next day after services at the church, four of us carried the little four-foot-long casket to the gravesite. As the family crowded the casket taking yet another good-bye, I stood back and looked at Lydia in her flip-flops, and the grandmother, Delores, in her hand-me-down dress that Maxine had hemmed just an hour before, and thoughts like *blessed are the poor*, and *suffer little children to come unto me*, ran through my mind. But then, as Father Laughlin led us in saying the Our Father, a beautiful yellow butterfly came out of nowhere and landed on the spray of flowers on the casket, where it rested as we prayed, and then flew silently away while little Tina pointed at it. Life is sometimes stranger than fiction and sometimes love transcends even death.

I think that anyone who has experienced the love of the Salkehatchie program will agree that the rewards are so great that you might be willing to give up a lot, or suffer a lot, or even die a little just to be able to participate.

St. John of the Cross once said, "In the twilight of life, God will not judge us on our earthly possessions and human success, but rather on how much we have loved." May God enrich all our lives with opportunities to share in love with our brothers and sisters.

Super Struggle
John Culp, 1991

Is it courage or stupidity? Is it helpful or showing off? Has the hard work, money, and time given been worth it? Who really cares if a home has a floor or a roof or windows? Can this family really benefit or will the children and parents continue to be trapped in dirt, rags, and ignorance? Why not spend a week at Lake Junaluska or maybe go to Jerusalem and see the Holy Land? This is good, too.

Some will say the work camp is such a good thing, but they will never allow themselves to experience the truth of these people's lives. I personally cannot live in poverty conditions very long because I, too, enjoy a comfortable home, running water, a bathroom with a shower, clean clothes, and good meals. The freedom to walk away, to leave this type of living, is a gift we sometimes take for granted. My feelings become disturbed when I see flies cover a child or one with signs of worms, an old person unable to rest because the roof is falling in, teenagers' minds receiving no incentives or nurture, retardation caused by poor nutrition, or isolated lives behind walls of prejudices.

God deliver me from the pains of people you made in your image and called good but evil strikes down. God doesn't deliver us—he sends us back to another week of dirt, sweat, hard work and turbulent feelings. The dream

I had about helping has become too real. Only through his grace have lives been changed. Young and old have shared gifts of love. "Trashy" people have become people of worth. My preparation is one of trying to cope with feelings of disgust and anticipation of more real misery in people's lives. But I know salvation and grace will be given to us through the lives we touch, and the incarnation will be in the lives of the people that we go to be with.

We really don't have to go. Christ will understand and forgive us, but I want to go because this is where life is. There we will discover God anew.

Salkehatchie and My Mom
Marcus Sizemore, 2004

I remember going to church on Salkehatchie Sunday every year since I was only four or five years old. At the end of each summer my church in Fort Mill devotes a service for Salkehatchie volunteers to share experiences

Faith can move a mountain.

and memories. I remember the year before I was old enough to go to Salkehatchie a fellow youth who had gone stood up and spoke to the congregation. He looked nervous and his voice was shaky. He told us about the home he worked on, the family he worked with, and what he did that week. I remember some of it was so difficult for him to talk about that he could not go on anymore. I wondered what had occurred that made it so hard to talk about. Plenty of other people had been to Salkehatchie and shared their experiences with the congregation before. I wondered, what made his experience different than the rest?

Though my dad had gone to Salkehatchie off and on again for several years, my mom and I had always agreed that we would go to Salkehatchie together. So we went the summer after I turned fourteen. Boy, was I in for a surprise! Salkehatchie changed my life.

I chose the house that I wanted to work on because I knew it would be a tough job to get done in only five days. What made it so tough? How could I have been so naïve, to have never taken the time to wonder if there were people living in South Carolina without running water, a bathroom, or electricity? Sure, I had been camping and even gone to summer camps where we had to "rough it," but those times lasted a week at most. These people were living without the things that I took for granted when I woke up each day.

Three women lived in the house: a mother and her twin daughters who were seniors in high school. One of the daughters had a baby boy. The first day I worked on the house I had no idea what I was doing but I knew there was some way I could help. That week we installed water and sewer lines, a new hot water heater, and electricity. We also added a room to the back of the house, turned a closet into a bathroom with a shower, toilet, and sink, added a side door, and installed a new kitchen counter and cabinet set with a brand new sink. The family loved it.

Perhaps most memorable was the new front porch we made. We poured concrete to make it and then we all signed our names in it. This was not done just because we wanted to; it was at the request of one of the daughters. I guess you could say we made a lasting impression on that family. We also left them a five-gallon bucket of paint and brushes; the next summer, their house was a new color. Salkehatchie not only helps families in need, but it helps people get motivated to help themselves.

Perhaps my dream deep down inside was to work with my mom at Salkehatchie once I became old enough to be a junior site leader.

My first year of Salkehatchie I was fourteen years old and I guess I kind of avoided my mom just because I didn't think it was cool for everyone to know I was her son. I'm twenty years old now and I regret that. We went to Salkehatchie together two years in a row, but we never worked at the same site. The summers of 1997 and 1998 were perhaps the most enjoyable and memorable times I ever had with her as a young adult. She enjoyed Salkehatchie and I could tell that she was glad that I came with her.

In the summer of 1999 my mom was sick and unable to go. I could tell that something wasn't right with her but she told me she would go next year. In the spring of 2000, right after my junior prom, she told our family that she had ovarian cancer. That was one of the worst days of my life. She kept the news all bottled up inside for two or three weeks just because she didn't want me to worry about her while I was at the prom. She put others before herself. I remember the exact day and exact moment like it was all a bad dream. The look on her face showed that she was about to tell us something that would hurt her more than it would ever hurt any of us. We were all at the dinner table and we had already eaten. She told us to have a seat and I knew from the tone of her voice that something was not right. As soon as she told us I just stared down at the table in disbelief. My dad cried, my brother cried, and my mom cried too. I tried to be the strong one and keep it all back. I comforted my dad, and I knew that he didn't want to lose his wife of nearly eighteen years.

That summer my mom began to go to chemotherapy about twice a month. She began to lose her hair and changed so much from the drugs and steroids that I felt sorry for her. She was in constant pain but continued to try and do all the things a mother does. Toward the end of my senior year her health took a turn for the worse. She was in and out of the hospital starting that spring. I don't know how she did it but she managed to get well enough that the doctors said she could come home and attend my graduation. That was a miracle in itself.

That summer I went to Salkehatchie with my little brother, Cliff. It was his first time. Everyone who knew my mom continued to ask me how she was. My brother noticed how many people there knew her. At summer's end I left home to attend the University of South Carolina, the place where both my parents went to college and my mom graduated cum laude. The day I moved into the dorm my mother was in the hospital. I was reluctant to go because I knew that she would miss me and I didn't want to be far from her side.

That fall I would go home about once a month to see my family. Right around Thanksgiving, my mom was back in the hospital with respiratory problems. I had not seen her in a while and she looked so sad. She was unconscious and on a breathing machine. I just wanted my old mama back. That year was a sad Christmas because that was the first Christmas I had ever spent without my mom. She was in an induced coma for over two months until I visited her around Valentine's Day and she was coming out of it. She would try and write things because she could not talk due to the tracheal tube she had down her throat to help her breath. I still have those scribbles that she tried to make look like words with the little strength she had. She asked me a few questions and even asked me what classes I was taking and how I did in the fall. Even in the hospital and in pain, my mother was worried about me, her oldest son.

Late in February of 2002, there was talk that she might be able to come home for the first time in at least three months. She came home and was in a very, very good mood. I was thrilled. Perhaps my mom had beaten the cancer like I had prayed she would. She was not 100 percent but she was glad to be with her family. One day I came home from college and spent a little time with her by myself. This was the day when I thought about my future, my real future, for the first time in life. She told me that she didn't want to miss out on things that most mothers get to see. She wanted to see me and Cliff graduate from college and get married. She didn't want to miss out on the best things of a mother's life. I don't blame her. I didn't want her to. She said she couldn't wait until the day that she could say she was a grandmother (which she didn't want to be too soon down the road). This was hard for her to say and hard for me to take. I was eighteen years old at the time and she was only forty-seven. She must have known that she was nearing the end of her road. I hoped and prayed every day that she would get better and that she could beat her cancer. I couldn't even imagine not having my mom around anymore.

I was at college in May when my dad called and told me I needed to come home. He didn't have to tell me why. I knew I didn't have much time. I arrived at the hospital and nearly all of my family was there. My grandmothers, aunts, uncles, cousins, and even some of mom's closest friends were all there. I got to her bedside and bawled. I held her hand and perhaps the greatest miracle I have ever seen took place. She opened her eyes. She saw her sons for the very last time. I somehow knew that God was watching. My brother and I stared in disbelief and for one moment, I felt that everything would be all right.

She'll never get to see me graduate college. She'll never get to walk me down the aisle. She'll never get to see her first grandchild. I knew my mom for nineteen years and six days. I guess God had other plans for me and for her. She was the greatest mom.

The first months after her death were the toughest. I went to Salkehatchie by myself that year and it helped me. A Salkehatchie house in Lake City is dedicated to my mom. The family who lives there, the Fulmores, never met my mom, but they know that she was a great person. A friend from our church, who had worked with my mom the last year she was able to go to Salkehatchie, also worked on the Fulmore home.

That hot July day that we toured houses and dedicated the house to my mom, Jeralyn, the sun was shining down and a cool breeze came through. It sent chills down my spine and I knew that my mom would be proud. I did not work on that house but I really don't think I could have. It was hard to hold the tears back that day.

At the end of that summer, I spoke at Salkehatchie Sunday, as I had done before on several occasions. I spoke about the work that I did and the people we helped. But this time it was tougher. I had learned the true meaning of Salkehatchie. Salkehatchie is not a physical thing at all. Someone can put new roofs on poor people's houses all day long and not get anything out of it. Salkehatchie is not what you put into it but what you get out of it. My mom has been my inspiration to continue to participate in Salkehatchie. She put others before herself. I strive every day to do the same. I want to be an inspiration for someone. I want other people to know the joy and satisfaction you get out of putting others before yourself.

Without Salkehatchie I don't know how I would have gotten through the summer after my mom passed on. I have been going to Salkehatchie since I was fourteen and look forward to it every year. Some may say I'm obsessed. I say I'm in love with it. By God's grace, it has helped me through some tough times. The summer of 2002 it helped me find myself. It helped me realize that my mom was setting an example for others her entire life.

Salkehatchie is my way of setting an example. If I had to choose only one thing in my life to experience, I would choose Salkehatchie.

Abundant Blessing
Russell Smith, senior pastor,
Covenant First Presbyterian Church, Cincinnati, Ohio

Based on Ruth 4:1-22, this sermon was part of a series on "Ordinary People, Extraordinary God." The excerpt included here follows a recounting of Ruth's marriage to Boaz and Naomi's caring for her grandson, Obed, who would be grandfather of David, king of Israel.

David would be a blessing that Boaz, Ruth, and Naomi could never have expected. This is often the way that God, working through his faithful ordinary people, produces blessing in the lives of others. But God also compounds that blessing in an extraordinary way so it carries on in totally unexpected ways.

My mother grew up in Union, South Carolina. Just up the street from her family was the Culp family. Little John Culp was about the same age as my mother's baby brother Paul, who we call Buzzy. John Culp had a terrible speech impediment. He could hardly talk—stuttering was a terrible problem for him. You can imagine the cruelty of some of the neighborhood children as well. But Uncle Buzzy befriended John. John always was thankful for the kindness of Uncle Buzzy and my grandfather.

Through that kindness, God helped John have the self-confidence to overcome that speech impediment. John himself calls it a miracle. He was miraculously able to talk and show the world what a fine mind he had. That would be a fine story of blessing in and of itself, if it ended right there.

But you see, with his newfound confidence, John also felt a calling on his life—a calling to be a preacher. And John, through his study of the scriptures, put his faith into action by starting a rural mission organization. In the late 1970s, John took a team of teenagers and adults to the sea islands of South Carolina and spent a week repairing houses for the destitute. Other churches heard about this and joined his church in the project. Soon, they had a summer camp with more than a hundred people coming each year. And then there were multiple camps. They called it Salkehatchie Summer Service.

Teams of youth and adults would fan out across the state of South Carolina, spending a week working on renovating homes for the poor and needy. John's ministry has helped hundreds of families: the elderly, the handicapped, and the single working mothers. An example of a small kindness that God used to develop into an abundant blessing.

But this is a God-sized story. For you see, of all the teenagers who came to work in Salkehatchie camps over the years, dozens of them sensed a call on their lives to vocational ministry. And they went into churches and mission posts, multiplying the blessing even more. And God's people are nourished because their shepherds sensed a call while on a mission trip that was started by a pastor who was shown a kindness while he was a young boy. Again, an example of how God used a small kindness to develop an abundant blessing.

But again, this is a God-sized story. You see, in the summer of 1994, a young man attended one of John Culp's Salkehatchie work camps. He had participated in these camps for many years, but this year was different. He had just lost his job, and he was struggling with what direction his life would take. He went to the work camp not knowing what to do with his life, and he came back knowing that God was calling him to ministry. He took another job to raise money to pay for school, he went to school, and then became an ordained Presbyterian minister.

That young man was me. A kindness that my uncle and grandfather showed in the 1950s resulted in a blessing for me in the 1990s.

Of course I realize that there were other influences on John's life, just as there were other influences on my life and on all the other lives in the story. The point is not to show that one action was directly responsible for the later results. Rather, the point is to show that God is behind the scenes, and he so orchestrates events as to result in abundant blessing. It is God who ultimately encouraged John Culp's heart to go to ministry. It is God who ultimately directed all those people to work in Salkehatchie camps. It was God who worked on my heart. But it was God's good pleasure to use all these ordinary people to accomplish his extraordinary will.

I have heard it said, and I believe it true, that there is no waste in God's economy. God can and does take anything and transform it for his purposes. He took Naomi's despair and transformed it into an opportunity to bring Ruth to Israel so she could be a source of abundant blessing. He took John Culp's disability and transformed it into an opportunity for him to rely more fully on God speaking through him. If it is true for them, then it is true for us. No matter how hard the circumstances, no matter how painful the situation in which we find ourselves, no matter how deep our despair, our God is bigger than all that. Our God is able, in his own timing, to transform our pain into an opportunity for abundant blessing. That is why we can move from despair to hope, to expectation, to blessing, because we know the character of our extraordinary God.

So we've seen how God ultimately used this despairing widow, Naomi; this hard-working and faithful foreign girl, Ruth; and this kindly older man, Boaz, to produce abundant blessing for Israel in their descendent David. But remember, this is a God-sized story, and so the blessing doesn't end there. You see, centuries later, they would have an even more famous descendent. Look at the Gospel of Matthew, 1:1-6. In this genealogy we see that Boaz and Ruth are specifically mentioned as ancestors of Jesus. This section lists three Old Testament women: Tamar, Rahab, and Ruth—all foreign-born women who were heroes in their own right, each one a distant ancestor of Jesus. God used these unexpected ordinary people to ultimately provide the greatest blessing of all for all of humanity.

Jesus's birth, life, death, resurrection, and ascension were God's crowning achievement. Through Jesus, God takes the initiative to cleanse the guilt from his faithful. Through Jesus, God shows his love for us. Through Jesus, God opens the doorway for us to have a direct relationship with him. Through Jesus, God wins the ultimate victory over sin and death. Through Jesus, God provides the abundant blessing we all yearn for. Through faith in Christ, we receive the fullness of God's abundant blessing—eternal life to enjoy relationship with him.

Our God, our extraordinary God, used the lives of these ordinary people to produce an abundant blessing for all people. And he still uses ordinary people to accomplish his extraordinary will. Just consider: If he so used Ruth, Naomi, and Boaz, how will God use you? How will he take your faith and your actions of kindness and compound them to produce abundant blessing that you cannot anticipate?

You think about that. Amen.

Send the People Away!
Richard Allen, minister for outreach and development, United Methodist Christ Church, New York City

Sermon based on Mark 6:30-44

They started out tired. They needed a vacation. There were so many folks around that they couldn't hear themselves think. Have you ever driven a van full of middle schoolers? It was like that. The text for the morning is pretty blunt: "... so many people were coming and going that they"—Jesus and the disciples—"did not even have a chance to eat." Then Jesus says those great vacation words: "Come with me by yourselves to a quiet place and get some rest." So they go, but the crowd follows. And it begins to get dark. The disciples come to Jesus. They want—they need—some quiet time. They are delicate and couch the request in a concern. "This is a remote place," they said, "and it's already very late. Jesus, please, Lord, send the people away."

Send the people away. I know the feeling. It's a feeling of being overwhelmed, of being drained, of feeling totally depleted, not only of helping, but of even caring whether you ever help anyone again or not. Send the people away. For their good, for my good, for the good of us all, get rid of them.

I had never much noticed that phrase before, but this week it jumped out at me. And since we read nearly as much into the Bible as we read from the Bible, maybe the word I heard is a word from my own heart. Perhaps there is something drying up in me. That's neither a complaint or an excuse. We all get like that from time to time.

I think Jesus knew that even disciples get like that from time to time. I even think that Jesus sometimes felt drained, frustrated, empty. Read the Gospel of Mark sometime and notice its rhythms: Jesus with the crowd, then Jesus alone. Then with the crowds again, then alone again. Jesus—even Jesus, especially Jesus—took time apart to charge his own spiritual batteries. Interesting, isn't it, that Jesus would have to seek his own solitude, but we try to live as if prayer were merely an option and that quiet time is somehow wasted time. Jesus knew the disciples needed time with him, so he suggested it: "Come with me by yourselves to a quiet place and get some rest."

How striking that this lesson falls, as it does, in the midst of the vacation season. So I say to you—and to myself—that Jesus still calls us in the midst

Preparing the Salkehatchie tradition of leaving a cross at each home.

of our burdens: "Come with me," he says, "... to a quiet place." I notice it in myself, that a change of place and a change of routine does the routine much better. So often we forget the lesson of Bishop Gerald Kennedy, a modern powerhouse, who said, "I can do a week's work in six days, but not in seven. And I can do a year's work in eleven months, but not twelve." There's a time to put down even the most important task so that you can really pick it up again. When that time comes, holding on to the job even tighter won't help you keep your grip on it. Life is full of ironies, and this is just another. Sometimes only turning loose allows you to hold on. "Come with me by yourselves to a quiet place," says Jesus, "and get some rest."

The trouble is, it doesn't work. Folks follow Jesus and the disciples and the quiet place fills with voices. Have you ever noticed how quiet it is to ride alone in your car? I'm sad for those I see on the highway with ears stuck into cellular phones. It may be an efficient use of time, but it's sad. And the interstate is one of those rare places where the body can go into cruise control and the spirit can take a moment's refreshment. The silence is full of noise. The disciples steal away with Jesus, and so does the crowd.

It's understandable, then, that the disciples get fed up. "Send the people away," they tell Jesus. They want them gone. They are overwhelmed with the noise and with the needs. They have had it with the confusion, the bickering, the blowing noses, and the babies crying. "Send them away. ..." The disciples were overwhelmed.

Last week, the youth talked about Salkehatchie and what it was like for them. You could hear in their words something we all felt. It was overwhelming. It is frustrating to tackle such big jobs with too little time, too little money, too little trained help. When I saw my site for the first time, I said, "This is not so bad. We can do this. We'll be done early. All we have to do is a roof. And a little trim. And maybe some plywood will have to be replaced. And a little painting. And we put up a few pieces of Sheetrock. Just that. And a little cleaning up. It's not so bad." I said all that out loud, and because I am well trained in denial, I even thought it. It's not so bad.

But reality began to sink in as the week progressed. The roof was worse than we thought. The kids were less skilled than I assumed, because I usually assume that everyone else knows what I know. When Mandy stepped through the attic Sheetrock and landed on the floor, I began to realize that some of these kids did not know what I know. And the porch roof needed to come off, the bugs were more pervasive than earlier imagined. The sun was hot. Worst of all, we began to realize that no matter what we did, it might not make that much of a lasting difference in the lives of the people who lived there. One of the adult counselors nearly walked home to Surfside one day when she took a break from killing roaches and overheard one of the women say, "There's more to life than working." This counselor is a good and true disciple of Christ our Lord. But she was saying what those earlier disciples said way back then: "Lord, send the people away. ..." In effect, let them take care of themselves.

I say that not to be critical of my co-counselor. She merely spoke what we were all thinking. And we were thinking what all of the church sometimes thinks: "Lord, it's not working and it's not worth it. I've got mine, now let these other poor people get theirs. Any way they can. Just get me out of the picture. I've had it." If we're really honest, we become overwhelmed. There are so many problems in the world and I have so little in my own reserves. "What can I do? Lord, send them away!"

Listen to what's going on for the disciples in the lesson. They are tired, hungry, annoyed, and probably growing very angry that their vacation with

Jesus has been interrupted. Notice again what they say: "Send the people away so they can go to the surrounding countryside and villages and buy themselves something to eat." The disciples aren't worried that they themselves won't have anything to eat. They don't say, "Hey, Jesus! Let's go get some bread. We're hungry and we don't have anything." Why not? The text doesn't say. I believe they didn't talk about their own needs because they knew their own needs were already met. I think that they stopped off to buy bread on the way. After all, they knew where they were going and how long they planned to be there. They were going into the wilderness to be alone for a while. They had their camping supplies with them and they knew it.

And, for me, that's precisely the point. The disciples had just enough to last them, and not a bit more. They weren't about to share. There wasn't enough. That says something about us, too. For we are all inclined to think that we would become more generous once we have taken care of our own needs. Occasionally that may be true, but I rarely see it—in myself or in others. Generosity, the true spirit of sharing, is born in scarcity or not at all. We don't share from our own abundance; we share from faith there's never enough. But if we can let go of what we have and in God's abundance. If we're all worried about having enough, trust God to make it enough—it is enough. And it's a question of holding on or turning loose.

Jesus takes what the disciples have and blesses it, and suddenly there is enough for everyone. Holding on becomes less important than turning loose.

Christ invites us to turn loose today and trust this grace to sustain us and our neighbors in the wilderness of life. Christ invites us to know our own needs, but to trust God's sustaining grace. We are all poor. Our sharing comes from a trust in the depth of God's abundant store. Amen.

Reflections
Arlene Bowers Andrews

Annie's Dog
1999

So we brought the puppy home. My car doesn't smell so bad after all (it smells more like dirty laundry than dirty dog). My sister-in-law is still speaking to me. And, above all, my niece doesn't have to live with the fear that an innocent creature was mauled to death because her hard-hearted aunt didn't want to deal with a stray animal.

The fourteen-year-old son at the Snipes home, where Annie worked, raises pit bull dogs to fight one another. The home is far down a country road, situated beside a vast cotton field and pinewoods. The pit bulls were tethered in the woods for the Salkehatchie week, at a distance from the house, but Annie went down to see them. One, in a pen, was covered with scars. The son told Annie they were mean to the dogs to make them tough. Annie said that when he or anyone came near the dogs, they got upset; one even foamed at the mouth.

The puppy that wandered into the Snipes family's yard just before Salkehatchie week is a little black dog, a pure-bred Lab according to Annie, though most likely she is a pure God-knows-what. Annie saw a member of the family kick the puppy, and the son told her he was thinking about raising it to be in fights with his pit bulls. Annie knows a Lab would never fight like a pit bull and that the confrontation would be an intentional massacre. She was appalled that anyone would regard this as entertainment. From the first day, she set out to save the puppy - she planned to take it home and place it for adoption. She spent the week swiping food from our camp meals. I didn't have the heart to note that this would only make matters worse if we could not take the puppy, because it would become attached to the place where the food was.

I, of course, being less gifted in the area of compassion, was adamantly opposed to the idea of bringing a dirty, flea-infested, worm-ridden, urinating and defecating wild dog along for a three-hour ride home in a car with five people and all their gear. I also thought of Annie's mother's response; they already had four people and a dog in their house in a city neighborhood. So when Annie announced on Monday that she was bringing the dog home at the end of the week, I started suggesting alternatives.

"Ask one of the site leaders who lives in this county where to take a stray dog."

I asked someone and found out their animal control program has a prompt euthanasia policy. That would not do.

"Ask if any site leader knows someone who would like to adopt a puppy. ... Ask Mrs. Snipes, who cooks in the cafeteria at the school, if she knows anyone who wants a puppy. ... Ask the people who serve us lunch at the church ... ."

Annie, being a shy and determined person, did none of these. Thursday I told her clearly there was no room in the car for a dog.

As we were driving away from the camp on Saturday morning, Annie said quietly, "We are going to get the dog now, aren't we?" My mouth dropped. We were packed like sardines.

"Annie, where would we put a dog?"

"On my lap."

"She'll need to pee and poop; it will stink and ruin my car."

"No, she hardly eats anything."

"She'll get carsick."

"I doubt it. She'll probably sleep—that's what she does all day."

I stopped the car and looked around for help. I had three other kids in the car.

"What do the rest of you think?"

They ganged up on me.

"There's plenty of room. ... Annie really wants to take the dog ... . You can't leave it here, they're mean to it. ... It will be fine."

So we got a box, put Annie's dirty towels in it to absorb the pee and poop (in the event they should occur), drove twenty miles out of our way, and rescued the dog.

They were right. I was wrong. The puppy was precious—as soon as I looked in her sweet, appealing black eyes, I loved her. Who wouldn't? She stayed in her box on Annie's lap the whole way, slept most of the time, didn't pee or poop, and didn't smell nearly as bad as the sweaty, foul odor wafting up from the four laundry bags that held the kids' work clothes.

There I was, so quick to see the worst in this situation. I tried my best to avoid this presumably rank creature when, in reality, the creature smelled and behaved far sweeter than I. The puppy was created to bring out the love in us. Annie did that, unconditionally. She also showed the Snipes's son what love and compassion can do; I can only pray that he understood what he saw. She saved me from the guilt of my own cold-heartedness. Would I have been any less evil than the guys who set up the fights, if I had driven away and left the puppy to her fate? I think not.

The puppy's name is Alice.

Children's Sermon
1993

How many of you had a bath yesterday or today?
Do you like to take a bath?
Every day, or every few days, you get to take a bath.

Let me tell you about some children I know who couldn't take a bath, even if they wanted to! Their names are Mary and David. I met them when some young Christians—teenagers—went to help them through Salkehatchie Summer Service. Jesus said for us to help poor people, and that's what we do at Salkehatchie.

We went to Mary and David's house. They couldn't use the bathtub because it was clogged up, full of muddy water that had been used over and over. There was a place for a sink in the bathroom. A pipe was sticking up out of the floor, but there was no sink! The toilet was clogged, too, and full of dirty water. The kitchen sink worked, but it leaked behind the faucets. Every time you turned the water on, water poured under the sink and onto the floor and on feet. The floor in front of the sink was wet and rotten, with holes in it.

Mary and David live with their mama, but she didn't know how to fix the bathtub and sinks and toilet. Do you know how? I don't either. Plumbers know how. But the mama is poor and has no money to pay a plumber.

So Mary and David were really dirty. They never got to take a bath. Sometimes they got washed off with water from a bucket.

You might think it's fun to never take a bath. But David was already sick with fever because he had a little cut on his toe and it got infected. A doctor from Salkehatchie Summer Service got him some medicine.

Our Salkehatchie teenagers pulled out the broken kitchen sink and the toilet, and a Salkehatchie plumber came and told them how to fix everything. Now Mary and David and their mama have a new bathtub with a shower and a bathroom sink. Their toilet flushes, and they have a new kitchen sink and new kitchen floors.

We worked for a week and finished on Friday afternoon. We left Mary and David's house for a while and when we came back, we had all our Salkehatchie friends with us. Mary and David were clean. They had taken a bath and washed their hair and put on clean clothes. They sang "Jesus loves me" for all our friends. My body was really, really dirty because I had not had time for a bath; I had been fixing and cleaning all day. But when they sang, I felt clean in my heart.

Jesus loves us, whether our bodies are clean or dirty. But when we love Jesus back, we feel really clean.

Water
1999

"Let justice roll on like a river, righteousness like a never-failing stream!"—Amos 5:24

Water is a pervasive theme at Salkehatchie.

Will it rain? Hopefully not on Mondays or Tuesdays, because that's when the roofs have been ripped off and the ceilings beneath are exposed. We cover the roofs with gigantic tarps, but a vigorous storm can lift the tarps right off. You can paint over mildew-stained old ceiling boards, but drenched old ceiling boards crumble and collapse. So if it rains while the roof is exposed, the crew has a whole new job: replacing ruined ceilings.

Drink water.

Of course, rain causes many of our families' troubles. Over the years, roofs erode, alternately hammered by heat and swollen by ice. Shifting temperatures, windstorms, and aging induce cracks. Water seeps in; the cracks enlarge. The water sits under the shingles on the roof boards and ceiling boards, evaporating slowly. Saturation brings forth rot that, like a sponge, absorbs water rather than allowing it to roll down. Water drips into the house. First, cracks appear in the ceilings, then huge gaping holes. Mildew grows along the walls, and the floors repeat the process: water seeps in; the floor cracks, rots, develops holes, and then the floorboards collapse.

Miss Helen tells us how at night, while she was in bed, rain would fall on her face. She and other families in similar situations create artistic, musical compositions of buckets and pans, strategically placed to ward off the worst of the dripping rain. Often they have carpets on their floors, which is essential for warmth in the winter, but they get wet and breed mildew and odors and all sorts of critters (mostly related to cockroaches).

Drink water.

If the house has running water, more likely than not it also has plumbing problems. The floor rot is even worse where this occurs, especially under kitchen sinks, around toilets and bathroom sinks, and wherever the water heater may be. Sometimes, water runs, but gets discharged directly under the house because the sewage lines are broken. So when we are there, the water is turned off while the plumbing is disassembled. This is likely to last for days, because plumbing takes forever. As soon as you fix one pipe, the next one malfunctions—it's like dominoes.

While the water is off, no real cleaning can be done, unless you can borrow some water from a neighbor. You get creative about doing certain jobs without water, like carefully killing mildew with undiluted chlorine bleach; removing paint or linoleum glue from hands with sandpaper; keeping paintbrushes moist by wrapping them in plastic rather than soaking them in water; mixing rainwater from a jar or bucket with powder to make floor crack filler; or wiping up spills with rags that have already wiped up spills. Of course, the toilets don't work, so in the unlikely event that someone needs to go to the bathroom (sweat relieves fluid retention), a trip to a convenience store or nearby church may be required.

Drink water.

I cannot fathom why, in the richest country in the world, citizens still live in houses that have no plumbing. Typically, they have outhouses in their backyards and pumps that tap into wells. Our crews can put an electric pump on the well and run pipes into the house. Sometimes, we even have to arrange for a new well to be dug. One year, my son Brook worked at a house that didn't even have a well. The lady who lived there got water by walking a few yards into a thicket where a spring gurgled. It was rather muddy, but it was water. She used chamber pots and the adjacent woods for her bathroom facilities. She had done this all her life, which was close to eighty years. Brook's crew built her an outhouse and ran a water line to the county service so she'd have drinking water. The young people on the crew watched, in tears, as for the first time ever she turned a spigot and clear water splashed forth over her wrinkled hands.

Drink water.

A rusty old pump, primed with a few cups of water and jerked vigorously twenty or thirty times, will bring forth cool, clear water. Most young Americans cannot imagine having to go to such effort when they want a sip of water. At one home, the dear old resident asked us not to install an automatic pump for her well, because she feared she could not pay the electric bill. She did accept an outhouse to replace the many slop buckets she used.

Drink water.

With any luck, water-filled clouds will cover the sky, bringing cooler temperatures. This works best when it doesn't actually rain. It's a hassle to interrupt work to gather things and put them in the house or under a tarp because a shower passes by. When the sun comes back out, no one can find what they need because everything was hastily tossed somewhere. The roof is not a great place to be when a storm threatens and lightning flashes. Every year I bring rain ponchos but I've never had to actually use one, except as a picnic tablecloth. When it does rain, we let the soothing, cool waters pour over our bodies.

Drink water.

When we return home, we touch a button on a washing machine and water gushes

From any source, water works miracles.

forth to wash load after load of filthy laundry. Sour gray clothes, covered in sweat, soot, paint, tar, and the dust of disintegrated house parts gather into a growing pile day by day during the seven-day mission. We wash and dry them and tuck them into special containers in the attic, ready for next year.

Drink water.

After a long day's labor in the blistering sun, nothing feels better than a long soak in a tub filled with lukewarm water, mineral salts, and bath oil. Dream on. What we get at our Salkehatchie camp is a chance to stand in line behind ten other salt-encrusted filthy people on whom sweat has dried. All together, the group has about an hour, perhaps ninety minutes, to get clean and refreshed for evening activities. In a cabin with ten campers, once your turn arrives to enter one of the two shower stalls (assuming they are both functional), you wear your plastic thongs into the shower (or you'll take a foot fungus home with you). The plastic shoes also guard against getting shocked when you touch the spigots. The water runs intermittently hot and cold - you stand back during the hot moments and jump in during the warm interludes. The cold moments are generally tolerable. When you step out, more likely than not the concrete floor is covered with an inch or two of water. In a good year, the two toilets stay functional all week despite their heavy usage. In a bad year, if the toilet goes, the shower is also out, because plunging the toilet causes a sewage backup into the shower. When that happens, you get in line at the next cabin, which means you now have to wait in line behind twenty people.

Drink water.

The ground temperature during our Salkehatchie week in July generally reaches a daily high of 95 to 100 degrees Fahrenheit. On the roof, the heat index can reach 120 degrees. You start to sweat early in the morning. By midday, you have a bandana or other head wrap to prevent salty sweat from dripping into your eyes. I find that in the hottest part of the day, I start to fantasize about cool bodies of water. When I was as a child, our neighbor built a pool with cinder blocks. It was only about three feet deep, but we would pile in on a hot day and the water would wrap around our bellies and arms and feel so cool.

The advantages of constantly pouring water out of your skin are a) you rarely have to go to the bathroom during the day, which is good because you rarely have bathroom facilities available; and b) for a week after you return home, you have the softest skin you've ever had. All the impurities just under the skin have been washed away. Such a spa treatment would probably cost big bucks.

Drink water.

One of the biggest safety concerns during Salkehatchie week is that a person will become dehydrated, which is bad enough by itself, but we also worry that a dehydrated person will become disoriented and fall off a roof or make a mistake with a power tool. We keep at least two large coolers at the site. One is filled with ice water, the other with Gatorade. We insist the water is the more essential of the two. We put water in plastic bottles for the roof crew and toss empty and full bottles back and forth. Our sites are served by a team of angels in the form of two women who drive from site to site each morning and each afternoon with fresh ice and water. Sometimes they bring frozen sugar water in the form of popsicles. Sometimes we get cold watermelon.

Jesus said, "Whoever believes in me will never be thirsty" (John 6:35). I know this in a spiritual way, but in a physical way, at Salkehatchie, this is true, too. As soon as we think about wanting water, it is there for us.

The book of our faith begins and ends with water. In the beginning, when God created the heaven and the earth, the water seems to already be there. The Spirit of God moved over the waters. At the end, the prophet John calls, "Let the one who is thirsty come; and let the one who wishes take the free gift of the water of life" (Revelation 22:17). Throughout the book, we hear of the incredible power of water. God uses it to destroy the entire earth, except for Noah and his chosen. Water wipes out the Pharaoh's army and saves the emancipated Hebrew slaves. Moses strikes a rock and draws water for a parched wilderness tribe. The exchange of water bonds Isaac to Rebekah and begins a mighty nation. The psalmist seeks still waters for comfort. Jesus, in his humility, washes the feet of his followers. Jesus controls the power of water, turning it to wine and calming a stormy sea. Yet when his time was done, in the midst of his sacrifice, he said, "I am thirsty."

One of the most meaningful associations I have with water at Salkehatchie comes from the year John Culp baptized a little boy named Sammy at our site. Sammy was about nine months old. He lived with his great-grandmother (who had Alzheimer's disease and stayed at a state institution some of the time), his grandmother (who couldn't read), and his mother (a seventeen-year-old young lady who had dropped out of school and had been earning her living as a prostitute at nearby truck stops). Sammy's mom was now working as a store clerk. If there was a man in Sammy's life, he didn't show up during the week we were at Sammy's house. Sammy was the apple of his gramma's eye, and dearly loved by his mom. At his gramma's request, when the entire camp came during the final tour of sites on Friday, John donned a white robe and performed the sacrament of baptism for Sammy.

The services for the sacrament of baptism in our church include reminders of the significance of water in our faith. When nothing existed but chaos, God swept across the dark waters and brought forth light. After God saved his people from the flood with an ark, he made a covenant of protection through the water crystals in clouds that form a rainbow. He sent his son to live among people by way of nurture in the water of a woman's womb. Jesus was baptized by water, and so all Christians go through the rite of baptism to mark the transition from old life to new.

In our church, when an infant or child is baptized, the congregation makes a promise. One of our pledges is that we will "surround this child with a community of love and forgiveness, that he may grow in his service to others." I can still remember standing on the road in front of Sammy's house while he was baptized, reciting that pledge and wondering how I was going to keep it, given that I live one hundred thirty miles away. The opportunity arose for me to work on the South Carolina First Steps program, which provides support resources in all counties for early childhood development programs. I dedicated my work to Sammy and called upon people to reach out to neighbors like him, to provide family support and care in a way that will enable them to thrive. I made a promise, sealed by water, that I would help build a community for Sammy. My fourteen-year-old niece gave her first year of Salkehatchie Summer Service at Sammy's home; years later, she chose early childhood education as her college major.

Water trickles in the form of tears. Jesus wept from sorrow. During one Salkehatchie week, a lady cried in anguish on Monday evening when she entered her home after it was ripped apart. She saw revealed the true nature of the rotten devastation that had been hidden by her futile covers, plastic sheets, carpets, buckets, and wood patches. On Friday, the eyes of a man with neurological disability filled with joyful tears as he shuffled up his new ramp and wandered around his clean, dry, pretty home. As a crew left its site for the final time, a six-year-old boy tried to control his trembling lips as forlorn tears trailed down his cheeks and he waved good-bye to his new, dear friends. A tough young eighteen-year-old volunteer who hadn't cried in years moaned, "Oh, no, I'm going, too," as he joined his site crew in tearfully hugging and bidding bittersweet farewell to the sweet lady of the home they virtually rebuilt.

Salkehatchie Summer Service is named for the Salkehatchie River, which winds through the South Carolina Lowcountry to the Atlantic Ocean. Water, the mighty force, perhaps the most powerful physical force on earth, surrounds us in subtle, healing ways.

Freedom

If the Son sets you free, you will be free indeed.—John 8:36

Our family always does Salkehatchie Summer Service during the week of the Fourth of July. From the past, I vaguely remember fireworks, parades, extended family cookouts, and trips to the lake. At Salkehatchie, the holiday is like any other day of the week, except we have red, white, and blue decorations on our lunch tables.

Being at Salkehatchie helps me reflect on the freedom I have that other people don't have. I am not shackled by ill health, poverty, or a low-wage job with no vacation benefits. I am free to take the time and spend the money to do Salkehatchie. I am free from fear that someone will shoot bullets through my windows, that no one will hire me, that my car won't work, or that I will have no water in my house. I am free and able to get in my car and go to a doctor or to get groceries whenever I want. I don't have to beg a ride from a neighbor or think of a way to barter services for a ride. I am free to say what I want around anyone, without the fear that someone powerful in the community will take offense at my words and then turn off my water. I am free from nagging thoughts that people may despise me and treat me unfairly because of my race. I am free to walk away from my everyday responsibilities and spend time in service to others.

I think of equality and how hard I work at my job for substantial compensation, while others work just as hard or harder with little or nothing to show for it. Mr. and Mrs. McKenzie, who successfully farmed all their lives and raised their own children plus six foster children, had no health or house insurance. Mr. McKenzie required a series of heart surgeries, which put the family half a million dollars in debt. Then lightning struck their house and burned half of it. The family didn't even have the resources to clear away the burned timbers and debris. A proud man, self-sufficient until these catastrophes humbled him, Mr. McKenzie could barely be on the site while the youth worked to clear it, because he felt such shame at receiving help. He stayed in the background, coming out only in the evening after the crew was gone. By the end of the week, as the debris began to vanish and the half-house was enclosed and gleamed with new paint, his pleasure at the progress slipped through his stern, withdrawn face. He knows he is equal to all of us; he doesn't understand why life does not treat him equally, and neither do I.

I was raised in a military family and have a passion for the principles for which our country stands. I am a patriot, I love a parade, and I cannot sing patriotic songs without tears flowing down my face. I love being a citizen of the United States of America and relish the privilege that comes with that association all around the world. My heart aches to know that people in other countries hate or resent us and I pray constantly for wise rulers of our nation who can show the rest of the world how to value freedom, equality, and justice. Unfortunately, I cannot justify why our leaders sometimes behave arrogantly and put our image at risk, and I cannot in any way understand why our leaders let American citizens live in squalor. Ours is the richest nation in the world. We can provide Mr. McKenzie with health insurance; he deserves it as much as I do. We can also make sure every American has running water and functional toilets. And we can provide public transportation systems, like all other developed nations do, so that our people can exercise their freedoms.

So, for all our values, I know that life in the USA can be unfair. I certainly don't deserve more freedom and benefits than others. I do what I can to work within our democratic system to make things more fair. Meanwhile, Salkehatchie week is a time when we do become more equal. At camp, we generally go by first names, and people rarely share the labels they often have. Few know who has more wealth or power or influence than others. Even the ministers, who carry an inherent authority among our workers in other contexts, tend to be humble, blending in with the crowd at camp. We quickly learn that even though our material status is different, our spiritual status is equal to that of the families whose homes we serve.

Paul wrote, "There is one body and one Spirit, just as you were called to one hope when you were called; one Lord, one faith, one baptism; one

God and Father of all, who is over all and through all and in all" (Ephesians 4:4-6). We are all unified in the one. We may not be equal according to material standards, but we are equal in worth to God. We each have different resources and gifts, but when we live in Christian community, we each contribute what we have. And we carry each other's burdens (Galatians 6:2). As Paul went on to say, "the whole body, joined and held together by every supporting ligament, grows and builds itself up in love, as each part does its work" (Ephesians 4:16). We rise above the unfairness and inequality in the world.

And so Salkehatchie offers us hope about how we could live in freedom and equality, if only we would be willing to live in Christian love. Maybe the day will come when we see to it that material resources are more equitably distributed, all the time, everywhere within our land. Until then, we can practice and learn through our annual pilgrimages to Salkehatchie sites. There, we may discover what it feels like to let the Son set us free.

Loaves and Fishes

How many of your friends have the equipment to suck out a septic tank? At Gayle's site, they plunged and plunged to fix the toilet, and then realized the septic tank was as full as could be. They hadn't planned for this and had no idea how to make arrangements to get it unclogged. One of the guys on the crew said, "My dad has a friend with a septic cleaning service." What a coincidence that this young man was on this site. It so happened that his dad's friend was from a town only twenty-five miles from the site. Another coincidence. So, thanks to the wonders of cell phones, the dad was called, the friend was called, and a man with a "Your Number Two Is Our Number One" sign on his truck showed up at the site.

One spring, Neil received a check for $500 from a lady whose husband had died. She wanted the money to be used in his memory at Salkehatchie Summer Service in Marlboro County. Neil didn't know just how to use the money. Then it became clear that at one of the sites, a new well would have to be drilled. When the driller came and announced the cost, it was $500. What a coincidence!

In 2004 when this book was originally written, just $1,500 was allocated to each Salkehatchie home.[1] All supplies for roofing, plumbing, bathroom fixtures, lumber, flooring, windows, insulation, and any other structural supplies have to come from that fund. Smoke detectors are donated, but we have to use part of the $1,500 to feed the crew lunch on Friday. Supplies for painting and decorating have to come from somewhere else.

Reader, think about your own home. Imagine that a dreaded storm wreaks havoc and you have no insurance. What could you possibly accomplish with $1,500? Well, you could call together your community and get free labor. You could beg for donated supplies. You could borrow tools. You could bargain shop for the cheapest (though reliable) materials. You could use scrap materials that make things functional, albeit unattractive. You could call on people throughout the community for advice or help for special needs. You could squeeze every ounce of creative thought from your brain and those of your friends and discover new ways of making things work. You could be sure every purchase is absolutely essential and watch every penny to be sure none are wasted. You would probably realize that none of this would happen without good communication and relations among your site crew, the friends and family who support them, and material suppliers in the community. And you still couldn't fix your house with just $1,500.

Unless you pray. And somehow, each time you think you're going to exceed your budget, there's still money in the till. Someone donates a few dollars or critical items. Turns out you didn't need as much material as you anticipated, or what you did need cost less than you thought. Miracles happen.

Every year the task at hand seems financially impossible. Every year the work gets done, often with money left over. The principle of loaves and fishes clearly prevails at Salkehatchie.

---

1. As of 2003. In 1978, each crew had $1,000. As prices increased over the years, the allocation has increased.

Being Done

Time goes faster, the older we get. One day equals 0.27 percent of a one-year-old's life, but is only 0.0055 percent of a fifty-year-old's life. That means a day is fifty times more in a one-year-old's life than in a fifty-year-old's life. Is there an end of time? Is time human-bound? What is an end? What is eschatology?

"We're not going to finish!" My first year at Salkehatchie, I lived in anxiety the entire week, believing that we would leave this family with a house in worse condition than when we arrived. Each day, the list of tasks to be completed seemed to grow longer rather than shorter: roofing, window repair, building and screening a porch, Sheetrock, painting. There were supplies to be acquired and tired young workers to be inspired. I had no faith, no comprehension of what was evolving as we worked. My site leader was Dave Stewart, a laid-back potter by profession. He kept saying, "It's finished when it's done."

Salkehatchie art: A septic tank cover.

One year, my daughter Emily worked on a site with a small crew and an enormous job. They kept discovering more work when they peeled off the roof. Burned rafters needed replacing. Someone fell through a ceiling every day of the week, creating new jobs—major jobs. Four young people lived in the house and labored every day, all day, with the crew. John, the fourteen-year-old young man of the family, worked late into the evening on Wednesday with two site leaders. He paused to put a CD in a player, and as he listened to the music, tears streamed down his face. The families tend to feel with us the anxieties, hopes, and awe at the enormity of the changes that are to occur in so short a time.

Our daughter Emily wanted to make the house where she worked as lovely and organized as possible, and she kept seeing things that needed to be done and felt frustrated that they could not do it all. When we toured the houses on Friday, I saw a series of darling rooms decorated to the style of each occupant and smiling faces throughout the family. Emily, though, was sad to leave them and discouraged about what was undone.

We never have enough time or materials to do everything. When we walk away, the houses always could use more fixed windows, more floor repairs, more painting, more adaptations for handicap access. I worked on homes where we just closed the doors to some rooms and didn't even try to go in there. Often site leaders stay through Saturday to fix essentials, like getting the plumbing to work.

No, there's never enough time to finish. Time presses us. A massive amount of work must be accomplished in fewer than five workdays—between six o'clock on Monday morning and about two o'clock on Friday afternoon. The families seem less pressed for time than we are. One resident said to me, "God never hurries, but he's always on time." The psalmist knew this too, when he wrote, "From everlasting to everlasting you are God. ... For a thousand years in your sight are like a day that has just gone by, or like a watch in the night" (Psalm 90:2-4).

I keep the habit of marking time. I buy a watch for five bucks every few years and wear it at Salkehatchie, where it gets encrusted with sweat, soaked in bug repellent, and coated in paint. When it stops ticking, I get another.

The week has a beginning and an end. In between, time takes on strange dimensions. John Culp claims Neil Flowers once walked around a house for three days before he started to do anything—it was such a mess he couldn't figure it out. We take time to plan on the weekend before we begin, but when we arise on Monday morning, it's as if the race is on.

The Good Book says there is a time for everything ... a time to tear down and a time to build (Ecclesiastes 3:1, 3). Monday is a day of rapid progress because we do demolition and removal on the larger jobs. By Tuesday, we are chipping at walls and floors and starting to replace. At Salkehatchie, the rule is "Don't rip anything out after Wednesday," but everyone violates it. The kitchen sink cabinet may not come out until Thursday, but if you're just starting that job on Friday morning (and I have), you're definitely in panic mode.

Almost everyone has waves of panic at some point during the week, when a realization sets in that, short of a miracle, this house will stay disassembled. That feeling of doom almost always occurs on Wednesday afternoon, and again Friday morning, with waves in between. So much to do, so little time.

What is time, anyway? St. Augustine said, "What then, is time? If no one asks me, I know what it is. If I wish to explain it to him who asks me, I do not know."

Psychologically, each person has a capacity for time perception, the awareness of time passing, as some kind of change occurring in a sequence with some duration. One event follows another. The individual perceives a sense of duration between start and finish of an event, but the perception is related to the person's attitude toward the event. Thus, one person who enjoys using a circular saw and making precision cuts may perceive that a stack of boards for constructing a ramp was cut in no time, whereas another person, bored with the same job, may think it takes forever.

When one of our site crews met an elderly homeowner at their house, she cheerfully chastised them. "I prayed and prayed to God for help, and I knew you would come. What took you so long?" We felt like perhaps we hadn't been reading our mail from God or had failed to heed a call.

Physicists have explored the notion of time and regard it as a fundamental premise of human consciousness. Without it, thought and action would be chaotic. People exist in a continuum of past, present, and future. Sir Isaac Newton believed time is like a container within which the universe exists and change takes place. Physicists measure time in standard intervals, such as a millennium, a day, and a second (the basic unit). These measures are based on solar time, the earth's rotation relative to the sun. Time is related to space and serves as a basic construct in understanding humans' relationship with the physical universe.

I suppose one could measure the physical time it took to harm the families and break the houses we visit. Most roofs will deteriorate in fifteen years, rot in twenty, collapse in thirty. We can fix them in two or three days, depending on the size, degree of damage, and number of roofing crew. Often, the sequence and duration of the family wounds are harder to discern. In some of the families, you easily perceive the effects of four hundred years of slavery, a hundred years of legal discrimination, and forty more years of uncertainty and struggle. A history of racism and colonialism created poverty so entrenched that our work, mighty though it is, feels like a Band-Aid on a gunshot wound. In other families, the wounds are fresher, precipitated by disease, mental illness, bad luck, or poor life choices.

What we bring may not be a cure, but it is timeless. The love flows forth in ways that cannot be explained. As the poets noted, "I know that everything God does will endure forever; nothing can be added to it and nothing taken from it" (Ecclesiastes 3:14), and, "In the beginning you laid the foundations of the earth, and the heavens are the work of your hands. They will perish, but you remain." (Psalm 102:25-26). The roofs will deteriorate again, the floors will rot and collapse, and the debris will decompose. But the love of God that is shared during Salkehatchie week will grow and spread. It has no end.

Salkehatchie is intergenerational. We cradle the babies in our site families and frolic with neighborhood children. Our teen workers literally bounce with energy. Our fourteen-year-old workers follow our eighteen- and twenty-two-year-old workers, taking their cues from them about everything from how to hold a hammer to how to take a break. Many young adults have grown up doing Salkehatchie each summer, and a few happy couples even met at camp and later married. The middle-aged workers generally do the organizing, then step back and let the younger folks lead as much as possible. The families we serve have members of all ages, but most have septuagenarians and octogenarians, folks who cannot risk standing on a chair to change a light bulb, much less crawl under a house to wrench plumbing or climb up on a roof to lay shingles.

Our timing is often critical: we arrive, a man goes to the doctor on Tuesday and he is told he has a brain tumor that will require surgery within two weeks that will leave him unable to walk. We are able to make the house handicapped accessible and replace his deteriorated bed before he has surgery so that when he returns, life will be easier for him in his home.

For most of us, Salkehatchie Summer Service takes one week out of a year, plus a couple of days on either end for preparation. Many people believe they don't have that much time to give, but it's only about 1/52 of a life's year. So little time, really.

Even though we are keenly aware of time, I wonder if being done is ever an appropriate goal at Salkehatchie. At some time on Friday we pack up our tools, say good-bye, and leave. But the work is never done. When Jesus said, "It is finished" (John 19:30), it was really the mark of a new beginning. Perhaps, instead of saying "we're done" as we leave the family, we should say, "let's begin."

Salkehatchie is intergenerational.

Chapter 6

The Ripple Effect: Spreading The Light

At Salkehatchie I learned ... to appreciate and love the things I take for granted. Money and material objects don't matter in life. The things that matter are love, family, friends, and one's relationship with God.

Poverty around the world is a devastating issue to think about. There are not only people in need in South Carolina, but all over the world. Maybe one day I'll be fortunate enough to do missionary work in a faraway country.

—*Youth volunteer*

The Salkehatchie River still looks a lot like it did in 1974, when John and Peggy drove across and decided to start a camp. The Spirit of God still moves over those waters, just as it did at the beginning of time. Still, people live in homes with no plumbing. We wonder, "What's it all about?" And we yearn to know the sunshine of God's love, the hope of eternal happiness. Humbly, we hesitate when we hear Mother Teresa's words that, as followers of Christ, we are that sunshine, we are that hope. Salkehatchie Summer Service, and other programs like it, gives each one of us the opportunity to boldly say, "Yes, I will be the light. Here I am, send me!"

In this book we have tried to illustrate how Salkehatchie mediates the journey from confusion to confidence about our solidarity with God. Seeds of change, planted during the weeklong immersion experience, come to fruition in the other fifty-one weeks of the year and throughout the lives of the many participants. Whether they be volunteers or site families immersed in the experience, supporters in the church and neighborhood, or bystanders who witness what happened, Salkehatchie Summer Service essentially touches one heart at a time. It is an intensely personal experience, although it happens in community, in a fellowship of believers. Each person who is touched then touches another. Surely, over time, as the light spreads, the world will see less indecent housing, more positive youth development, and a more caring church.

Salkehatchie has a broader impact beyond the week at camp. A biblical foundation inspires the work and the transformation that can occur as a participant begins to comprehend the meaning of the biblical messages with his or her whole being—physical, emotional, mental, social, and spiritual. When people get it, it's as if their hearts are on fire and they share it with others. The message spreads.

> Do not conform to the pattern of this world,
> but be transformed by the renewing of your mind.
> Then you will be able to test and approve what God's will is—
> his good, pleasing and perfect will.—Romans 12:2

A clear calling

One youth participant put it this way: "There are two facets to this mission. We serve the poor. The other thing we do is help people who are not poor to understand their God-given responsibility to help their brothers and sisters."

Certain parts of the Bible can be hard to understand, but the parts about poverty are crystal clear and abundantly redundant. Over and over, through the various prophetic voices of those who wrote the word, across centuries of history about the faithful, and throughout the gospel, God adamantly calls his followers to reach out to the poor. While Salkehatchie may seem to focus on material poverty, the tenets of the Christian faith and the lessons of Salkehatchie address matters of spiritual poverty and wealth as well. We accept Paul's statement that, "For you know the grace of our Lord Jesus Christ, that though he was rich, yet for your sake he became poor, so that you through his poverty might be rich" (2 Corinthians 8:9). We celebrate our spiritual wealth through the love of Christ.

The Bible is clear that being materially poor is not a great place to be and that believers should work to get people out of material poverty. Early in the moral codes, God spoke directly to Moses to require feeding the poor (Leviticus 19:10; 23:22) and opening hands wide to the poor and the needy (Deuteronomy 15:11). We are not to blame the poor for their poverty (1 Samuel 2:7-8) and certainly are not to take from the poor (Isaiah 3:14-15). The Psalms affirm that God will protect and respond to the poor (Psalms 12:5, 35:10, 86:1). Those who consider the poor are blessed (Psalm 41:1) and woe to those who harm the poor (Amos 2:5-6).

Jesus came to bring good news to the poor (Luke 4:18) and he blesses them, assuring the poor that they will inherit the kingdom of God (Luke 6:20). In story after story about his life, throughout the Gospels, Jesus models compassion for others. He unequivocally declared that the greatest commandment is to love God with all our heart, soul, and strength, and to love our neighbors as ourselves (Matthew 22:37-39). He also affirmed, in splendid detail, that the followers of God are to reach out to the stranger, the sick, the hungry, the thirsty, the poorly clothed, and the prisoner (Matthew 25:31-46). After he tells the story of the Good Samaritan, he tells the crowd, "Go and do likewise" (Luke 10:37). Hebrews 13:2 says that if we reach out to a stranger, we may very well meet an angel. That's so true at Salkehatchie.

The early Christians, who were often poor themselves because of persecution, were all about showing compassionate love (1 John 3:17), particularly to the weak (Acts 20:35), the fatherless and the widows (James 1:27), and the poor. As Paul told early church leaders, "All they asked was that we should continue to remember the poor, the very thing I had been eager to do all along" (Galatians 2:10).

The Bible also says a lot about the rich and those who pursue material wealth, much of it unfavorable. While many Bible stories and lessons speak of material prosperity as a blessing (see Deuteronomy 15:4; Ezekiel 36:11) and many of God's core followers (like Abraham, Joseph, and King David) were wealthy, a close reading shows that the promise of prosperity is often a promise of freedom from want; that is, satisfaction of needs, rather than indulgence.

The problem with indulgence and pursuit of plenty, of course, is that it interferes with our pursuit of a close relationship with God (Luke 16:13). This proverb says it all: "Give me neither poverty nor riches, but give me only my daily bread. Otherwise, I may have too much and disown you and say, 'Who is the Lord?' Or I may become poor and steal, and so dishonor the name of my God" (Proverbs 30:8-9). As the poet observed, "Whoever loves money never has enough; whoever loves wealth is never satisfied with his income" (Ecclesiastes 5:10). Jesus admonished his followers to set their hearts on God and ignore acquiring even basic essentials like food or drink, because a focus on God will lead to having basic needs met (Luke 12:29-34).

The people of ancient times were apparently as inclined as people of modern times to devote themselves to the process of material acquisition and to hoard things once they got them, rather than share them. Repeatedly, various voices in the Bible admonish us to keep our lives free from the love of money and be content with what we have (Hebrews 13:5; Philippians 4:11); to avoid wearing ourselves out to get rich (Proverbs 23:4; Luke 16:13); and to avoid hoarding and covetousness (Exodus 20:17; Luke 12:15).

The most profound message, of course, is found in the gospel, in the words of Jesus himself: "One thing you lack. ... Go, sell everything you have and give to the poor, and you will have treasure in heaven. Then come, follow me" (Mark 10:21). The early Christians took this literally and shared everything in common (Acts 2:44-45) and were wary of the temptation of wealth, believing "the love of money is a root of all kinds of evil" (1 Timothy 6:10). They advised one another to "Command those who are rich in this present world not to be arrogant nor to put their hope in wealth, which is so uncertain, but to put their hope in God, who richly provides us with everything for our enjoyment" (1 Timothy 6:17). When they said, "Now listen you rich people, weep and wail because of the misery that is coming on you!" (James 5:1), they echoed the condemnation announced by prophets like Jeremiah, who said, "They have become rich and powerful and have grown fat and sleek. ... They do not promote the case of the fatherless; they do not defend the just cause of the poor. Should I not punish them for this?' declares the Lord" (Jeremiah 5:27-29). Luke tells us that God favors the poor over the rich when he says, "He has filled the hungry with good things but has sent the rich away empty" (Luke 1:53).

Some say that as the rich get richer and the poor get poorer, the rich are benefiting from the poor. After all, some who are rich drive expensive cars and wear brand name clothes while paying dirt-low wages to people who sew their clothes, pick their vegetables, pluck their chickens, provide day care to their children and aging kin, cook their food, dispose of their (unbelievably excessive) garbage, maintain their sewers, or beautify their landscapes. Some complain about homeless people on the streets and fight hard to keep people with disabilities from living in their communities. In other words, the spoil of the poor is in their houses (Isaiah 3:14-15). Woe be to them.

Of course, few in the United States regard themselves as rich. Except that when you look at the entire planet through God's eyes, gazing at the material status and lifestyles of all the people of the world, Americans are shockingly indulged. Most Americans are undoubtedly among the materially rich of the world. Most middle- and working-class Americans are rich beyond comprehension from the perspective of many of God's children. More than half of the world's population lives in abject poverty. In the US, we tend to deny our wealth and avoid being regarded as among the rich from a biblical perspective. When we confront our denial and accept our abundance, we realize we have a dilemma: What does it mean that we have so much?

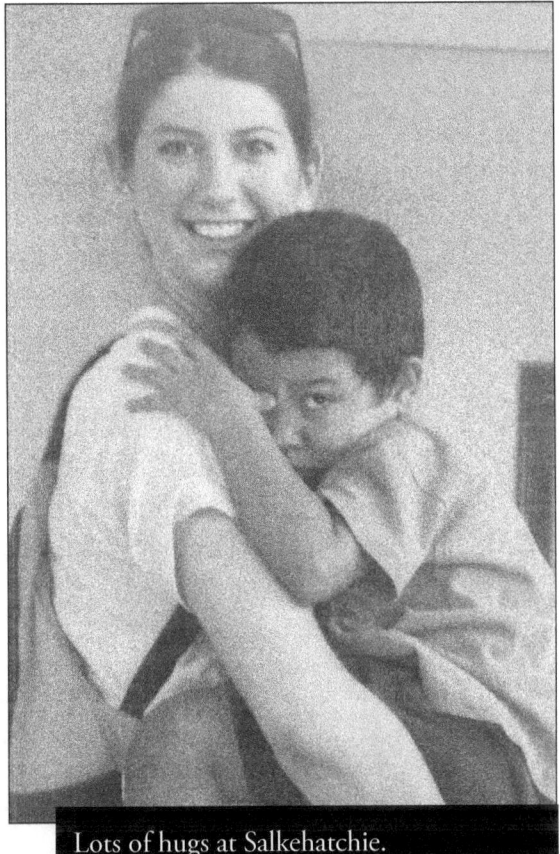
Lots of hugs at Salkehatchie.

The question can be answered in many ways and ultimately must be answered in each Christian's heart. Still, most would agree that a clear lesson from the biblical messages is that we should not pursue wealth for its own sake and that we do God's will with whatever we have, be it pittance or plenty. Almost every new volunteer at Salkehatchie gains an acute awareness of her or his material privileges and ponders what it means that they have been given so much while others have so little. They approach the notion of stewardship with a fresh perspective. And they particularly gain insight into their relationship to the poor. They learn to pass it on, and to share what they have with others.

As Jesus observed, it's not about what we have, it's about how we give. What the widow gave to God's house, which was a tiny amount but all that she had, counted for far more than the large amounts from the rich who gave only portions of their abundance (Mark 12:43-44). The Bible also tells us that when we give, we should not expect a payback. Luke says, "But when you give a banquet, invite the poor, the crippled, the lame, the blind, and you will be blessed. Although they cannot repay you …" (Luke 14:13-14). As we say at Salkehatchie, we are called to be servants, not heroes.

Jesus called his disciples to be the "light of the world" and he admonished them to "Let your light shine before others, that they may see your good deeds and glorify your Father in heaven" (Matthew 5:14, 16). The disciple James interpreted this for early Christians when he explained that work completes faith—without a demonstration, faith is dead. We are justified by what we do "and not by faith alone" (James 2:24). As Christ's disciples, we are the agents of His love and mercy. We are the physical body of Christ.

The Bible could not be clearer. Many young people at Salkehatchie have grown up with these teachings. Others are just discovering them. What we know, though, does not always steer a clear path to what we do. So often our actions are inconsistent with our beliefs. Salkehatchie gives us an opportunity to convert our beliefs into action.

> I am not saying this because I am in need, for I have learned to be content whatever the circumstances. I know what it is to be in need, and I know what it is to have plenty. I have learned the secret of being content in any and every situation, whether well fed or hungry, whether living in plenty or in want. I can do all this through him who gives me strength.—Philippians 4:11-13

On becoming disciples

We can define the purpose of Salkehatchie this way: to glorify God, which is the purpose of all Christians, and to make and nurture disciples of Jesus Christ, which is the purpose of the United Methodist Church.

Of course, that applies to all missions. With regard to Salkehatchie specifically, the recruitment material says:

> Salkehatchie is a pioneering servant ministry at selected sites in South Carolina involving high school- and college-age youth, adult community leaders, and persons of different cultures in upgrading housing, motivating community cooperative efforts by helping persons help themselves, and providing all participants with opportunities for personal growth and service.

We would add that the purpose is to teach youth and adults humility by stripping of their everyday comforts and helping them to realize their own privilege, thus freeing them from the bondage of materialism and opening their hearts to God's grace. Christ modeled this for us and called us to serve in humility, but we have few opportunities in the US to live this way. Salkehatchie creates such an opportunity.

Christians in the US live in a materialistic world that tempts them away from genuine relationships based on love. By creating a temporary service community that is in fact part of a large, connectional church community, Salkehatchie offers participants the opportunity to relate openly and caringly to one another and build bridges with people whose paths they do not cross in everyday life. Hopefully, what they learn about expressing themselves and building relationships at Salkehatchie carries over into their daily lives, helping them fight the temptations of disconnected existence.

Stuart Andrews reflected on being disciples in the Salkehatchie mode:

> In my life I have seen nothing, except Jesus himself, that has been more effective in making disciples of Jesus Christ than Salkehatchie. Dietrich Bonhoeffer said that the essence of Christian discipleship is to respond to Christ's call and die. Bonhoeffer did just that; he gave his life fighting Nazi oppression. Thankfully, the cost of discipleship at Salkehatchie is not so dear. But what is it that we begin to die to at Camp Pee Dee?
>
> What becomes of our desire to protect our time and resources

when we commit a week each year to participate in Salkehatchie?

What becomes of our indulgence when we learn we can climb out of bed at five o'clock in the morning in the service of others?

What becomes of our pride when we forsake an opportunity for credit about a job done on the site so that another person can enjoy the satisfaction of service?

What becomes of our resentment when we withhold judgment and pray for understanding of seemingly able-bodied family members who witness our service without offering to lend a hand?

What becomes of our self-righteousness when we witness an outpouring of faith from the heart of someone who has received so relatively few of life's material blessings?

What becomes of our spiritual complacency when we are inspired by the confessions, prayers, and praise of our brothers and sisters in reflections?

What becomes of the quiet, desperate fear that we don't have anything—no talent, passion, or resources—that God can use to change the world, after observing a Salkehatchie miracle?

What becomes of that desire to hide from God because we don't believe in him or in ourselves enough to contribute to the kingdom after making the contributions Salkehatchie asks of us?

What becomes of all these ways we try to protect ourselves? Do they die? Maybe not at first. Maybe never, completely. But day by day, year by year, Salkehatchie transforms us into disciples of Jesus Christ and unmistakably diminishes the powers and principalities that separate us from the love of God.

In order to gain the benefits of discipleship, we must be willing to let go and give up our old ways. Many people seem afraid to do this. Perhaps people need greater guidance about what to do. Many churches have taken stands and created opportunities for people to learn how to live their faith. For example, in 2003 Pope John Paul II declared, on behalf of Roman Catholics, that the church has a preference for the poor. Here, we share what the United Methodist Church has done to help people act on their beliefs.

John Wesley insisted that when we accept God's grace, we then should grow in it. He observed that when we respond to God's grace, through our faith we feel the urge to do good works. He called Christians to do works of mercy.[1]

By example, he lived modestly and gave what he could to the poor, visited prisoners, spoke out against slavery, helped create schools, and taught preventive health practices. True to the traditions Wesley started, the UMC has called for more equitable distribution of resources across the world. Its social principle on poverty (from the 2012 *Discipline*) states:

> In spite of general affluence in the industrialized nations, the majority of persons in the world live in poverty. In order to provide basic needs such as food, clothing, shelter, education, health care, and other necessities, ways must be found to share more equitably the resources of the world. Increasing technology, when accompanied by exploitative economic practices, impoverishes many persons and makes poverty self-perpetuating. ... To begin to alleviate poverty, we support such policies as: adequate income maintenance, quality education, decent housing, job training, meaningful employment opportunities, adequate medical and hospital care, humanization and radical revisions of welfare programs ... . Since low wages are often a cause of poverty, employers should pay their employees a wage that does not require them to depend upon government subsidies such as food stamps or welfare for their livelihood.

In addition, The United Methodist Church has positions supporting the development of decent housing and calling on faith communities and governments to assure decent housing for all. Its *2000 Book of Resolutions*, Statement 106, "Housing in the USA" affirms:

> The Social Principles statement of The United Methodist Church declares: "We hold governments responsible for ... guarantee of the rights to adequate ... shelter" (para. 164A). We reaffirm this right as well as the assertion of the 1972 General Conference that "housing for low income persons should be given top priority" (1972 *Book of Resolutions*).

---

1. He also called them to do works of piety, which are the disciplines of prayer, Bible study, and worship that bring us closer to God.

The statement calls upon the church and the government to pursue specific policies to assure effective cooperation among all levels of government to address housing conditions: expansion of subsidized rental housing; assurance of fair housing; support for housing for historically excluded populations, such as those with mental or physical disabilities and Native Americans; and financing policies to promote home asset development.

The *2000 Book of Resolutions* Statement 104, "Available and Affordable Housing," points to the global nature of the housing crisis:

> The need for adequate housing at affordable costs is critical. Millions of families around the world huddle together in densely overcrowded apartments, rural shacks, ancient house trailers, converted warehouses, and condemned or abandoned buildings. Because the remainder of us fail to recognize their plight or simply do not care enough, millions, through no fault of their own, live in inadequate housing that lacks such necessities as running water or plumbing. Still others, many of whom are children, have no shelter at all. While The United Methodist Church affirms the pervasive powers of families as "creators of persons, proclaimers of faith perspectives and shapers of both present and future society," it must continue its condemnation of policies that ignore the causal relationship between shortages of low-income housing and the lack of political will to ensure that safe and affordable housing is available to all.
>
> Whatever the form of community organization, housing protection, management, or ownership of a housing project, every effort should be made at each developmental step to ensure that those who are being aided are afforded the opportunity, and indeed, are required, to take every action necessary to direct the undertaking. Recognizing housing conditions and needs over time has brought about trends that cannot be ignored. Only through concrete actions and a commitment to the goal of fit, livable, and affordable housing will we begin to see the demise of unfit conditions and increased rates of home ownership. The time has come to take steps to promote the more equitable distribution of wealth and resources so that a decent place for a family to live becomes the foundation for dignity and self-respect.

These principles form the basis for local church and community action, including a variety of interventions ranging from neighborhood home repair crews to advocacy for broadscale public policies. Still, participation is low. The temptation to pursue wealth, consume stuff, and engage in extended leisure can be hard to resist. Back in 1996, The United Methodist Church's General Conference called for a "Rebirth of Compassion." Citing both the rise of self-indulgence, conspicuous consumption, anger, and violence, and Jesus' call to bring good news to the poor, the statement ends:

> It's hot. It's dirty.
> It's love.
>
> *—John Culp*

In this spirit, we call upon United Methodists throughout the land not only to feed the hungry and house the homeless, but also to work for policies that will end hunger and homelessness. We call upon our bishops to speak boldly for those who cannot speak for themselves—against economic policies that benefit the few at the expense of the many, against violence toward women and homosexuals, and against the continued militarization of a nation with no external threat.

We call on our people to support candidates for office who are committed to policies of full employment, universal health insurance, long-term health care, quality public education for all children, reduced military spending, and progressive taxation.

Finally, we call on our churches to reach out in love and compassion to all persons, regardless of race, economic condition, sexual preference, and religious persuasion, becoming beacons of love in a stormy sea of hatred, discrimination, and violence. Let us be signs of the coming reign of God in our midst—a reign marked by compassion and justice.[2]

---

2. "Call for a Rebirth of Compassion," *UMC Book of Resolutions of the United Methodist Church* (Nashville, Tenn.: The United Methodist Publishing House, 1996), pp. 472-473.

Salkehatchie Summer Service is a part of this connected community, the greater church. The service embodies the social principles that promote the Christian tradition of charity while moving beyond charity to justice and true transformation.

Transformation through the caring church

The buzzword these days is transformation. People talk of transformation when they speak of government, healthy lifestyles, occupying countries, service systems, spiritual development—you name it, it can be transformed. The word has a more revolutionary connotation than some of its predecessors, like reformation or change. The implication is that the object of change will begin one way and be entirely different after the transforming process. It's more substantial than evolution or development.

No doubt about it, Salkehatchie houses get transformed. At week's end, they are safer, drier, more hygienic, and warmer for winter. The families who live there smile more—much more—when our work is done than when we first begin.

Some lives are transformed, too. According to various families, volunteers, parents of youth volunteers, and others, some lives have radically changed as a result of Salkehatchie. "Awesome" is the term they use. That's the same term Luke used when describing the perceptions of the people who witnessed the Pentecost and subsequent work of the disciples: "Everyone was filled with awe at the many wonders and signs performed by the apostles" (Acts 2:43). Those who participated in Salkehatchie sense a mystical change and carry it home with them. Their friends and families notice it. They may approach their daily lives in a way that shows more care for others.

Some eventually make life-changing decisions brought about by their Salkehatchie experience. They join a Bible study, enter the ministry, join a foreign mission, or choose a service career.

Some participants may not feel transformed, but say they have still learned something. As one adult who served as a youth volunteer reflected, "I don't care if you went one year or twenty. Salkehatchie lives within you your whole life. You never forget that feeling." Few youth participate in Salkehatchie without gaining some degree of maturity. Mature moral development involves a sense of self relative to others, with a belief in responsibility toward the well-being of others. Young people enter their teen years in the narcissistic halo of childhood. We hope they leave it with a strong sense of how to determine their own needs (distinct from desires) and balance these needs with respect for the needs of others. They learn empathy, the understanding of how another feels, and the capacity to express that understanding. Salkehatchie gives them a rapid boost in the moral development arena. They are acutely aware of how they are superficially different from the families they serve while spiritually they are so similar.

This generation of youth has grown up being informed about basic virtues through programs known as character education. At Salkehatchie, this information comes to life.

A study in teamwork.

They learn that love is one of the most diverse forces in the universe, expressing itself as compassion, community, adoration, attachment, and a host of other feelings. In a world desperately short of mercy, they learn confession, forgiveness, sacrifice, and unconditional regard for others. They learn to replace prejudice with truth. They become agents of justice while barely beginning to discover the essence of what justice can be. They discover how hope happens. Over and over again, they tell us how all this has affected their faith in God.

They learn that when they accept grace, that free gift from God, they become inspired to share the gift with others. Thus grace, though free, is not cheap. It is a precious gift that must be handled delicately and responsibly. Church takes on new meaning through sweat and tears.

At Salkehatchie we use the word family in many ways—we work at the homes of families. We speak of the broad family of Salkehatchie participants as if we are veterans of a war or members of a tribe. College students greet strangers wearing Salkehatchie T-shirts and feel like distant cousins, though they have just met. Jesus said, "Whoever does God's will is my brother and sister and mother" (Mark 3:35). Jesus said this in a historical context when blood relatives tended to live near one another and share everything about their lives. To be family meant having a tight, interdependent bond lasting through thick and thin. Paul, writing to the early church, established the pattern of referring to church members as brothers and sisters in Christ. Salkehatchie participants spontaneously feel the way Paul obviously did.

The spirit of Salkehatchie is difficult to express in words. You see it in tears, hugs, facial expressions, body language, and jumps for joy. You see it in the artistic crosses that crews make and leave at the home sites. The crosses are often made of wood, sometimes rough, sometimes smoothly constructed and painted. They may be made of plumbing pipe, or bamboo, or other materials found at the site. They may be decorated with fabric or wrapped in silk flowers. The crosses imply: This house is part of a greater whole, the community of Christ's love.

One eighteen-year-old said, "You can't describe it. You have that kind of inner feeling. The way you grow spiritually, it's your own and you can't explain it to anybody."

Paul Rogat Loeb, in *Soul of a Citizen*, observes that whatever word we use for the mysterious force that animates us—heart, spark, spirit—its full potential cannot be realized in isolation.[3] It must be expressed, communicated and shared with others. Often, in the face of injustice, we fail to speak out, perhaps because we feel powerless or believe it's none of our business. Martin Luther King Jr. said, "Harm to one is injury to all."[4] Injustice hurts us all. Prophets who came before us shouted for justice—Isaiah, Jeremiah, Amos. John Culp likes to start his camps with video clips of Atticus Finch

---

3. Paul Rogat Loeb, *Soul of a Citizen* (New York: St. Martin's Press, 1999), 21.
4. Martin Luther King, "Who Speaks for the South" in *A Testament of Hope: The Essential Writings and Speeches*, ed. James M. Washington (San Francisco, Calif.: Harper, 1986), 93.

in *To Kill A Mockingbird* and Archbishop Romero defying the guerrilla troops who desecrated his church. Salkehatchie volunteers come from a long line of role models who were justice seekers.

Furthermore, everything is God's business. Being a Christian in prayerful communion with God gives us the right, as the body of Christ, to enter the business of injustice. And so we do. We declare, "Here we are. Send us." As Luke observed, "The Spirit of the Lord is on me, because he has anointed me to proclaim good news to the poor. He has sent me to proclaim freedom for the prisoners and recovery of sight for the blind, to set the oppressed free, to proclaim the year of the Lord's favor" (Luke 4:18-19).

Not only do we step in, but also we do amazing things. In particular, the youth are expected to assume significant responsibility. If they don't do it, it will not get done. One site leader says he had no idea how to put vinyl siding on a house, but a fifteen-year-old volunteer did, and she taught the whole crew. Another leader developed dizziness early in the week. He turned over responsibility for leading the roofing job to a fifteen-year-old, who led the crew to do a fine job. The youth rise to our expectations of them.

No matter how much we accomplish, we are humbled by the fact that there is still much more to be done. The work has imperfections, just like us. Nothing is plumb; we scab (make things fit with whatever materials are at hand); we create functional spaces and things in odd shapes. Our work is just a drop in the bucket when we consider the extent of the problems faced by people in poverty.

We become acutely aware of how meager our efforts are as we watch, year after year, the increasing number of prisons that pop up in rural communities where crops used to grow. As we leave the Salkehatchie homes where children live, we wonder who will end up behind bars, and what we can do to help their families prevent it. We pray earnestly that the limited time we have with families will inspire hope about the transforming power of love and that the families will find fresh strength and resources to conquer their challenges. We take comfort in Paul's words about dealing with affliction: "Therefore we do not lose heart. ... So we fix our eyes not on what is seen, but on what is unseen, since what is seen is temporary, but what is unseen is eternal" (2 Corinthians 4:16, 18). We accept that God "comforts us in all our troubles, so that we can comfort those in any trouble with the comfort we ourselves receive from God" (2 Corinthians 1:4).

Participants know that, somehow, they must convince others to become part of the transformation. Each participant has witnessed change. At the houses that are falling apart, they learn that chaos can be transformed to order and darkness to light. They may trade electronics for the peace of the natural world, gain confidence after quaking with anxiety, or discover that the mundane can be profound. They may rise above the exclusionary perception of us and them, White and other, rich and poor, old and young. They may accept humility after a life of privilege. Many yearn to tell the story so that others may know.

Einstein spent a lifetime trying to understand the concept of light. It has many properties. Some light is radiant—it glows from the inside out. That's like the light of the Spirit that fills our lives and shows when we act like followers of Christ. Light is also reflective—it shines on an object and radiates it to reveal it for what it is. So, as Salkehatchie participants radiate God's love, they shine light on the dark and ignored places of the world. The truth gets revealed for what it is and we hope those who see the light will believe and act.

Youth development

From the beginning, Salkehatchie Summer Service has aimed to promote positive youth development. In January 2004, the American Academy of Political and Social Science released a report that summarizes state-of-the-art scientific knowledge about how to help young people develop in positive directions.[5] The authors of various articles identified effective practices to enhance each child's talents, strengths, interests, and potential. They discussed setting high expectations and promoting the child's personal attributes.[6] These attributes include: lifelong commitment to being a learner, positive

> Go back home and live it.
>
> —*John Culp*

---

5. Christopher Peterson, ed., "Positive Development: Realizing the Potential of Youth," *Annals of the American Academy of Political and Social Science* 591, no. 1 (January 2004): 202-220.
6. Peter L. Benson, *All Kids Are Our Kids* (San Francisco: Jossey-Bass, 1997).

values, and positive identity; and social attributes such as caring, honesty, responsibility, restraint, and commitment to equality and social justice. They report that science has affirmed that young people who have spiritual faith and moral convictions and who participate in religious activities are more likely than others to develop in a healthy direction and stay out of trouble.

Programs aiming to promote positive youth development revealed that they have these objectives:[7]

- Promote bonding (emotional attachments to family, peer group, school, community, and organizations such as one's church, culture)
- Foster resilience (capacity for adapting to change and stressful events in healthy and flexible ways)
- Promote competence
    - Social competence (attitudes and skills in relating to others)
    - Emotional competence (ability to identify, express, and respond to feelings in one's self and others)
    - Cognitive competence (ability to solve problems, make decisions, understand expectations of others, use logic, and think analytically)
    - Behavioral competence (effective nonverbal and verbal communication and action)
    - Moral competence (ability to assess and respond to what is right and wrong by society's standards and how to handle moral dilemmas)
- Foster self-determination (ability to think independently and act accordingly)
- Foster spirituality (relating to God and one's own spirit)[8]
- Foster self-efficacy (perception that one can achieve one's own goals through one's own actions)
- Foster clear and positive identity (a coherent sense of self across settings)

---

7. R. F. Catalano et al., "Positive Youth Development in the United States: Research Findings on Evaluations of Positive Youth Development Programs," in *Annals of the American Academy of Political and Social Science* 591, no. 1 (January 2004): 98-124.

8. The authors acknowledge that social scientists have only recently begun to appreciate spirituality and that this is hard for them to define.

- Foster belief in the future (internalized sense of hope, optimism)
- Provide recognition for positive behavior (positive response to youth's behavior by people in the youth's environment)
- Provide opportunities for prosocial involvement (to help others)
- Foster prosocial norms (adoption of healthy beliefs and clear standards for behavior)

Salkehatchie was established long before this list evolved, but it embodies all of these objectives. Whether the objectives are achieved varies from person to person, year to year. Certainly, though, each camp attempts to promote these traits in each participant, young and old.

Salkehatchie has also discovered that adult leadership is critical to making it work. It's not just what you do, but how you do it. The Reverend Fred Reese observed that these leadership factors contribute to Salkehatchie's effectiveness:

- Spirit of commitment, concern, and compassion
- Sense of mission and urgency
- Casual, gentle, nonjudgmental way of relating to young people
- Getting group input on how to repair the house
- Use of local people to help with interpretation and sensitivity to local resident's problems
- Willingness to sacrifice
- Openness to innovation and criticism
- Involving the family
- Patience

Salkehatchie adult volunteers gather to share ideas about how to guide the youth and support one another. Adults who regularly attend Šalkehatchie rest assured that the future is in great hands. Salkehatchie youth are people with vision, sound moral reasoning, effective problem solving, compassion, and social connectedness. They know how to live communally and responsibly. And they know submission to God. They rebuild their own houses, their spiritual temples.

These themes are reflected in what youth say after they return home:

... Before I went to Salkehatchie, I really didn't want to go. As the week went on, I was very glad I went.

... At Salkehatchie I learned that money and material objects don't matter in life. The things that matter are love, family, friends, and one's relationship with God.

... I think it is good that we don't think about the dirt, grime, and bugs. We humble ourselves enough to do the menial tasks necessary.

... This week has taught me to overcome prejudices and fears and to treat everyone as you wish to be treated.

... The week that I thought would never end is now over, and I'm already looking forward to next year. Never before has one week touched me in such an awesome way. Everyone that registers for Salkehatchie goes to give to the poor and improve as a person; but what they don't realize, and what I didn't realize, is that you end up receiving more than you give. It's strange but true!

... After this week, I feel closer to God than I have ever felt.

... I would not trade this week for anything.

When we asked young people, "Why do you keep coming?" they said:

> A farmer went out to sow his seed. ...
> Still other fell on good soil.
> It came up and yielded a crop,
> a hundred times more than was sown.
>
> —*Luke 8:5, 8*

… It's like a family reunion.

… Salkehatchie kind of gets in your soul, in your blood, and ever since I can remember amazing things happen at Salkehatchie—things that I never thought that I could do, or something that I didn't expect to happen, or a lesson I thought I'd never learn. There is always something that helps me grow.

… It enables me to grow. It's something I don't want to leave. I come here and I am not ready for it to be over.

… One word would be empowerment because you come away feeling power because I really put a roof on that house or whatever.

… You just can't describe it. You have that kind of inner feeling and the way you grow spiritually, it's your own and you can't explain that to anybody.

… I think that it's like a community. I don't think there is much that we really do on our own here. First, God is always with us. But second, you're always with people that you have formed these bonds with. It is almost a bond that exists from the moment you walk in the door because you're all here for the same reason.

… I have never felt alone at Salkehatchie. I have always felt secure, like you can take risks that maybe you wouldn't take in other situations because of the community that is formed.

… We would be lying if we said we hadn't felt frustrated at Salkehatchie. I think in a lot of ways it does break you down, and it opens you up to see how God can work through you. … It opens us up to ask for teamwork, to pull together and do something amazing.

… A lot of people will say that they wait all year to get to Salkehatchie. I think without Salkehatchie, I couldn't have made it through the rest of the year. I would have given up a long time ago.

> After a week at Salkehatchie, I feel refreshed enough to take on the rest of my life.

Similarly, adult counselors give their reasons for coming back, again and again:

> ... I like being able to see the people year after year as they grow up. It's like watching flowers bloom. Kids who were scared to death, who would hardly say anything, are now leaders of their teams. And it's the one place that you can see and feel God in your hands.

> ... The best thing is watching people feel God. It could happen in an adult. It could happen in a homeowner. It could happen in a youth. When they get it, they get it. Some youth just come and have a great time. It didn't seem to touch them or mean anything. And then one year they come and suddenly, "Oh, yeah. This is powerful."

And so, young and old, the people come. They spend a week in an environment that is very different from their routine existence. They say they come because there they feel closer to God, more trusting of their fellow humans, courageous, humbled, supported, and empowered. They want to be transformed.

Spreading the Spirit

In the big scheme of things, no one accomplishes much at Salkehatchie, only a little. But we do plant seeds. And those seeds grow. The spirit of Salkehatchie stays with some participants long after they stop participating. The light of Salkehatchie has shone in their lives. And they pass it on.

In 2004, Sister Margaret Donner, one of the nuns who inspired John back in 1978, wrote this:

> Salkehatchie has from the very beginning been close to my heart, and I can't believe how it has grown. For me it's a new kind of Pentecost, for only the Holy Spirit can bring peoples together in these simple, helpful, sacrificing ways which enkindle a new fire of love

and communion.

For our little community in Gifford, bridgebuilding was of utmost importance—connecting the gifts and talents of some with the needs of others. Salkehatchie is a summer service project, but it's much more; it's a channel for bridge building on so many levels. Who will ever know how Salkehatchie has touched the hearts of all these people: the young people, the adult volunteers, the people whose houses are being repaired, their neighbors, the community, the churches which prepare the lunches, the pastors, those who read about it in the paper, people like myself who happened to be in the right place at the right time. Connections are formed which will never be forgotten, because lives are transformed.

"Were not our hearts burning within us?" (Luke 24:32) John, what a gift it was for me the day you came to our door! I thank God for you, for Salkehatchie, for all the lives touched and transformed by your "yes."

One of the aspects of Salkehatchie that I especially like is the "Reflection Time." What we do in life is important, but how we remember it is just as important. So to reflect on that one moment of our journey (how we felt about something that happened that day, a word that was spoken, a smile given, etc.) could determine how we carry this experience into the future. It may even determine the direction of our journey. Just to put young people or anyone in touch with a reality other than their own, which Salkehatchie often does, can open all kinds of doors to the future.

Love, Sister Margaret

On the occasion of the twentieth anniversary of Salkehatchie Summer Service, in 1997, Emory Campbell of Penn Center gave this tribute:

> For more than fifteen summers we have looked forward to the commanding voice of Rev. John Culp piercing the peaceful dawns at Penn Center with a spiritual call to his youthful disciples: "Let's go!"
>
> Sometimes you had not slept all through the night, due to overheated rooms, nonfunctioning showers, etc. But your tolerance for discomfort had been increased by your commitment to do Chris-

tian work. And, morning after morning, summer after summer, you rose to the occasion.

The occasion has been a ministry that has paralleled Penn Center's ministry: To help the least among us have a more comfortable life.
- YOU have found places we had not seen.
- YOU introduced us to families in our own backyard.
- YOU have given us the opportunity to share our problems at your annual conference.
- YOU've helped us get grants from the Blind Trust.
- YOU inspired us to organize a Habitat for Humanity, where we have built eleven homes for local families.
- YOU have helped us to get a SIP worker for the past fifteen summers.
- YOU have even repaired Sam Doyle's house, one of the island celebrities.
- YOU have truly been a friend in need to the community of St. Helena and the surrounding area.
- YOU are indeed a friend of Penn Center forever.

We regret that we have nothing tangible to give each of you today, but we would like to share the following spiritual food with

Site family gets into the act.

you, our friends:

First, Galatians 6:9: "And let us not be weary in well doing: for in due season we shall reap, if we faint not" [KJV].

And, second, 1 Corinthians 15:58: "Therefore, my beloved brethren, be ye steadfast, unmovable, always abounding in the work of the Lord, forasmuch as ye know that your labour is not in vain in the Lord" [KJV].

We love all of you and hope there will never be a summer at Penn Center without Salkehatchie.

Sometimes, longtime volunteers cannot attend camps, but they still carry the spirit of Salkehatchie in their hearts. US Army Captain Bill Matheny, veteran of many Salkehatchie summers, sent the following letter to Black Swamp Camp:

02 June 2003
Baghdad, Iraq
Dear Salkehatchie Summer Service Workers,

I hope this letter reaches you well and in good spirits. You are all about to undertake the Lord's work. I would like to thank you for your commitment to him, and I ask that you show the same commitment and compassion throughout the week at your house.

For those of you who don't know me, my name is Bill Matheny. I have had the privilege of attending Summer Salkehatchie for seven years, although not consecutively. This year I will be unable to work with you at Black Swamp. The Lord placed me in Iraq to help the civilians here. I have found that being here reminds me of working with the families helped by Summer Salkehatchie. I want to pass along some of the things I have learned through Summer Salkehatchie and my experiences here [in Iraq].

The Iraqis were, at first, very wary of our presence and unsure of our intentions. For the first week, they saw us as destroyers. The Iraqis were unsure of our ability to repair what we had done. Your [Salkehatchie] family will wonder if you will return after having dismantled their home within a matter of hours. Talk about the plans you have for their home. Reassure them that you will be back early the next morning.

The Iraqis are a humble, gracious, and hospitable people who are truly grateful for the gifts they have been given. Even in time of uncertainty, they thank God for their good fortune and his grace. We have formed strong relationships with the families in the neighborhood my company patrols.

You will find that most of the families have very strong religious beliefs and will see your service as a gift from God. You will become close to the others working on your site and, God willing, the family you have come to help. Both your faith and theirs will be strengthened by the experiences at Summer Salkehatchie.

We have involved the Iraqis in the rebuilding of Baghdad. This has empowered them with great pride in both their abilities and their city. Try to get your family involved in the work being done to their home. They will be hesitant at first, but the reward greater than [you can imagine].

No matter where you stand with the Lord, use this time to strengthen your relationship with him. You are surrounded by people who care for you and your well-being. Their wealth of knowledge is a valuable tool that should not be ignored. Also use this week as a chance to strengthen your relationships with friends, both old and new. The friendships that grow there will last you a lifetime.

I hope that you enjoy your week at Black Swamp. If this is your first year, I hope that you will enjoy your experiences and will return next year, so that we may have the opportunity to meet. For everyone else, I pray that you will also have a fulfilling experience this year. I am envious. I wish that I could be there to share in your week. You are always in my thoughts and prayers. With my love always ...

In him,
Bill

Adults who attended Salkehatchie as youth still carry the spirit with them, even though they no longer participate. One young woman, a podiatrist, wrote John to say:

> Podiatry School taught me to treat foot fractures, infections, ingrown toenails. ... But Salkehatchie taught me to treat the whole person and how to truly care about people. The human spirit is so

precious and fragile.

Jay Gore, who attended many years as a youth and young adult, reflects:

> Salkehatchie's not going to mean anything to people who don't have the Spirit and don't have the ability to allow it to really affect them. You have to be so open. I will say that my friends and I thought we were the studs of the universe when we'd go to Salkehatchie. But it's not just about hanging out with other people your age and acting cool and running around after reflections. You have to let it affect you. It's about sacrifice. You have to take the experience home with you and integrate it into your life. ... We're part of this rat race, and you have to separate and really dig ... and look at yourself harder. It's had a huge impact on my paradigm about life and people.

When we asked Jay how he would encourage others to come he re-

> The seed that fell among the thorns stands for those who hear, but as they go on their way they are choked by life's worries, riches and pleasures, and they do not mature.
>
> —*Luke 8:14*

sponded, "I'd just say, 'Go, man. It's unexplainable until you get there and go through it.'"

The workers at the building supply and hardware stores say, over and over, "What you are doing is so important. I wish more people would do this." They know the frantic pace at which we work and are quick to fill our orders. They give deep discounts, donate paint, answer questions, and help solve complex problems.

People in the community notice the dirty workers. One woman spontaneously sent this letter to Steve McCormick, Lancaster Camp director:

> I wanted to write to let you know how God has used you to touch

my life this week. I am not a homeowner that was part of your missions this year. I am someone who sat back and watched with my

> There's people down this road.
>
> *—John Culp (as he wanders along dirt roads, looking for homes)*

eyes and listened with my heart. You taught me a few valuable lessons I don't think I will ever forget.

I work across the street from one of your job sites and have had the privilege of watching your teams from my desk. I have gotten angry, I've laughed, I cried, I prayed and repented, and I have greatly been blessed. For months I've watched the family you worked with. When you came, I thought how undeserving they were of your kindness. That is when the Lord reminded me of how unworthy and undeserving I am of his love and kindness. (Hard pill for me to swallow.) They need him as much as I do! As I watched the roof come off the top of that house and saw all the rottenness underneath, I saw my life being uncovered and God shining his light in to the dark and hidden places so that he could restore and rebuild me the way he wanted to. I had to praise his name for letting me see this. Then there was another day, as I sat at my desk working, that I saw the guys on the roof dancing, laughing, and having fun. They were doing a job, but this wasn't like work because it was being done as a cheerful giver. It was like the 100-degree temperature was barely noticed.

Customers and employees have all been commenting on the project and its people and I couldn't help but feel my spirit stir when I thought about how it touched [the lives of] other people, lives that weren't Christians. Especially since it touched me so deeply and I am a Christian. I've had to thank God this week for all the little things that seem so unimportant (like for putting a window in front of my face so that I could see him move in such an awesome way). Thank you all for being such a wonderful testimony of his love and a great witness to those you never knew were watching. One of the other things I learned this week was that if I keep my eyes open, along with my heart, and my mouth shut, the Lord has a lot to say to me.

What do you think? Thanks again for adding to my life.

K—

A church hosted four Christian visitors from Russia, a woman and three youth. One hot week, they worked on Salkehatchie sites. Six months later, after their return home, the leader wrote to say, "Of all the things we saw and did in the US, I remember Salkehatchie most."

Salkehatchie participants let their lights shine. Some people see it and recognize it for what it is. They, in turn, carry it with them into their communities. They pass it on.

Hard hearts

Other people fail to see the light and let it pass. John Culp says, "They don't understand." His son Wes, a young adult, is more explicit:

> People don't really care, to be honest. If you were to sit here and start pouring your guts out about somebody not having a bathroom, people don't want to hear that. They'll tune you out.

All of us who have worked at Salkehatchie have had that experience. We start to talk about it, and the listener's eyes glaze over. They nod politely, say "Uh-huh," and change the subject. Some people routinely skip church on Salkehatchie Sunday. Maybe they don't want to know.

We reflect about why some people seem not to care. Some engage in no service to others of any kind or make only small gestures. They don't take time to pray for youth at Salkehatchie or listen to them when they return. Some may be simply self-indulgent, happy in a cocoon of pleasure. Others may be overwhelmed by their own misery. Some are addicted to the pursuit of wealth. Perhaps, in a world that is more political than spiritual, some are afraid they will be criticized for having a bleeding heart. In *Amazing Grace*, Jonathan Kozol bemoans what he sees as the hardening of attitudes toward poor people.[9]

---

9. Jonathan Kozol, *Amazing Grace: The Lives of Children and the Conscience of a Nation* (New York: Crown Publishers, 1995).

Or maybe it's because many people avoid pain. They reduce it to something experienced only in the media. They make light of it, leaving it nameless and faceless. People who avoid pain will not join the journey of those who are suffering in real life. Jesus forewarned that this would happen when he observed, in the parable of the sower, essentially, that the seeds of people obsessed with life's temptations produce nothing (Matthew 13:22).

Some do care about poor people but think we're just putting Band-Aids on gaping wounds. They do not understand the totality of the experience. Others, especially intellectuals, seem to know a lot about poverty, but they cannot name one poor person they know. They have no faces to connect with their statistics. They have never had a mystical experience and allow no room for miracles in their proposed solutions to the problem.

A Salkehatchie smile.

When disparities among groups are wide, like they are among groups in the US, people with extra resources tend to be farther removed from those in need, so their willingness to share gets reduced. People who feel relatively deprived tend to suffer more stress and unhappiness and are at risk of falling into the despair of hopelessness.[10] Much remains to be done to promote economic and social justice while bringing the light of hope to those who are deprived.

---

10. For a fine review of the effects of poverty on psychological well-being, see Bernice Lott, "Cognitive and Behavior Distancing From the Poor," *American Psychologist* 57, no. 2 (February 2002): 100-110.

The people of the US still have not elected officials who will create major government programs to address affordable housing, particularly repair of old homes. The current theme in government housing policy is to help low-income families with employed wage earners purchase homes, which is an excellent way to build assets. This works for people with the ability to work and manage any challenges they may have. Faith-based programs such as Habitat for Humanity and the Nehemiah Corporation have contributed enormously to making home ownership a reality for people with limited means.

But for the poorest of the poor, who are unemployable or struggling to manage their challenges, few widespread and effective policies or programs for stable, affordable, decent, safe housing exist.[11] A few programs offer loans for repair of homes, but the owner has to be able to repay the loan, an impossible challenge for many. Many grant programs require work to be done to code standards but allot insufficient amounts for that to happen. No government or private source helps with mobile home repairs (18 percent of the homes in South Carolina are mobile homes).[12] Faith-based programs like the United Methodist Relief Center in Charleston, South Carolina, the Appalachian Service Project, and Salkehatchie have taken on one home at a time. As much as these programs accomplish, their impact is a drop in the bucket of need.

It cannot be that people don't know about people living in unsafe and unhealthy houses. All they have to do is look as they drive by or read the newspaper. During each of the twenty-eight years Salkehatchie volunteers have served, multiple articles have been written in state newspapers about the work. The service has inspired journalists to write editorials and special feature articles about the housing needs of poor people. Perhaps the message simply has not been said often or clearly enough.

Certainly the people of the United States could assure that each person has a safe, decent place to live. Over and over, Salkehatchie crews have gone to homes with no bathrooms where the families proudly display pictures in the living room of their children and grandchildren who serve in the US

---

11. The Rural Housing Service of the US Dept. of Agriculture has limited programs, as does the US Dept. of Housing and Urban Development (HUD). Some states have programs designed to assure indoor plumbing (e.g., Virginia's Housing and Community Development program). These barely touch the extent of the need.

12. 2003 South Carolina Profile of Housing Characteristics (Washington, D.C.: US Bureau of the Census, 2004)

military. They defend our principles of freedom and equality, yet their home living conditions are far from equal. Is it really so much to ask that every American citizen have a flush toilet that works?

Why do so many people in the US ignore the poor, or even worse, blame them and try to punish them? Most Americans regard themselves as Christians. The Pew Research Council periodically conducts a random telephone survey of American households and asks questions about their religious perspectives. The March 2002 poll revealed that 82 percent of respondents report their religious preference is Christian (the other percentages were: 1 percent Jewish, 10 percent no preference, 7 percent other). The survey also revealed that Americans say they are strongly supportive of helping those in need. Almost eight in ten, or 79 percent, say people should do more to help the needy, even if that entails some personal sacrifice. More generous government assistance to the poor is favored by 67 percent. Two-thirds would be willing to forego tax cuts to do more to help the needy.[13]

The Bible, a guidebook for Christians, is clear: People with means are to share their resources with the material poor. Most Americans say they are Christian and many of them say people should do more to help the needy. So the attitudes of many are consistent with the Bible's teachings. So why are one in four of their African American and Hispanic neighbors still living in poverty? Why do 3.5 million people in the US experience homelessness in any given year?[14] As a group, the American people have far more material resources than they could possibly ever need.

Somehow, what people say they believe and what they do are disconnected.

One of the side effects of living in a powerful nation that loves individual freedom and honors the pursuit of happiness is that we are surrounded by a prevalent myth that people can choose not to be poor. We want to believe that we are all equal and that we live in a classless society where everyone can be what he or she wants to be. Some believe that people who are poor got that way by doing something immoral, so therefore they are less worthy than those who are not poor, and they do not deserve to be helped.

Psychologist Bernice Lott describes the tendency of nonpoor people to

---

13. "Americans Struggle with Religion's Role at Home and Abroad," (20 March 2002) Pew Research Center, http://pewforum.org.
14. National Coalition for the Homeless Web site: http://www.nationalhomeless.org.

distance themselves from and exclude poor people, dehumanizing them and believing they don't have the same feelings as they do. They are stereotyped as lazy, unmotivated, promiscuous, dishonest, addicted, stupid, violent, and uninterested in learning.[15] In fact, studies show remarkable diversity among poor people. Many (as we discover at Salkehatchie) are faithful, hardworking (holding two or three jobs), creative, and effective problem solvers in the face of incredible challenges. Lott observes that when nonpoor people have

> Follow God's example, therefore, as dearly loved children and walk in the way of love, just as Christ loved us and gave himself up for us as a fragrant offering and sacrifice to God.
>
> —*Ephesians 5:1-2*

personal contact with poor people, they are more likely to understand them and less likely to cast judgment and blame them for their situations.

Perhaps when people say, "People should do more to help the needy," they mean other people, not themselves. Of course this would be contrary to the teachings of their Christian faith, because nowhere does the Bible say only some people should help the poor. Some church leaders have raised alarms about the current tendency for people to seek a consumer church rather than a servant church. In a consumer church, people can enjoy entertaining music and messages without sacrificing much from their existence in the secular world. This is quite different from the missional or servant church, which regards the church (in Christ) as the core of existence and teaches that it is the role of the member to carry the mission into their existence in the secular world.

So we don't understand. Those involved with Salkehatchie don't understand why people in the richest country in the world will tolerate their neighbors living in houses with no toilets. We don't understand why a building inspector would mock the work of a Salkehatchie crew and insult the director, moving him to tears of pain and rage. Why do we have so much when others have so little? We don't deserve it. We don't understand why a

---

15. Lott, "Cognitive and Behavior Distancing."

widow, living in the house her husband was building but never completed before he was killed on his job, has to cope with rain coming through her ceiling while she listens to million-dollar jets take off from a nearby military base.

Perhaps it's not meant to be understood—at least not fully. Salkehatchie is about trying to find meaning, but it's also about so much more: feeling raw emotions, believing with blind faith, opening ourselves to new relationships, reaching for our physical limits, giving up ourselves, and living in a community, a partnership of believers. Given our lack of understanding, we accept the mysteries of life and the frailties of humankind and trust in God to show us the way when we are lost. We know we have much to do to build bridges within and across all our communities.

God is always ahead of us

Salkehatchie Summer Service is one part of a mighty collective effort by Christians across the world. Consider this reflection:

> Antioch. Cordova. Smyrna. Pleasant Hill. Salem. New Hope. Ebenezer. Hebron. Bethel. As we wind our caravan of vans and buses through the deserted rural roads of Marlboro County, touring the

Home is ... being at grandma's side.

home sites where we will work, we pass these little United Methodist churches, scattered around the countryside. We can drive for miles, along forests and fields, glancing at the occasional house or barn, watching the kudzu go by, and suddenly, there it is: the black cross with the red flame behind it, symbol of another United Methodist church. They sit alongside the road, isolated, neat and tidy, most often with an adjacent cemetery surrounded by a rusty iron fence, far from any homes. We see churches of other denominations, too. A county history book, published in 1897, mentions many of these churches.[16] They are obviously still viable one hundred and six years later.

As our herd of one hundred seventy United Methodists and friends swarm over the county, we are reminded that many people of faith have come before us. Our work will supplement their ongoing local ministry. We are comforted to know that we are part of a connectional church that extends its presence far and wide. We and other Salkehatchie Christians are here, as well as in most of the counties of South Carolina and in Georgia and North Carolina. While we do Salkehatchie Summer Service, other Christians are serving in similar ways in places like south central Los Angeles, Nicaragua, Zimbabwe, South Korea, Palestine, and far places of the world.

We are reminded that no matter where we go, God is there before us. He is there in all the agony of poverty, under the house where we slither to see what is causing the plumbing problems, on the blistering hot tin roof, in the room where we find signs of drug abuse, and even in the stench of the old freezer that hasn't worked for a year, but still holds its rotten contents. It's hard to imagine that Christ is in such places, but the Bible says, "I am with you always" (Matthew 28:20). So if we are there, he is, too.

When we were children, our church said a version of the Apostle's creed that included the phrase, "He descended into hell," after the statement that Christ was crucified, dead, and buried. It's still included in a footnote to the creed in the Methodist hymnal. That

---

16. J. A. W. Thomas, *A History of Marlboro County with Traditions and Sketches of Numerous Families* (Atlanta: Foote & Davies, 1897; Marlboro, S.C.: Marlboro Historical Society, 1971).

phrase was disconcerting, because it implied that Christ must be punished after death, and it's hard to understand why that would be. An interpretation of the phrase by Frederick Buechner offers fresh insight. His comment is essentially that, of course, Christ went to hell—he would make his way through the dark to save whoever he can.[17] Christ would go anywhere that people need light and love.

God is there in our agony, grief, and depression. He is also there when the sun breaks through the clouds after the storm, in the smile of the faithful old woman who feels the joy of the young workers around her, and in the harmony of the youth singing together. God is before us, beside us, and behind us.

Those little country churches may look physically isolated, but a community of believers surrounds them, as does the Holy Spirit.

Sharing the light

We sing the hymn, "Here I Am, Lord," whenever we gather for Salkehatchie events.

> ... I who made the stars of night, I will make their darkness bright. Who will bear my light to them? Whom shall I send?
> [Refrain] Here I am Lord. Is it I, Lord? I have heard you calling in the night. I will go Lord, if you lead me. I will hold your people in my heart.[18]

One by one, thousands of people come together each year in scores of communities to make the darkness bright and hold the people in their hearts through Salkehatchie Summer Service. They don't always know what they will do or why, they just know that as Christians, where there is darkness, they are meant to be there. Where there is despair, they can bring hope. Where there is doubt, they can bring faith.

"They won't understand what Salkehatchie is all about," John Culp says. And people who participate don't fully understand, either. The apostle

---

17. Frederick Buechner, *Listening to Your Life* (San Francisco, Calif.: Harper, 1992), 222-223.
18. Dan Schutte, "Here I Am, Lord" in *The United Methodist Hymnal* (Nashville, Tenn.: The United Methodist Publishing House, 1989): 593.

Paul said this, too: "For we know in part, and we prophesy in part; but when completeness comes, what is in part disappears. ... For now we see only a reflection as in a mirror; then we shall see face to face. Now I know in part; then I shall know fully, even as I am fully known" (1 Corinthians 13:9-10, 12).

One day, we'll understand. Until then, as Paul said, we have faith, hope, and love. That's what Salkehatchie is all about.

The Salkehatchie Sending Forth

God be merciful to us and bless us, look on us
>with kindness,
>>**So that the whole world may know your will, and that all nations may know your salvation.**

I have given you as a covenant to the people, a
>light to the nations,
>>**To open the eyes of the blind, to release the prisoners, and announce good news to the poor.**

You are the light of the world ... your light
>must shine,
>>**So that they will see the good things you do and give glory to God.**

God, through Christ, changed us from enemies
>into his friends and gave us the task of
>making others friends of Jesus, also!
>>**We are ruled by the love of Christ!**

Our love should not be just words and talk;
>>**It must be true love which shows itself in action!**

I heard the Lord say, "Whom shall I send?" Who
>will be our messenger?
>>**I will go! Send me!**

Go, then, to all peoples, everywhere, and make them my disciples!
>**We hear your call, O Lord! Amen.**

Appendices

Appendix A
Salkehatchie's Broader Context

The Salkehatchie River starts near the city of Barnwell, in a county that is now the location of the Savannah River Site, a major nuclear defense center, and Chem Nuclear, a waste facility. The proximity of the river's source to the nuclear industry takes on meaning in relation to the personal history of Salkehatchie's founder, John Culp, who initiated the first camps while pondering how to bring justice to a world threatened by divisions, including the massive nuclear arms race. Barnwell is also the location of Healing Springs, a natural water source attributed with healing powers by Native Americans, and the splendid Church of the Holy Apostle, an Episcopal architectural testament to the glory of God.

After leaving Barnwell, the river flows along the border of Bamberg and Allendale counties, each formed in relatively recent history (1897 and 1919, respectively). One gets a glimpse of the culture of these and the other counties in the Salkehatchie River basin by visiting their 2003 county historical websites. Each emphasizes the trauma of the nineteenth-century war that changed their community's destiny.

An excerpt from the Allendale County website illustrates a perception that prevails among some local residents:

> Sherman's crew burned the buildings at the old location of Allendale to the ground, and probably attempted to burn the ground itself. In Georgia they burned Atlanta and books, in South Carolina, they attempted to burn the very dirt. War may be hell, but Sherman, his associates, allies, and their ilk, have been wished there ever since by all in his path.[1]

Descendants of people liberated by the war and non-Southerners (the majority of Americans) often wonder why, one hundred forty years after the end of that war, certain Southerners continue to express vehement loathing for the deplorable acts of war perpetuated by their ancestors' enemy, along

---

1. South Carolina GenWeb-Allendale County, accessed 2 May 2003. http://sciway3.net/clark/allendale/history.html

with their concurrent tendency to honor the Confederacy. For the most part, those who wonder can be assured that the sentiment has little to do with just war ideology or pacifism. This "never forget" phenomenon persists as a core feature of the culture where Salkehatchie Summer Service was conceived, and co-exists with recent progress in overcoming historic racial exclusion. The legacy of post-Civil War segregation and discrimination explains why people of African descent disproportionately have houses that are falling apart when compared to their neighbors of European descent.

Several Salkehatchie camps were underway on June 30, 2000, when the Confederate flag flew on top the South Carolina state capitol building for the last time. It came down only after a bitter political fight. The flag was moved to the ground in front of the capitol and did not come down from there until July 10, 2015, again while Salkehatchie missioners were working. A majority of South Carolina elected officials did not support the flag's removal until after a White supremist massacred nine African Americans while they were praying.

After Allendale-Bamberg, the river forms the border between Hampton County, named for Confederate general Wade Hampton, and Colleton County, home of the Pon Pon Chapel, where John Wesley, founder of Methodism, preached in 1734 while on his mission tour of the American colonies. At that time, Yemassee Indians still lived in the area, but a smallpox epidemic in 1759 led to their extinction. John Wesley wasn't the only preacher around in those days. These counties and others in the river basin are dotted with Christian churches, mostly racially segregated, of many types: Anglican (Episcopal), Baptist, Methodist, Holiness, Christian Methodist Episcopal (CME), and others. Many churches trace their history to colonial times.

The Salkehatchie River merges with the Little Salkehatchie River, which originates in Bamberg County and winds through Colleton County, to form the Combahee River, the border between Colleton and Beaufort counties. Beaufort, a coastal county bounded by sea islands, has been a link between South Carolina and the wider world for almost five hundred years. Beaufort was visited by Spaniards in 1514, occupied by United States troops during the Civil War, influenced by the diverse population at a major military installation that trains Marines from all over the country, and invaded by affluent immigrants from everywhere who moved to Hilton Head and other islands. When compared to the inland basin counties, Beaufort teems with activity. Most notably, Beaufort County is home to the Gullah people, descendants of free and enslaved people from West Africa.

Emory Campbell, author of *Gullah Cultural Legacies*, answers the question, "What is Gullah?":

> In a brief word Gullah is a culture comprising a system of beliefs, customs, artforms, foodways, and language practiced among descendants of West Africans who settled along the coasts of North Carolina, South Carolina, Georgia, and Florida from slavery period to the present.[2]

During slavery, the harsh, humid climate of the sea islands and the related risk of malaria deterred White people from occupying the plantations for long periods.[3] Instead, they stayed inland, enabling slaves to maintain their ethnic identity and develop a hybrid West African culture. The African American people of the sea islands were (and still are) a relatively empowered people who practice self-determination and community cohesion. The visible signs of their culture are their distinctive poetic language (a blend of English and African speech patterns), seafood and rice dishes, unique arts (including woven baskets and fishnets), and richly expressive forms of worship, song, storytelling, and dance. Less tangible characteristics include their commitment to church and family, sense of connectedness to each other and the earth, staunch self-sufficiency as a group, and comprehension of the unity of past, present, and future.

The East Coast includes more than one thousand sea islands, almost all accessible only by boat until recently, when bridges began to be built. Some free African Americans lived on the islands before emancipation. They were farmers and fishers, like the first disciples. After slavery, more African Americans purchased island property and farmed it relatively autonomously until the 1960s, when the advent of air conditioning led White investors to value the area for resort development.

Years of political neglect changed with the building of bridges and

---

2. Gullah Heritage Consulting Services brochure, Hilton Head, S.C., n.d., xi.
3. For an interesting, sometimes chilling (because of its unemotional accounts of beatings and killing of slaves) record of plantation life from the perspective of an owner who lived on St. Helena's Island, read Theodore Rosengarten's *Tombee: Portrait of a Cotton Planter* (New York: Morrow, 1986).

introduction of public services such as water and sewage facilities. Resort development brought higher tax bases, and parcels of land used by African American farmers began to be taxed at exorbitant rates, on the basis of highest potential use (i.e., commercial resort). Indigenous families simply could not afford the taxes. Emerging civil rights helped African Americans move off the islands to faraway places. Thousands of acres of land were lost by Gullah people and they became dispersed. New opportunities and privileges and regrettable losses threatened the existence of the Gullah culture. The Gullah people had to fight back and save their culture.

On St. Helena Island, one of Beaufort's barrier islands, the fifty-acre historic Penn Center preserves the Gullah culture, protects the environment, and promotes local self-sufficiency. Started by Quakers in 1862, during the federal occupation of then-Confederate Beaufort, the center has been a continual major resource for African American and interracial education. During the years of Reconstruction, post-Reconstruction, Jim Crow segregation, the civil rights movement, and late-twentieth-century action for economic justice, Penn Center served as a bridge, sometimes a lifeline, between the people of the South Carolina Lowcountry and the rest of the world.

When public accommodations were closed to African Americans, and mixed-race groups had few places they could gather, Penn Center was a haven where people could come to study, organize, and retreat. In the 1960s, Penn Center hosted Rev. Dr. Martin Luther King, the Southern Christian Leadership Conference, and other civil rights activists, including those organizing throughout the South for school integration and voter participation. In 1971, in anticipation of the US bicentennial, a little museum was started at the center, and its role in cultural preservation began.

While Penn Center was helping African Americans and integrationists work for a new South, White southerners were also grappling with the "race question" in their own segregated communities. In the 1960s all-White southern congregations of many faiths, including Methodism, were asking the "ominous" question, "What will the ushers do if 'colored' people come on Sunday morning?" Nowadays, such a question seems laughable, but in those times, this was a profoundly distressing dilemma for White segregationist Christians. Some churches planned to heartily greet their visitors. Others planned to quietly seat them at the rear or in the balcony. Several planned to discretely walk them back outside the door and direct them to the nearest African American church.

Through the 1950s and 1960s, when many White southern segregationists were fighting tooth and nail to resist integration, some White and African American Christian ministers and lay people were practicing ways to bridge their historic gaps and lead others to do the same. The media tended to focus on "outside agitators" from states outside the south who came to help create change, but the substantial work for integration came from within local communities.

In the 1950s Rev. Fred Reese, pastor to a Methodist Upstate congregation, traveled monthly to Columbia to participate in the state Christian Action Council interfaith committee on race relations and to chair the state Human Relations Council. They supported lunch counter sit-ins and other public displays of integration. His all-White congregation heard about what was happening in Columbia and disapproved heartily, but they had no idea Fred was involved. He didn't tell them what he was doing because he knew they would expel him from his position as their pastor, and he knew they needed his ministry. He also had a family to support.

Fred, one of the earliest Salkehatchie participants, actively participated even when he was older than seventy-five years old.

In 1975, when United Methodists first started deliberating ideas for a summer youth mission, the South Carolina Lowcountry was just beginning to practice racial integration. In 1954 the US Supreme Court had ordered school integration in a case known as Brown v. Board of Education of Topeka, Kansas et al. The case was a combination of five lawsuits from different communities. One, Briggs v. Elliott from Clarendon County, South Carolina, was not listed first but it was the one argued by attorney Thurgood Marshall and became the cornerstone of the final Supreme Court decision.[4]

In spite of this South Carolina-based victory, most school integration did not begin in earnest until almost a generation of students later, in 1970. Throughout the south, efforts by African Americans to integrate encountered massive White resistance. In 1964 Congress passed the Civil Rights Act and the Voting Rights Act. Federal lawsuits and economic boycotts forced local communities to change their ways, though pioneer integration-

---

4. The Santee Salkehatchie camp is hosted at the Scotts Branch High School in Summerton. The building is new, but it carries the same name as the school where the historic effort to integrate took place.

ists paid high prices. For example, in 1968 SC National Guardsmen killed four students at South Carolina State College who were trying to integrate a bowling alley. South Carolina schools did not desegregate until 1970, after the US Fourth Circuit Court of Appeals ordered full desegregation and the federal government demonstrated in several southern communities that it would send in federal troops to enforce the law. Still, in the spring of 1970 angry parents in Lamar, Darlington County, overturned two school buses in protest.

Progress persisted and by the fall of 1970 local communities elected three African Americans to the South Carolina General Assembly for the first time since Reconstruction.[5] Finally, by the fall of 1971, throughout the state, African American and White students studied side by side, swam together in public pools, ate in the same restaurants, and generally began to live as part of a communal society. South Carolina was legally desegregated, if not integrated.

In 1978, when Salkehatchie Summer Service took off, Whites and African Americans in the Lowcountry of South Carolina were still new at relating to one another on grounds of equality. The first Salkehatchie youth volunteers were among the pioneers who, for the first time in South Carolina history, attended class and played sports at desegregated public schools. Many adult volunteers had been raised in segregation and had only recently ventured to join hands across racial lines. Many African American residents of the homes that needed repairs had never had social relations with White people in their communities and certainly not in their homes.

Salkehatchie was a bold initiative, given the times. Even though schools, workplaces, and public places have become integrated in the years since Salkehatchie began and people increasingly embrace one another across racial lines, many people still live in social segregation. Overt racial conflict rears its ugly head too often.

Vestiges of forced segregation traumatically cropped up in the summer of 1989, when African American Salkehatchie workers were told they could not swim at a pool in Saluda County.[6] The camp leaders had reserved the pool at the Saluda Swim and Tennis Club, owned by the Jaycees, for a refreshing dip after a long day's work on the site homes. When they ar-

---

5. Twenty-two years later, in 1992, James Clyburn became the first African American South Carolinian in the US Congress since Reconstruction.

6. Trip DuBard, "Discrimination by Habit," *Herald* (July 30, 1989).

rived, the pool manager pulled the camp leader aside and said, "We can't let them" (indicating the three Black youths) "swim here." Ostensibly, the club had maintained a Whites-only policy because the 1933 deed that granted the property to the club designated it for White recreation. Of course, the entire group left without swimming, and the United Methodist bishop and national Jaycees called for immediate integration of the pool.

Within two weeks, the pool was integrated, but not until the United Methodist youth were emotionally devastated by this blatant show of racism.

Even with civil rights enforcement, equal opportunity, and tolerant social mores, African Americans have had to bear the cost of the legacy of slavery and discrimination. After centuries of intergenerational poverty, home ownership is a precious asset, one that needs to be protected. Salkehatchie aims to do just that, while helping young people understand the oppression of poverty.

Appendix B
Twenty-Five Years of Salkehatchie Growth: 1978-2003

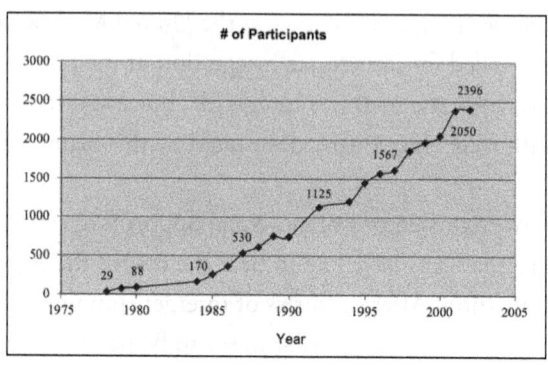

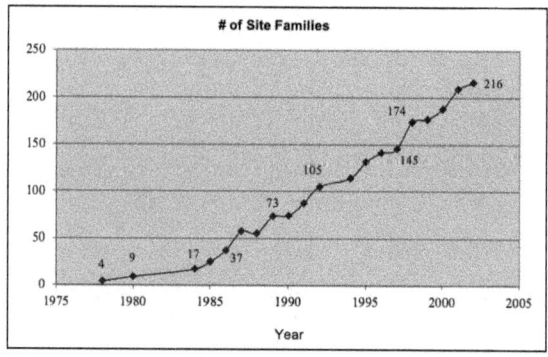

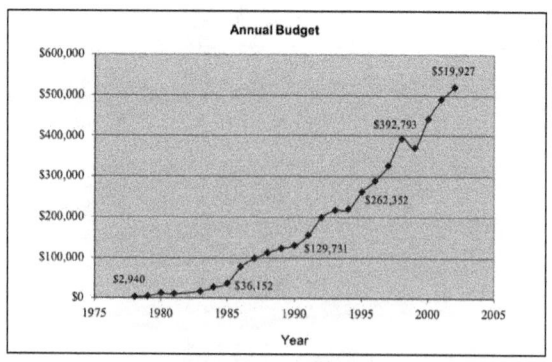

Appendix C
Location of Salkehatchie Camps by Year
(and County of Camp Headquarters): 1978-2004

1978 (1 Camp)
Gifford-St. Mary's;
Hampton-Jasper (Hampton)

1979 (1 Camp)
St. Mary's (Beaufort)

1980 (1 Camp)
St. Mary's (Beaufort)

1981 (1 Camp)
St. Mary's (Beaufort)

1982 (2 Camps)
Penn Center (Beaufort)
Santee (Clarendon)

1983 (2 Camps)
Penn Center (Beaufort)
Santee (Clarendon)

1984 (3 Camps)
Penn Center (2) (Beaufort)
Santee (Clarendon)

1985 (3 Camps)
Epworth-Phoenix, Laurens (Newberry)
Penn Center (Beaufort)
Santee (Clarendon)

1986 (5 Camps)
Epworth-Phoenix, Laurens (Newberry)
Horse Creek (Aiken)
Penn Center (Beaufort)
Santee (Clarendon)
Winyah Bay* (Georgetown)

1987 (8 Camps)
Black Swamp (Hampton)
Columbia (Richland)
Epworth-Phoenix, Laurens (Newberry)
Horse Creek (Aiken)
Penn Center (2) (Beaufort)
Santee (Clarendon)
Winyah Bay (Georgetown)

1988 (8 Camps)
Black Swamp (Hampton)
Columbia (Richland)
Epworth-Phoenix, Laurens (Newberry)
Greenville (Greenville)
Horse Creek (Aiken)
Penn Center (Beaufort)
Santee (Clarendon)
Winyah Bay (Georgetown)

1989 (9 Camps)
Abbeville (Abbeville)
Anderson (Anderson)
Black Swamp (Hampton)
Columbia (Richland)
Epworth-Phoenix, Laurens (Newberry)
Horse Creek (Aiken)
Penn Center (Beaufort)
Santee (Clarendon)
Winyah Bay (Georgetown)

1990 (11 Camps)
Abbeville (Abbeville)
Anderson (Anderson)
Black Swamp (Hampton)
Columbia (Richland)
Epworth-Phoenix, Laurens (Newberry)

Horse Creek (Aiken)
Hugo (Charleston)
Penn Center (Beaufort)
Rock Hill (York)
Santee (Clarendon)
Winyah Bay (Georgetown)

1991 (13 Camps)
Abbeville (Abbeville)
Black Swamp (Hampton)
Colleton (Colleton)
Columbia (Richland)
Epworth-Phoenix, Laurens
  (Newberry)
Fairfield (Fairfield)
Horse Creek (Aiken)
Hugo (Charleston)
Penn Center (Beaufort)
Rock Hill (York)
Santee (Clarendon)
Wateree-Camden (Kershaw)
Winyah Bay (Georgetown)

1992 (15 Camps)
Abbeville (Abbeville)
Anderson (Anderson)
Black Swamp (Hampton)
Colleton (Colleton)
Columbia (Richland)
Edisto-Edisto Fork (Orangeburg)
Epworth-Phoenix, Laurens
  (Newberry)
Fairfield (Fairfield)
Horse Creek (Aiken)
Hugo (Charleston)
Penn Center (Beaufort)
Rock Hill (York)
Santee (Clarendon)
Union (Union)
Wateree-Camden (Kershaw)

1993 (14 Camps)
Anderson (Anderson)
Black River-Kingstree (Williamsburg)
Black Swamp (Hampton)
Columbia (Richland)
Epworth-Phoenix, Laurens
  (Newberry)
Fairfield (Fairfield)
Horse Creek (Aiken)
Hugo (Charleston)
Johns Island (Charleston)
Penn Center (Beaufort)
Rock Hill (York)
Santee (Clarendon)
Union (Union)
Wateree-Camden (Kershaw)

1994 (16 Camps)
Black River-Kingstree (Williamsburg)
Black Swamp (Hampton)
Columbia (Richland)
Epworth-Phoenix, Laurens
  (Newberry)
Fairfield (Fairfield)
Foothills-Landrum (Spartanburg)
Horse Creek (Aiken)
Hugo (Charleston)
Lake City (Florence)
Lexington (Lexington)
Pee Dee (Marlboro)
Rock Hill (York)
Santee (Clarendon)
Union (Union)
Wateree-Camden (Kershaw)
Winyah Bay (Georgetown)

1995 (19 Camps)
Black River-Kingstree (Williamsburg)
Black Swamp (Hampton)
Charleston (Charleston)
Columbia (Richland)
Epworth-Phoenix, Laurens
  (Newberry)
Fairfield (Fairfield)
Foothills-Landrum (Spartanburg)
Horse Creek (Aiken)
Hugo (Charleston)
Lake City (Florence)
Lexington (Lexington)

Oconee (Oconee)
Pee Dee (Marlboro)
Penn Center (Beaufort)
Rock Hill (York)
Santee (Clarendon)
Union (Union)
Wateree-Camden (Kershaw)
Winyah Bay (Georgetown)

1996 (22 Camps)
Black River-Kingstree (Williamsburg)
Black Swamp (Hampton)
Charleston (Charleston)
Columbia (Richland)
Epworth-Phoenix, Laurens
    (Newberry)
Fairfield (Fairfield)
Foothills-Landrum (Spartanburg)
Horse Creek (Aiken)
Hugo (Charleston)
Lake City (Florence)
Lancaster & Chester (Lancaster)
Lexington (Lexington)
Oconee (Oconee)
Pee Dee (Marlboro)
Penn Center (Beaufort)
Piedmont (Anderson)
Rock Hill (York)
Santee (Clarendon)
Swamp Fox (Marion)
Union (Union)
Wateree-Camden (Kershaw)
Winyah Bay (Georgetown)

1997 (22 Camps)
Asbury Hills (Greenville)
Batesburg-Leesville, Lexington-Saluda
    (Lexington)
Black River-Kingstree (Williamsburg)
Black Swamp (Hampton)
Columbia (Richland)
Epworth-Phoenix, Laurens
    (Newberry)
Fairfield (Fairfield)
Foothills-Landrum (Spartanburg)

Horse Creek (Aiken)
Hugo (Charleston)
Lake City (Florence)
Lexington (Lexington)
Oconee (Oconee)
Pee Dee (Marlboro)
Penn Center (Beaufort)
Rock Hill (York)
Santee (Clarendon)
Savannah-Baker Creek (McCormick)
Swamp Fox (Marion)
Union (Union)
Wateree-Camden (Kershaw)
Winyah Bay (Georgetown)

1998 (25 Camps)
Bamberg (Bamberg)
Batesburg-Leesville, Lexington-Saluda
    (Lexington)
Berkeley (Berkeley)
Black River-Kingstree (Williamsburg)
Black Swamp (Hampton)
Catawba-Fort Mill (York)
Columbia (Richland)
Epworth-Phoenix, Laurens
    (Newberry)
Fairfield (Fairfield)
Foothills-Landrum (Spartanburg)
Horse Creek (Aiken)
Hugo (Charleston)
Lake City (Florence)
Lexington (Lexington)
Oconee (Oconee)
Pee Dee (Marlboro)
Penn Center (Beaufort)
Rock Hill (York)
Sand Dollar (Charleston)
Santee (Clarendon)
Savannah-Baker Creek (McCormick)
Swamp Fox (Marion)
Union (Union)
Wateree-Camden (Kershaw)
Winyah Bay (Georgetown)

1999 (22 Camps)
Bamberg (Bamberg)
Batesburg-Leesville, Lexington-Saluda
  (Lexington)
Black River-Kingstree (Williamsburg)
Black Swamp (Hampton)
Catawba-Fort Mill (York)
Columbia (Richland)
Epworth-Phoenix, Laurens
  (Newberry)
Fairfield (Fairfield)
Horse Creek (Aiken)
Hugo (Charleston)
Lake City (Florence)
Lexington (Lexington)
Oconee (Oconee)
Pee Dee (Marlboro)
Penn Center (Beaufort)
Rock Hill (York)
Santee (Clarendon)
Savannah-Baker Creek (McCormick)
Swamp Fox (Marion)
Union (Union)
Wateree-Camden (Kershaw)
Winyah Bay (Georgetown)

2000 (27 Camps)
Bamberg (Bamberg)
Batesburg-Leesville, Lexington-Saluda
  (Lexington)
Black River-Kingstree (Williamsburg)
Black Swamp (Hampton)
Blythewood (Richland)
Catawba-Fort Mill (York)
Columbia (Richland)
Epworth-Phoenix, Laurens
  (Newberry)
Fairfield (Fairfield)
Horse Creek (Aiken)
Hugo (Charleston)
Johnson-Edgefield-Trenton (JET)
  (Edgefield)
Lake City (Florence)
Lancaster & Chester (Lancaster)
Lexington (Lexington)
Oconee (Oconee)
Pee Dee (Marlboro)
Penn Center (Beaufort)
Piedmont (Anderson)
Rivertown-Conway (Horry)
Rock Hill (York)
Santee (Clarendon)
Son City (Beaufort)
Swamp Fox (Marion)
Union (Union)
Wateree-Camden (Kershaw)
Winyah Bay (Georgetown)

2001 (33 Camps)
Bamberg (Bamberg)
Batesburg-Leesville, Lexington-Saluda
  (Lexington)
Black River-Kingstree (Williamsburg)
Black Swamp (Hampton)
Blythewood (Richland)
Catawba-Fort Mill (York)
Circuit Rider-Johnsonville (Florence)
Columbia (Richland)
Edisto-Edisto Fork (Orangeburg)
Epworth-Phoenix, Laurens
  (Newberry)
Fairfield (Fairfield)
Foothills-Pendleton (Anderson)
Horse Creek (Aiken)
Hugo (Charleston)
Johnson-Edgefield-Trenton (JET)
  (Edgefield)
Lake City (Florence)
Lancaster & Chester (Lancaster)
Lexington (Lexington)
Loris (Horry)
Oconee (Oconee)
Pee Dee (Marlboro)
Penn Center (Beaufort)
Rivertown-Conway (Horry)
Rock Hill (York)
Santee (Clarendon)
Savannah-Baker Creek (McCormick)
St. Matthews (Calhoun)
Sumter (Sumter)

Swamp Fox (Marion)
Timmonsville (Florence)
Union (Union)
Wateree-Camden (Kershaw)
Winyah Bay (Georgetown)

2002 (34 Camps)
Andrews (Georgetown)
Bamberg (Bamberg)
Batesburg-Leesville, Lexington-Saluda
 (Lexington)
Black River-Kingstree (Williamsburg)
Black Swamp (Hampton)
Blythewood (Richland)
Catawba-Fort Mill (York)
Circuit Rider-Johnsonville (Florence)
Columbia (Richland)
Edisto-Edisto Fork (Orangeburg)
Epworth-Phoenix, Laurens
 (Newberry)
Fairfield (Fairfield)
Foothills-Landrum (Spartanburg)
Greenville (Greenville)
Horse Creek (Aiken)
Hugo (Charleston)
Johnson-Edgefield-Trenton (JET)
 (Edgefield)
Lake City (Florence)
Lancaster & Chester (Lancaster)
Lexington (Lexington)
Loris (Horry)
Oconee (Oconee)
Pee Dee (Marlboro)
Penn Center (Beaufort)
Rivertown-Conway (Horry)
Rock Hill (York)
Santee (Clarendon)
Savannah-Baker Creek (McCormick)
St. Matthews (Calhoun)
Sumter (Sumter)
Swamp Fox (Marion)
Union (Union)
Wateree-Camden (Kershaw)
Winyah Bay (Georgetown)

2003 (36 Camps)
Andrews (Georgetown)
Bamberg (Bamberg)
Batesburg-Leesville, Lexington-Saluda
 (Lexington)
Bishopville (Lee)
Black River-Kingstree (Williamsburg)
Black Swamp (Hampton)
Blythewood (Richland)
Catawba-Fort Mill (York)
Circuit Rider-Johnsonville (Florence)
Columbia (Richland)
Edisto-Edisto Fork (Orangeburg)
Epworth-Phoenix, Laurens
 (Newberry)
Fairfield (Fairfield)
Foothills-Pendleton (Anderson)
Greenville (Greenville)
Horse Creek (Aiken)
Hugo (Charleston)
Huntersville (Mecklenburg County,
 North Carolina)
Johnson-Edgefield-Trenton (JET)
 (Edgefield)
Lake City (Florence)
Lancaster & Chester (Lancaster)
Lexington (Lexington)
Loris (Horry)
Oconee (Oconee)
Pee Dee (Marlboro)
Penn Center (Beaufort)
Piedmont (Anderson)
Rivertown-Conway (Horry)
Rock Hill (York)
Santee (Clarendon)
Savannah-Baker Creek (McCormick)
St. Matthews (Calhoun)
Sumter (Sumter)
Swamp Fox (Marion)
Wateree-Camden (Kershaw)
Winyah Bay (Georgetown)

2004 (41 Camps)
   Andrews (Georgetown)
   Bamberg (Bamberg)
   Bishopville (Lee)
   Black River-Kingstree (Williamsburg)
   Black Swamp (Hampton)
   Blythewood (Richland)
   Catawba-Fort Mill (York)
   Chester (Chester)
   Circuit Rider-Johnsonville (Florence)
   Columbia (Richland)
   Cowpens (Spartanburg)
   Darlington (Darlington)
   Edisto-Edisto Fork (Orangeburg)
   Epworth-Phoenix, Laurens (Newberry)
   Fairfield (Fairfield)
   Foothills-Landrum (Spartanburg)
   Greenville (Greenville)
   Hugo (Charleston)
   Huntersville (Mecklenburg County, North Carolina)
   Johnson-Edgefield-Trenton (JET) (Edgefield)
   Lake City (Florence)
   Lancaster (Lancaster)
   Lexington (Lexington)
   Loris (Horry)
   Native American (Orangeburg)
   Oconee (Oconee)
   Pee Dee (Marlboro)
   Penn Center (Beaufort)
   Piedmont (Anderson)
   Rivertown-Conway (Horry)
   Rock Hill (York)
   Santee (Clarendon)
   Savannah-Baker Creek (McCormick)
   Spartanburg (Spartanburg)
   St. Matthews (Calhoun)
   Summerville (Dorchester)
   Sumter (Sumter)
   Swamp Fox (Marion)
   Union (Union)
   Wateree-Camden (Kershaw)
   Winyah Bay (Georgetown)

TOTAL CAMPS IN 1978 = 1
TOTAL CAMPS IN 2004 = 41

* Some camps in Georgetown County changed names several times over the years. This list uses the current name of Winyah Bay for clarity. Former camp names were Bull's Bay, Pawley's, and Waccamaw Neck.

www.ingramcontent.com/pod-product-compliance
Lightning Source LLC
Chambersburg PA
CBHW050851160426
43194CB00011B/2115